The Politics
of Healthcare
in Britain

D0207036

The Politics
of Healthcare
in Britain

Stephen Harrison
and Ruth McDonald

SAGE Publications
Los Angeles • London • New Delhi • Singapore

First published 2008

SAGE Publications Ltd
1 Oliver's Yard
55 City Road
London EC1Y 1SP

SAGE Publications Inc.
2455 Teller Road
Thousand Oaks, California 91320

SAGE Publications India Pvt Ltd
B 1/I 1 Mohan Cooperative Industrial Area
Mathura Road
New Delhi 110 044

SAGE Publications Asia-Pacific Pte Ltd
33 Pekin Street #02-01
Far East Square
Singapore 048763

Library of Congress Control Number: 2007939449

British Library Cataloguing in Publication data

A catalogue record for this book is available from the British Library

ISBN 978-0-7619-4159-0
ISBN 978-0-7619-4160-6 (pbk)

Typeset by C&M Digitals Pvt Ltd, Chennai, India
Printed in Great Britain by The Cromwell Press Ltd, Trowbridge, Wiltshire
Printed on paper from sustainable resources

Contents

Preface

Our aims in this volume are to introduce readers to a fairly wide range of descriptive and analytical material about the past and present politics of healthcare in Britain. Our working definition of 'healthcare' is conventional; the majority of our material relates to the funding, organisation and delivery of diagnostic and therapeutic services to individuals, rather than to broader conceptions of public health. Our working definition of 'politics' is conventional too, though it perhaps merits some explanation. The funding and provision of healthcare in Britain, and indeed all western countries, is a central concern of public policy irrespective of widely differing degrees of public funding and public ownership of healthcare institutions. This concern extends beyond these matters of finance and provision to the extent of shaping other aspects of politics and public policy, an observation summed up in Moran's notion of the 'healthcare state':

> There is more to health care politics than health care policy; the scale of health care institutions means that they have ramifications for the modern state well beyond conventional health care arenas. Like any state, the health care state is about governing; and in the act of governing states shape health care institutions, and are in turn shaped by those institutions ... Health care systems pose problems for statecraft; but they also offer ways of solving problems, often problems whose origins lie beyond health care systems themselves. (Moran, 1999: 4–5)

This description is certainly apt in a Britain where not only does public expenditure on healthcare and direct provision of such care massively outweigh what is privately funded or privately provided, but also where this arrangement is routinely used by governments to enhance their political legitimacy. This connects with contemporary ideas about 'governance' which emphasise that, despite the formal provisions of national constitutions, states and governments do not simply govern in a top-down fashion. Rather, they seek to steer society through a variety of channels, some of which are indirect (Pierre and Peters, 2000: 4–5). In order to govern in this sense, governments must by various means enlist the efforts of other social actors. In Britain, the latter of course include 'official' public bodies, such as the institutions of the National Health Service (NHS), numerous professional, academic and other interest groups, and less easily definable 'social movements' (such as the 'patient movement' or the 'evidence-based medicine movement') based as much on shared identities as shared interests (Byrne, 1997). Mapping and analysing the interactions between governments and such actors are a central focus of this volume.

The third element of our book title locates our work in the context of Britain, that is England, Scotland and Wales. There have long been organisational differences (and differences of official terminology) between the three countries (Williamson and Room, 1983). As we show in Chapter 7, these have widened in recent years as a result of devolution to the Scottish Parliament and the Welsh Assembly (Greer, 2004), which is also beginning to result in differences in patient entitlement. Elsewhere in the book, however, we have confined our official terminology to that of the English NHS, whilst trying to ensure that the overall thrust of our analysis is applicable to the whole of Britain. The continuing rapid rate of NHS organisational change precludes any attempt to include definitive organisation charts and even the Department of Health no longer seems to attempt this. In order to avoid becoming mired in the minute history of changes in the titles of statutory bodies, we have generally referred simply to 'health authorities' where the context does not require precision.

A textbook such as the present volume does not have the same sort of aims as the research papers and conceptual reviews on which, as full-time researchers, we spend most of our time. The latter are tightly written in order to make at the most a few points; they therefore tend to employ a narrow range of concepts and literature that relate closely to the argument and/or evidence that is being deployed. In contrast, a textbook has the wider aim of informing readers about the general state of its subject matter. It must introduce a selection of relevant theories, concepts and evidence but it will necessarily leave loose ends and confine itself to indicating general lines of analysis and argument rather than pursuing them rigorously to a single conclusion. In order to meet this wider textbook aim, we have adopted a particular and distinctive structure for each of our substantive themes, that is Chapters 1 to 6. Each has four main sections; the first introduces a range of concepts that we take to be central to the particular theme, the second section provides a summary history of the theme, and the third summarises recent and contemporary developments. The final section of each chapter consists of discussion of how a small sample of theories might be used to address questions relevant to the chapter's theme. It is important to stress that these discussions do not constitute serious 'tests' of the theories; our purpose is rather to suggest to the reader how such abstract material can be related to substantive accounts. Our book would have been unacceptably long had we not been selective in our choice of themes. Important casualties of this selection process have included the politics of public/environmental health, the politics of pharmaceutical manufacture and regulation, and the politics of social care. On community care, see Means et al. (2003) and for public health, see Baggott (2000) and Lewis (1986). On pharmaceuticals, see Abraham (1997), Abraham and Lewis (2001), Davis (1997) and the edited European collection by Mossialos et al. (2004).

Some excellent health policy texts are very limited in theoretical coverage, either employing it only implicitly or treating it as primarily critical. We have taken the opposite view here, employing a wide range of conceptual and theoretical material, drawn mainly from political science and sociology but with important contributions from economics. Some readers may feel that we have been too eclectic, and that we should have undertaken a consistent political analysis, or that important intellectual traditions have been neglected. Others may feel that there is altogether too much conceptual material. We hope, however, that most will find our approach stimulating in terms of generating questions and analyses of their own. Our policy of providing extensive citations and a reading guide is designed to support further study.

Chapter 7 is designed to work in a different way from the other chapters. It follows from our textbook philosophy, summarised above, that we cannot provide a final chapter to summarise the book and neatly tie up the loose ends. Instead, Chapter 7 addresses the risk that our thematic approach diverts attention from potential interaction and tensions between themes. We therefore consider three such tensions that may set the scene for future political and policy conflicts.

Readers will note that our book is extensively referenced in relation to specific points made in the text. The text also sometimes indicates sources for more detailed coverage or overviews of such points. In addition, at the end of each chapter we provide a brief guide to further reading which relates to issues covered in that chapter.

With regard to reading materials on health policy and politics more generally, of the numerous UK health policy texts available, the current editions of Ham (2004) and Baggott (2004) offer wide-ranging and complementary coverage. The two-volume official history of the NHS (Webster, 1988, 1996) is comprehensive from before 1948 to 1979; a shorter but still detailed account of the first 50 years is Rivett (1998). Specifically political histories of the NHS are the current editions of Klein (2006) and Webster (2002). The creation of the NHS in 1948 is the subject of studies by Willcocks (1967) and Pater (1981). The detailed history of NHS organisation through to 1998 can be pieced together from the various editions of Levitt (1976; 1979), Levitt and Wall (1984, 1992) and Levitt et al. (1995, 1999). The history of the Department of Health is selectively covered in Rayner (1994), Day and Klein (1997) and Greer and Jarman (2007). The successive editions of the *Compendium of Health Statistics* (most recently Office of Health Economics, 2007) provide useful tabular and graphical data about the NHS and British healthcare, with some international comparisons.

Academic authors incur numerous intellectual debts, most of which they quickly forget as others' ideas become incorporated in their own thought. The following list of acknowledgements is no doubt grievously incomplete, and we apologise for omissions: Andrew Gray (formerly University of Durham), Huw Davies (St Andrews), Tim Milewa (Brunel University), Christopher Pollitt (Catholic University of Leuven) and our University of Manchester colleagues Kath Checkland, George Dowswell, Mick Moran, John Pickstone and Martin Roland.

Whilst writing this book we have both experienced rather closer contact with the NHS than we would have wished (as patient and carer respectively) so we are grateful to Karen Phillips and Anna Luker of Messrs Sage for their continued patience in the face of our numerous postponements of the manuscript delivery date. Finally, thanks for both support and appropriate diversion are due to our partners Annie Dearman and Tim Payne respectively, and in SH's case to Vic Gammon and the gang at Ryburn 3-Step (www.ryburn3step.org).

Steve Harrison
Ruth McDonald

Chapter 1

The Politics of Healthcare Resources and Rationing

Summary of chapter contents

- Third party payment in healthcare: what is it and why is it used?
- The consequences of third party payment
- Managing healthcare supply and demand
- Ways of interpreting third party payment: neo-Marxist and public choice theories

The phrase 'out of pocket payment' denotes the manner in which we purchase most goods and services in developed economies. We may literally take cash from our pockets, write cheques on our bank accounts, or employ debit or credit cards. Even if we are using credit cards, the end result is the same; we pay personally from our own resources, now or in the future. There is no necessary reason why health and medical care cannot be purchased in the same manner, and indeed most of us purchase a range of non-prescription 'over the counter' remedies from pharmacists, spectacles from opticians and so on, purchases that account for a little over 7 percent of all UK healthcare expenditure. A further proportion of such expenditure (some 3 percent) is accounted for by private (non-NHS) healthcare purchased out of pocket from doctors, other professional clinicians and hospitals. This figure does not include expenditure on private healthcare insurance (almost 4 percent of the total), which is one example of an alternative approach to healthcare purchase termed 'third party payment', to signify the involvement of a third party (in this example, the insurance company) in the transaction in addition to the patient and the clinician or hospital. The NHS is a larger example (some 86 percent of the UK total healthcare expenditure) of third party payment in

1

which central government acts as the third party, employing tax revenues (rather than insurance premiums) to fund healthcare for UK residents. Third party payment systems of one type or another are the international norm in the healthcare field and although out-of-pocket payment usually exists alongside it, the former usually dominates in terms of public policy and expenditure. As the above figures (estimated from Office of Health Economics, 2003: Tables 2.1, 2.22) show, the latter is certainly true of the UK. The first section of this chapter examines the concept of, and rationale for, third party payment, together with some of the consequences of its adoption as public policy. The second section is an historical sketch of how these consequences have emerged and been addressed in the UK since the foundation of the NHS in 1948, whilst the third section gives a more detailed account of what might be called the 'big ideas' for managing healthcare supply and demand that have emerged in the last few years. The final section of the chapter examines a number of theoretical questions about the basis and consequences of third party payment.

Key concepts in third party payment

The principle of third party payment is that financial contributions are collected from groups, irrespective of the immediate healthcare requirements of the individuals who compose them. Such groups may represent a more-or-less complete national population, or narrower groups such as the members (voluntary or compulsory) of social or private insurance schemes. Contributions are collected by 'third party payers' such as government or quasi-independent agencies or insurance companies, which employ the resources thus obtained to resource or reimburse healthcare providers (individual clinicians and/or healthcare institutions such as hospitals) for the care of individuals considered to be sick. Third party payment thus separates payment for care from its immediate consumption, and to varying degrees separates the financial contribution that the individual makes from the volume of care that they actually consume. In a *tax-financed* system, the government acts as third party payer by employing resources collected through the tax system to pay for citizens' care. Since the taxation system collects revenues to support public expenditure on a wide range of services, health's share may not be hypothecated ('earmarked'), thereby allowing governments to shift their expenditure priorities between different programme areas. In a *social insurance* system, the third party payers are social insurance funds, the number of which varies between countries (Mossialos et al., 2002). They may be non-governmental bodies whose history lies in trade union and voluntary effort or may be managed by the state, but in either case their resources will remain hypothecated ('earmarked') for healthcare and other specified services and not be merged with other revenues. Membership of a fund may be compulsory for some or all citizens. Members make periodic contributions to the fund, typically based on a percentage of earnings. Employers may also contribute, and non-earners may have their contributions to the fund met as a social security entitlement. The fund in turn pays the clinician or hospital for services provided to members, often at rates negotiated annually between organisations representing the various interests in the healthcare industry. A *private insurance* system treats the cost of healthcare as an insurable risk for an individual. Coverage might be voluntary, or routinely provided as a condition of employment for some workers. In this context, the third party payer is the insurance company, health maintenance organisation, or nonprofit friendly society, to whom the flow of money takes the form of premiums or subscriptions paid by policy holders, which provide the resources to pay for their care. The state may support private health insurance, for instance by allowing employers to provide health insurance as an employment benefit and to treat the premiums as a tax-deductible business expense. Britain and Sweden are typically treated as textbook examples of tax-financed systems (often termed 'national health services'), with Germany as an example of social insurance and the United States as an example of predominant private insurance (Freeman, 2000; Harrison and Moran, 2000; Moran, 1999). A fourth possibility is that governments with substantial direct revenues, such as the income of several Middle Eastern states from oil production, may simply provide healthcare facilities from these revenues.

There is no necessary relationship between a particular funding mechanism and the ownership of hospitals and other healthcare providing organisations. Public funds can be used to purchase care in private hospitals (as in Germany and, as we note in Chapter 4, increasingly in the UK) and private insurance could be used to purchase care in public hospitals (as frequently occurs in Britain). Nor is there any necessary relationship with the manner in which clinicians are remunerated; fee-for-service, capitation or salaries may be used either singly or in combinations. The characterisation of countries in terms of particular types of third party payment can conceal important similarities. For instance over 40 percent of US healthcare expenditure is accounted for by tax-financed public programmes such as Medicare (for older people) and Medicaid (for poor people). It might also be argued that the more compulsory social insurance becomes, and the fewer the different funds involved (as in contemporary Germany), the more it resembles tax financing. Moreover, the categories are not discrete; contemporary France retains many of the institutions of social insurance but increasingly funds them via general taxation (Jacobzone, 2004: 81–2). The most important similarity between these various systems is the underlying principle that third party payment detaches the act of payment for healthcare from that of receiving it when considered necessary.

Uncertainty and equity: rationales for third party payment in healthcare

Third party payment separates the individual's financial contribution from the volume of care that they consume though, especially with private insurance, there may be a relationship between the amount required to be paid and the volume *predicted* to be used by an individual. Third party payment pools (or 'socialises') resources to smooth out the uncertainties of individuals' health states requiring more expenditure than they are able to make, either as income maintenance (Lewis, 2000: 91) or, more usually, in the form of healthcare. Though judgements about their relative merits may be made, all third party payment systems socialise at least some of the financial risks of ill-health across a group that is distinct from current patients. Unlike out-of-pocket payment, third party payment never limits the value of benefits provided to the sum of an individual's contributions. Indeed, all things being equal, it would be better to save the money in one's own bank, thereby receiving interest and avoiding administration costs, than to participate in a scheme that limited benefits to the value of past contributions.

Third party payment is therefore a partial answer to the problem of an individual's uncertainty about their future healthcare needs (Barr, 2001). None of us can be certain of such needs; even those with 'good genes' and healthy lifestyles may walk under the proverbial bus. It would therefore be difficult for anyone to be confident about being able to afford future necessary healthcare from income or personal savings. Third party payment has the rationale of insulating individuals against unknown risks of both illness itself and of unaffordable costs of treatment. Third party payment can also be a partial answer to the problem of equity, that is to the empirical tendency for the poor and the sick to be the same people, as clearly demonstrated by the existence of wide social class differentials in both mortality and morbidity (*Population Trends 86*, 1996: 15–20). Despite having the greatest healthcare needs, under out-of-pocket payment such people would be least able to afford to have them met. However, the extent to which this is ameliorated by third party payment will depend upon how widely the risks of ill-health are spread and it is clear from the descriptions above that different variants of third party payment achieve this to different extents. Tax-financed systems pool the risks across a whole national population and, other things being equal, spread the risk most equitably. Private insurance, and any system of social insurance which employs a multiplicity of third party payers, are likely (other things being equal) to be less equitable since there exists the probability that poorer, sicker people will be found in some risk pools and richer, healthier people in others. The former group may therefore receive a poorer range of benefits than the latter. Moreover, any type of third party payment system (including, as we shall see below, the NHS) might in practice make charges for, or impose access restrictions upon, certain treatments.

Although these matters seem technical, they are also deeply political in that they manifest different normative assumptions about what risks should be pooled. A private insurance system seeks to compensate for the relatively narrow range of uncertainties related to the individual's health over his or her own lifetime and within his or her own social group. In contrast, a tax-financed system, in socialising risk across a single national population, additionally seeks to compensate for a broader range of socioeconomic inequalities. The latter has a *universalist* rationale, implying a notion of citizenship which includes social rights (Marshall, 1950) in which effective participation by individuals in society is to be secured by state action (Flynn, 1997).

The policy consequences of third party payment

Third party payment systems risk the inflation of demand over time. Such demand increases may be conceptualised in terms derived from the economic concept of 'moral hazard'. *Consumer moral hazard* arises only where some or all of the costs of care are met by the third party payers; it encourages a higher rate of use than would occur if full costs had to be met at the point of use (Pauly, 1968), since the demander assumes that the cost of their usage will be spread over a large number of taxpayers, fund members or policy holders. However, if large numbers of people behave in this way, then total demand (for healthcare and hence for the resources to provide it) *will* rise. Consumer moral hazard in third party payment systems for healthcare is the consequence of divorcing payment for services from their use. Third party payment makes it easier for people to obtain care than would otherwise be the case, but at the same time tempts them to increase their demands. An important qualification to this is that cost and price are not synonymous; the non-money costs of obtaining care can be significant. At the minimum the user must take steps, such as telephoning for an appointment, rearranging a working day, travelling to the surgery or hospital, and perhaps sitting for some time in a crowded waiting area, in order to gain access. Costs can be higher. We may react adversely to the drug which is prescribed or the needle may hurt as it pierces the flesh and the prospect of gastroendoscopy or sigmoidoscopy is hardly pleasant.

Provider moral hazard (or 'supplier-induced demand') arises from information asymmetries; the consumer's lack of knowledge of a highly technical service coincides with a provider's interest in increasing provision and allows the latter to affect demand. Whilst patients do make generalised demands in the sense of arranging a visit to the doctor or being taken to the Accident and Emergency Department, it is typically (though not invariably) the physician or other clinical professional who translates it into a specific demand for antibiotics, pathology tests, a specialist appointment, or a surgical operation. Some accounts cast such professional motivation in material terms. If the clinician is remunerated on a fee-for-service basis, there are clear incentives to maximise supplier-induced demand unless the total fees are 'capped' in some way. The same incentive may exist if the institution which employs the clinician is itself remunerated by the third party payer on any basis which is sensitive to the volume of patients or treatments. From such a perspective, a system in which clinicians were salaried would have the opposite effect of 'underprovision', since there would be no economic incentives to perform beyond the level necessary to retain one's job. However, this seems an unnecessarily narrow perspective on incentives; Donaldson and Gerard (1993: 33) have argued that where providers are salaried and do not themselves have to bear the costs of treatment, simple ignorance of costs may lead to overprovision. There may be professional ethical incentives to provider moral hazard; even if the hospital's budget is not volume-related and clinicians are remunerated by salary or capitation fees, demand might still increase as a result of the clinician's desire to behave ethically, that is to do the best possible (according to their own imperfect opinion) for his or her patient. Supplier-induced demand does occur in out-of-pocket payment systems, but might be limited by the patient's inability or unwillingness to pay; in a third party payment system such limitations are attenuated by the patient's and clinician's mutual knowledge that a third party will meet all or part of the money costs of care (Reinhardt, 1985). Thus, demand in a third party payment system might be expected to increase over time since neither consumers nor providers have the incentive to moderate it. This does not imply the assertion that healthcare demand in such systems is infinite; it is unlikely that demand for healthcare could escalate to the point where all other demands were excluded. It is rather that no real-world third party payment system as yet seems to have experienced an autonomous levelling off of demand.

Whilst the two forms of moral hazard provide the immediate basis for the inflation of demand in third party payment systems, there are a number of secondary factors which may affect the propensity of patients and clinicians to increase their demands. One obvious candidate is the constant invention and development of new medical technologies, many of which are extremely expensive. The pharmaceutical and medical equipment manufacturing industries are important sectors of the economies of the UK, USA and Germany and significant exporters. The term 'technology' encompasses 'drugs, devices and medical and surgical procedures used in medical care and the organisational and supportive systems within which such care is provided' (Office of Technology Assessment, 1978: 2). New approaches to psychotherapy, new packages of care for the elderly, and new multi-professional approaches to the care of stroke victims are therefore new technologies, and indeed may carry costs just as high as new drugs. The mere existence of technologies does not create a demand, which depends upon patients and/or clinicians perceiving that they might be beneficial. Moreover, the inventors and manufacturers of medical technologies have an economic interest in maximising their sales which, if it can be linked to public and professional perceptions of a condition as a 'disease', leads to the 'medicalisation' of conditions not previously thought of in such terms. In the words of Moynihan and Smith (2002), 'many of life's normal processes – birth, ageing, sexuality, unhappiness and death – can be medicalised', including pharmaceutical treatment of male baldness on the grounds that it might lead to panic, mental health problems or poor job prospects, and the transformation of personal shyness into the condition of 'social phobia', treatable by antidepressants.

Another secondary source of demand for healthcare is demographic shift; many countries have an ageing population in both absolute and relative terms, brought about by increasing life expectancy and a falling birth rate. Indeed one major study has suggested that although policy makers have tended to assume that further increases in life expectancy (currently a little under 76 years for British males and 81 for British females: Wanless, 2002: 42) can only be modest, there is apparently no absolute limit to life expectancy (Oeppen and Vaupel, 2002). Older people currently consume greater amounts of hospital care per capita than do younger people; the 75–84 year age group consumes four times as much NHS resource per capita as does the 16–64 group, a comparison that rises to seven times for the 85 and over age group (Glennerster, 2003: 58). However, there are disputes about whether increases in the older groups as a proportion of population necessarily imply continuing increases in demand. Policy makers in the UK have tended to assume that any such increases will be modest (see, for instance, Wanless, 2002: 42–3) and recent evidence suggests that proximity to death is a much more important determinant of hospital usage than age *per se* (Dixon et al., 2004; Seshamani and Gray, 2004). On the other hand, there is likely to be a very substantial increase in the demand for 'long-term care' for older people in residential and nursing homes and in their own homes over the next 30 years (Comas Herrera et al., 2003). Moreover, as the above discussions of moral hazard and medicalisation suggest, there is not necessarily a linear relationship between individuals' health and their demand for care – it has been reported that UK residents' expectations of 'unhealthy' life before death are increasing faster than their total life expectancy (Hebert, 2004).

The net financial impact of new technologies and demographic shift on a health system will depend partly upon whether the former reduce demand elsewhere in the system, either by substituting for other interventions for the same condition or by helping patients to attain a state of health in which they perceive themselves to need less treatment than would otherwise be the case. Klein has linked the effects of demographic and technological change in a pessimistic conclusion:

> *Even if the limitations of medical technology in curing disease and disability are now becoming apparent, there are no such limitations on the scope of health services for providing care for those who cannot be cured. Even if policies of prevention ... were to be successfully introduced, their very success in extending life expectancy would create new demands for alleviating the chronic degenerative diseases of old age. In other words, no policy can ensure that people will drop dead painlessly at the age of eighty, not having troubled the health services previously. (Klein, 1983: 182)*

It is also worth noting that developing technology (for instance, in anaesthetics or 'minimally invasive' surgery) can make interventions safer and subject to increased demand (Seshamani and Gray, 2004: 67).

A final secondary factor is *public demand*, which operates against a background in which healthcare is a prominent public and political issue in the UK, the USA and many other countries. One element of this is the much greater public availability of information about healthcare, with particular emphasis on high profile media reportage about new technologies. The Internet has begun to contribute substantially to the availability of such information (Coiera, 1996). Alongside this growth of information is an apparent increase in the level of activity by patient pressure groups, as we shall see in Chapter 5, usually organised around a particular disease or health condition (Wood, 2000). Such groups (which may also provide advice and other services to their members) are often supported by health professionals from appropriate clinical specialties and, naturally enough, press the appropriate health service bodies for what they perceive to be better services, including new technologies, for themselves. In the UK, these demand factors operate against a background of considerable public support for the NHS as an institution, even though they may be critical of their own experiences as patients. To cite one set of findings from numerous similar examples, 63 percent of respondents to a 2000 opinion poll rated the NHS as the single 'most important national institution', placing it in first place followed by Parliament (12 percent), the police (11 percent), the BBC (4 percent), and (at around 3 percent) the Royal Family, the Bank of England and the Benefits Agency (ICM poll, cited in the *Guardian*, 18 April 2000: 19). In thinking about patient and public demand, it is important to remember that it reflects the *perception* of the demander that healthcare would be good for them. Consequently, consumer moral hazard in healthcare is not necessarily avoided by reference to research into the clinical effectiveness or otherwise of treatments, a matter to which we return in Chapter 3.

Managing healthcare supply and demand

Faced with demands for healthcare fuelled by the kind of factors outlined above, third party payers may not simply respond with increased resources, and indeed one recent study has shown that there is no straightforward relationship between public opinion and NHS expenditure (Soroka and Lim, 2003). More generally:

The modern health care problem can therefore be seen as a reflection of the way healthcare financing has been collectivised, through the sort of risk pooling arrangements outlined above and through the way this process of collectivisation, by breaking the direct link between consumption and payment, removes or weakens budget constraints on consumers of health care resources. The problem facing health care systems is therefore how to reimpose, or reinvent, those constraints, in a world where the collectivisation of finance has to be taken as a given. (Harrison and Moran, 2000: 496)

In response to this situation, governments adopt various (not necessarily mutually exclusive) means of matching supply and demand. These can be roughly classified into *supply-side adjustments*, that is those which aim to increase the resources available for healthcare, and *demand-side adjustments* which aim to reduce or stabilise demand for services. Supply-side adjustments may take the form of measures to increase the flow of revenue to third party payers (tax or contribution increases, or co-payments), or to encourage a higher level of out-of-pocket or private insurance expenditure as assumed substitutes for third party payment. In publicly funded healthcare systems, other supply-side measures include toleration of public sector budget deficits and reallocation of public expenditure priorities so as to increase healthcare expenditure at the expense of other public programmes. In any system, policy makers may seek to improve the productive efficiency of the healthcare sector by a range of management and organisational measures aimed at codifying clinical practice and modifying the incentives facing actors in the system, a strategy further examined in Chapter 3. Examples include tighter management in general as well as some more specific techniques such as 'managed competition' (Bruce and Jonsson, 1996) and 'managed care' (Robinson and Steiner, 1998).

In contrast, demand-side adjustments are aimed at reducing or containing demand for care, a process for which we employ the term 'rationing', whilst recognising that this usage is not without its critics, including UK politicians. Some demand-side measures operate *implicitly* so far as the patient is concerned. Examples include cost barriers which partially offset the effect of consumer moral hazard. Such costs may be financial (thus charges for services are a deterrent), but spatial, psychological and procedural barriers may also be effective; remote or highly centralised facilities, user-unfriendliness and strict 'gatekeeping' criteria tend to reduce demand. Other demand-side measures are *explicit*, that is consist of more-or-less clear rules about patient entitlement; for instance, such rules may exclude certain procedures or drugs. The desirability of implicitness and explicitness is much debated. Some proponents of implicitness (Hoffenberg, 1992; Mechanic, 1992; for a philosophical discussion, see Calabresi and Bobbit, 1978) have justified their position on the grounds that explicit decisions are too brutal for society to contemplate, whilst others (Hunter, 1993; Klein et al., 1996) have concentrated on their conceptual and practical difficulties. Proponents of various degrees of explicitness (Harrison and Hunter, 1994; New and LeGrand, 1996) often stress transparency as a prerequisite of fairness.

Whether implicit or explicit, rationing mechanisms are necessarily underpinned by one or more of a range of criteria that may themselves be explicit or implicit and may reflect a range of political and other normative positions. Five criteria are perhaps the most widely advocated. First, the *rule of rescue* gives priority to persons in acute or life-threatening conditions, thereby locating moral content in trying rather than in succeeding. This is likely to generate significant opportunity costs in terms of 'wasted' effort, though it might be argued that this is a legitimate public preference (Goodin and Wilensky, 1984). Second, *deserts* are sometimes used as the basis of an argument for exclusion, often in the context of a health state which is considered to be self-inflicted (for instance by smoking or participation in dangerous sports). Third, prospective *effectiveness* of a healthcare intervention is widely argued to be a common-sensical rationing criterion (Evans, 1990). The existence of uncertainties about effectiveness undermines a good deal of the force of arguments that *whatever* is effective should be pro-vided, though the 'prudent insurance principle' (Dworkin, 1994) provides a thought exper-iment for dealing with such difficulties. Fourth, *cost-effectiveness* and *cost-utility* are espoused by those who maintain that the cost, as well as the degree of effectiveness, of interventions should be considered. This position has given rise to a number of artificial measures of health outcome such as Quality (or Disability) - Adjusted Life Years, whose theoretical properties are utilitarian in the sense that they aim at the maximisation of health gain in return for any given level of expenditure. Finally, as noted above, third party payment systems are under-pinned by a desire to enhance *equity*, that is to ameliorate the position of people who cannot afford the care from which they might benefit. *Equity* and *equality* are therefore concerned with the distribution of services or of health status respectively, a criterion which may trade off against cost-effectiveness.

An historical sketch of supply and demand in the NHS

As noted above, policy measures may focus on either the supply of resources to the NHS or on various means of reducing or containing demand. These are treated separately here, but it should be noted that in practice, governments often develop parallel policies so that both supply and demand are addressed simultaneously.

The supply of NHS resources

Many of the ideas that were to constitute the social policy of the postwar Labour government had previously been brought together in the wartime Beveridge Report (Beveridge, 1942). Although the need for a health service occupied relatively little space in the Report (which concentrated largely on social security), it contained the key assumptions that doctors would limit unnecessary demands for healthcare (Webster, 1988: 36) and that the impact of mak-ing medical services freely available would be to produce a population that would be health-ier than before in absolute terms. As a result, it seemed, the workforce would be more productive and in due course, the costs of the proposed health service would fall (Beveridge, 1942). Early experience of the NHS, established in 1948, suggested a different picture. For each of the first few years, it proved necessary for the government to obtain supplementary estimates from Parliament in order to meet the unanticipated level of demand (Klein, 2001: 26; Rivett, 1998: 110; for a detailed account, see Webster, 1988: 133–43). Contemporary interpretations saw the situation in terms of the bursting of a 'dam' of accumulated demand from people previously unable to afford care, and especially dentures and spectacles (Rivett, 1998: 80; Webster, 1988: 134). This experience led to the Labour government's decision to legislate in 1950 for prescription, dental and optical charges. Labour introduced the latter before losing office in 1951, though prescription charges were not introduced until 1952, after the election of a Conservative government (Rivett, 1998: 46, 55, 110) and were briefly abolished between 1966 and 1968 (Office of Health Economics, 2003: 39).

As early as 1949, it was argued that NHS cost estimates had ignored the effects of an ageing population and of perpetual technological advance. Moreover, contrary to Beveridge's assumptions, there was not a finite quantity of ill-health into which the NHS would make inroads. Rather, cures for particular diseases simply meant that patients survived to suffer from other, more expensive ones (Roberts, 1949, 1952). However, the Guillebaud Committee on the cost of the NHS, established by the government in 1952, reached the conclusion that the unexpected increases in NHS expenditure were largely the consequence of failure to account for inflation and that after 1951 NHS expenditure had actually fallen as a proportion of gross national product (Committee of Enquiry, 1956). The report did not recommend any further charges, and was unenthusiastic about existing dental and optical charges, recognising that they might act as a deterrent to patients who needed services. Guillebaud's reassuring conclusions can be seen as having set a positive tone for health politics for the next 30 years and perhaps even as having virtually removed the NHS from party politics (Klein, 2001: 25; Rivett, 1998: 114). By its tenth anniversary in 1958 the Labour and Conservative Parties were vying to gain political credit from, respectively, the NHS's creation and expansion (Klein, 2001: 48).

Yet even the founding Minister of Health of the NHS had entertained doubts about the value of 'the ceaseless cascade of medicine ... pouring down British throats' (Bevan, quoted in Webster, 1988: 145), whilst a later Minister of Health subsequently reflected both that rationing was inevitable and that explicit criteria should be employed, but that:

> the task is not made any easier by the political convention that the existence of any rationing at all must be strenuously denied. The public are encouraged to believe that rationing in medical care was banished by the [NHS], and that the very idea of rationing being applied to medical care is immoral and repugnant. Consequently when they, and the medical profession too, come face to face in practice with the various forms of rationing to which the [NHS] must resort [such as hospital waiting lists], the usual result is bewilderment, frustration and irritation. (Powell, 1966: 17)

It is therefore hardly surprising that no explicit attempts to manage demand were made, and prescription, dental and optical charges were seen as a temporary necessity rather than as an ongoing means of reducing demand. However, the 1950s and early 1960s were a period of economic austerity for the UK generally and of stagnation in the level of NHS resources more specifically. Table 1.1 shows changes in the latter, expressed both as a percentage of gross domestic product (GDP; roughly speaking, the national income) and in real terms, that is, adjusted for inflation. (It should be noted that these adjustments are made in terms of inflation across the whole UK economy rather than in terms of the usually rather higher

Table 1.1   NHS expenditure (UK, 1949 to 2003)

Calendar year & political party in office	% Gross domestic product	Real terms (adjusted by GDP deflator at market prices) Index (1949 = 100)
1949 Labour	3.46	100
1950	3.62	109
1951 Conservative	3.39	105
1952	3.20	99
1953	3.07	98
1954	3.00	100
1955	3.02	104
1956	3.07	107
1957	3.15	110
1958	3.21	114
1959	3.29	122
1960	3.37	131
1961	3.44	138
1962	3.43	138
1963	3.43	145
1964 Labour	3.43	155
1965	3.56	163
1966	3.68	173
1967	3.79	182
1968	3.81	189
1969	3.70	188
1970 Conservative	3.84	201
1971	3.91	208
1972	4.03	223
1973	4.00	235
1974 Labour	4.58	268
1975	4.85	281
1976	4.84	288
1977	4.63	283
1978	4.53	286
1979 Conservative	4.49	290
1980	4.88	310
1981	5.11	320
1982	5.09	324
1983	5.00	329
1984	4.96	335
1985	4.83	339
1986	4.88	355
1987	4.86	370
1988	5.05	404
1989	5.00	408
1990	5.10	420
1991	5.47	445
1992	5.80	472
1993	5.80	483
1994	5.84	507
1995	5.83	521
1996	5.71	525
1997 New Labour	5.64	535
1998	5.61	548

Table 1.1 (Continued)

Calendar year & political party in office	% Gross domestic product	Real terms (adjusted by GDP deflator at market prices) Index (1949 = 100)
1999	5.79	582
2000	6.00	628
2001	6.33	676
2002	6.72	732
2003	7.08	788
2004 estimated	7.46	856
2005 estimated	7.71	908

Source: Office of Health Economics (2005: Table 2.12). Cited with permission.

inflation in the prices of the narrower range of goods and services that dominate NHS expenditure: Office of Health Economics, 2005.) It is evident that the early years of the NHS saw decline on both measures after a high point in 1950. The NHS did not grow at the rate of the economy and it was not until the mid-1960s that the 1950 level was regained. Expenditure in real terms also fell in the first part of this period, regaining its 1950 level in 1957, and was static in the second half of the 1970s in the aftermath of the 1973 oil price crisis, the tripling of the government budget deficit and the consequent necessity for the UK to secure a loan from the International Monetary Fund (Ramsay, 2002: 16, 24). From this period onwards, government decisions on NHS expenditure were expressed as 'cash limits' rather than in volume terms (Likierman, 1988: 12). This means that budgets are stated as an amount of cash, alongside a stated assumption about inflation in the relevant period; it follows that if actual inflation exceeds the estimate, the budget is worth less in volume terms and vice versa.

Thereafter, NHS real expenditure grew constantly without any simple relationship to the political party in government or to the rate of economic growth. However, annual percentage increases by the 1980s had fallen to their lowest average since the 1950s (for a more detailed discussion, see Appleby, 1992: 31–52; Glennerster, 1992: 64–7) but were subsequently rather higher. As Table 1.1 suggests, the New Labour governments since 2000 have placed great emphasis on the expansion of NHS funding, and in 2000 the intention was announced to increase the UK percentage of GDP accounted for by health to the 'European national average'. The precise nature of this commitment was open to considerable interpretation; the timescale, the definition of 'Europe' (especially given the accession to the European Union of ten new members in 2004) and the question of whether the comparator is total health expenditure or simply public expenditure on health are obvious sources of interpretive flexibility (Appleby and Boyle, 2001). Table 1.2 shows that whilst UK total health care expenditure is rather low in relation to most comparable countries and to the (15-member) European average, the UK public proportion of this total is slightly higher in relation to the comparators. If the policy were to be interpreted as an intention for the UK to approximate to an EU pattern, the implication would be for UK *private* healthcare expenditure to increase. However, although it has since been officially stated that the aspiration was

Table 1.2 International comparisons of health expenditure (selected countries and groups of countries, circa 2003)

	Total health expenditure 2003 (% GDP)	Proportion of health expenditure publicly funded (%)
Australia (2002)	9.3	67
Austria (2002)	7.6	70
Belgium	9.6	71 (2002)
Canada	9.9	70
Denmark	9.0	83
Finland	7.4	77
France	10.1	76
Germany	11.1	78
Ireland (2002)	7.3	75
Italy	8.4	75
Japan (2002)	7.9	81
Netherlands	9.8	62
New Zealand	8.1	79
Norway	10.3	84
Portugal	9.6	70
Spain	7.7	71
Sweden (2002)	9.2	85
Switzerland	11.5	59
United Kingdom	8.4	85
United States	15.0	44
OECD weighted average	11.1	60
EU15 weighted average	9.4	76

Source: adapted from Office of Health Economics (2005: Tables 2.4, 2.8).

not a precise one (Ferriman, 2001) expansion in public funding for the NHS has continued to be announced through to 2007.

The main source of NHS revenue has always been taxation, modestly supplemented from national insurance receipts (Glennerster, 1992: 167), with the contribution made by revenue from patient charges constituting only about 2 percent of the total in recent decades (Office of Health Economics, 2005: Table 2.25), largely because of the wide exemptions available, including children, persons over 60 years of age, income support recipients, expectant and nursing mothers, and sufferers from specified diseases (Glennerster, 1992: 167). As a result, only some 15 percent of GP prescriptions are subject to charge (Glennerster, 2003: 50). (For a detailed discussion of NHS charges, see Appleby, 1992: 47–8; Glennerster, 1992: 167–9.)

One consequence of funding the NHS from general taxation is that governments are able to reassess their public expenditure priorities. Table 1.3 shows striking changes in the distribution of UK public expenditure between sectors over the last 50 years, and that the NHS has been a principal beneficiary. A comparison with defence is especially striking; in 1950 defence consumed double the expenditure of the NHS, by the mid-1970s the two sectors were of equal size, and by the mid-1990s, the NHS was twice the size of defence (14.2 percent versus 7.1 percent of total in 1995/96). Public funding also means that the NHS (along with other public services) can be supported by government budget deficit, that is borrowing from the

Table 1.3   Distribution of UK public expenditure by sector (percentages for selected years 1950–2000)

Year	NHS	Defence	Education	Housing	Social security	Other (inc. social services)
1950	11.8	21.3	9.2	8.4	16.7	32.6
1960	10.4	19.8	11.0	6.0	17.9	34.7
1970	10.7	13.2	13.6	7.1	21.1	34.2
1980	12.7	12.5	13.9	9.2	27.8	23.9
1990/01	12.5	10.0	12.4	2.7	31.2	31.2
2000/01	15.5	7.1	12.7	1.3	36.4	27.0
2004/05	17.7	6.0	13.7	1.6	34.9	26.1

Source: adapted from Office of Health Economics (2005: Table 2.27).

public and from institutions by means of marketable and non-marketable securities, such as 'gilt-edged securities' and National Savings issues respectively.

The efficiency with which health services are provided is clearly a factor that determines the supply of such services; if a given level of services can be provided for less resources, the balance of resources might be used to provide more services. We shall see in Chapter 4 that UK governments since the early 1980s have made extensive efforts to employ techniques of management and performance improvement to this end.

Government attitudes to private healthcare expenditure have varied sharply over time, though it is in any case far from clear whether increases in private expenditure really do reduce demand on the NHS (Glennerster, 1992: 70). Under pressure from non-professional health workers' trade unions, the Labour government in the mid-1970s sought the complete separation of NHS and private provision through the progressive closure of 'paybeds', that is private beds in NHS hospitals. Opposition by the medical profession led to a compromise in which only modest reductions were made, and indeed it seems probable that the policy also stimulated the expansion of private hospitals and private health insurance coverage (Klein, 2001: 131–3; Rivett, 1998: 296–7; for a detailed account, see Webster, 1996: 620–7). In contrast, subsequent Conservative governments terminated the phasing-out process in 1979 (Rivett, 1998: 349) and from 1990 to 1998 allowed income tax relief on private healthcare insurance premiums to people over 60 years of age, though with little evidence of any consequent expansion in the uptake of policies (Appleby, 1992: 22, 29; Klein, 2001: 162). The coverage of private health insurance has been growing since the mid-1970s and now stands at about 6.7 million persons (a little under 4 million policyholders) (Office of Health Economics, 2005: Table 2.29). The private insurance market is dominated by BUPA and PPP (both not-for-profits) and a commercial carrier, the Norwich Union; after a period of apparently fierce competition in the 1980s the market has grown only modestly. Perhaps the greatest significance of the private sector over the last decade has been its contribution (in excess of £300 million) to NHS funding through its use of paybeds and other NHS facilities (Hansard, 31 January 2002: column 556W).

For capital acquisition, the NHS after 1995 became increasingly reliant on Private Finance Initiative (PFI) schemes, later termed Public-Private Partnerships (PPP), generally receiving capital grants from public funds only where it had been demonstrated that private capital had been sought unsuccessfully (for technical details and a historical summary, see Heald, 1997; for a critique, see Pollock et al., 2004). The core of PFI/PPP is the conversion, from the perspective of public finance, of what would otherwise be capital expenditure into revenue expenditure. Private sector organisations, conversely, inject capital in the expectation of a revenue return. Typically, a consortium of private organisations is involved, including at least a construction firm, a bank, and a facilities management firm, all in a complex legal relationship. Schemes may involve design, building, financing and operation of new hospitals, or parts of them, typically with a 20 to 60 year payback period, perhaps involving the sale of NHS land and buildings to private companies. PFI/PPP can therefore be seen as the NHS purchasing services rather than capital assets (effectively converting capital to revenue), thereby spreading the cost over many years and taking advantage of the assumed relative efficiencies of private sector construction and management.

Managing demand in historical perspective

We have seen that the first 40 years of the NHS saw little explicit policy debate about the need to manage the supply/demand relationship. Direct government control over such a large proportion of UK health expenditure naturally facilitated expenditure restraint, especially since the introduction in the 1970s of a system of 'cash limits' under which the annual budget for many government activities, including most of the NHS, was established in cash terms at the beginning of the financial year and not adjusted for any subsequent changes in salary or other costs, or for increases in service usage (Glennerster, 1992: 57). Thus official policies for meeting demand were largely on the supply side; NHS resources could not be expanded as quickly as would be ideal, but progress could be made. This approach is generally consonant with the original legal basis of the NHS, re-enacted in subsequent legislation:

> It shall be the duty of the Minister of Health ... to promote the establishment ... of a comprehensive health service designed to secure improvement in the physical and mental health of the people ... and the prevention, diagnosis and treatment of illness ... (National Health Service Act 1946 s1(1))

Thus, unlike (say) social security, UK health legislation does not give specified entitlements to citizens. This raises the question of how demand was kept in balance with the uneven growth in resources. One means was the restriction of the prescription of new (and often technically difficult to produce) drugs to consultants (specialists). For instance, neither cortisone nor the antibiotic tetracycline could be prescribed by GPs until 1954 (Rivett, 1998: 55). But the Guillebaud Committee (see above) rejected any need for a more generally restricted prescribing list (Rivett, 1998: 113), a possibility that was not resurrected until 1984, and it seems likely that until the 1990s most of the burden of rationing was carried by a number of processes that were not officially recognised or explicit to patients.

First, doctors employed more or less pragmatic criteria to decide whom and whom not to treat. The concept of 'professional autonomy' is considered in some detail in Chapter 2, but we can note here that the NHS had been constructed on the principle that 'doctors ... must remain free to direct their clinical knowledge and personal skill... in the way ... they feel to be best' (Ministry of Health, 1944: 26). The role of professional autonomy in allowing clinicians to match supply and demand was identified by two American researchers of the NHS; their observations are neatly summarised by their own examples:

> *By various means, physicians ... try to make the denial of care seem routine or optimal. Confronted by a person older than the prevailing age of cut-off for dialysis, the British GP tells the victim of chronic renal failure or his family that nothing can be done except to make the patient as comfortable as possible in the time remaining. The British nephrologist [kidney specialist] tells the family of a patient who is difficult to handle that dialysis would be painful and burdensome and that the patient would be more comfortable without it. (Aaron and Schwartz, 1984: 101)*

This summary also neatly conveys the political advantages of implicit rationing. Despite the fact that treatment is being refused, the impression is nevertheless left that the best course of action has been adopted. Expressed more bluntly, implicit rationing cloaks a potentially highly divisive issue with political invisibility (Harrison, 1988: 124). It is important to note that, although Aaron and Schwartz's example is dramatic (since without dialysis, the patient with end-stage renal failure will not survive), the same pragmatism underlay more mundane clinical decisions.

A second implicit mechanism by which supply and demand were managed was, and indeed remains, the system that prevents patients from obtaining access to secondary (specialist) care other than on referral by a GP. Although this arrangement has pre-NHS roots as a means of preventing competition for patients between consultants and GPs (Lewis, 1986), its logic is also that the GP is able to deal with minor or routine conditions and possesses the knowledge to refer more difficult cases to the appropriate type of specialist (Rivett, 1998: 81–2). It is almost certain that without such a system, to which the metaphor of 'gatekeeping' has been applied, patient demands for specialist care would be greater. Moreover, there is also indirect evidence that GPs' referral decisions are not simply a reaction to patients' clinical conditions but are also informed by the length of the relevant waiting list; the greater the waiting time, the less likely a referral (Goldacre et al., 1987; Smethurst and Williams, 2001).

We noted above that patient charges for such services as prescription drugs and dental care contribute to NHS revenue. However, charges militate against some of the objectives of third party payment; the Guillebaud Committee considered that charges would act as a deterrent to patients, and indeed they were seen precisely as such by the postwar Labour government (Webster, 1988: 145). An additional area of charges derives from the fact that *social* care is provided by local government authorities. Some older and disabled people may be entitled to 'direct payments' to allow them to purchase care packages to suit themselves (Rummery, 2002) but other service users may be the subject of substantial (means-tested) user charges. Over many years there has been a tendency for the boundary between what is defined as healthcare and what is defined as social care to shift towards the latter, in effect introducing charges for continuing care where none previously existed (Clement, 2003), though this has not been an explicit policy.

It is clear, then, that demand management methods that are wholly or largely implicit to patients (and public) have been predominant since the creation of the NHS, and indeed continue to be so. Despite the very early recognition of the necessity of rationing outlined above, attempts by policy makers to discuss explicit priorities seem to have commenced only in the mid-1970s. The earliest prominent example was the consultative document *Priorities for Health and Social Services in England* (DHSS, 1976), which sought to 'establish rational and systematic priorities throughout the health and personal social services' (1976: 1) for the following three years (see also DHSS, 1977). The specific priorities proposed were services for older people and those with (in today's terminology) mental health problems and learning difficulties, with consequent restraint in the growth of acute services. The same period saw the development of explicit formulae for the geographical distribution of financial resources throughout the NHS (Resource Allocation Working Party, 1976), whose logic and general approach continues to inform such allocations today (for a summary, see Glennerster, 2003: 63–7). However, since the early 1990s, there has been an increased tendency for policy to be conceived in terms of more explicit approaches. A consistent thread within this discourse has been the notion of *effectiveness* as a criterion for making decisions about what clinical interventions and services the NHS should, and should not, provide. It seems likely that the inception of both the NHS Research and Development (R&D) Programme (see Chapter 3) and the NHS quasi-market (often misnamed 'internal market'; see Chapter 4) are associated with the prominence of these ideas, which also gave rise to a good deal of academic writing along the same lines. Despite this prominence, empirical studies of the NHS in the 1990s provide little evidence of the successful application of the explicit criterion of clinical effectiveness, suggesting that such decisions encounter difficulties both of robust research information that can be applied and of legitimacy in seeming to deny services to patients (Harrison and Wistow, 1992; Klein et al., 1996: Ch 5). Thus the usual outcome was for denials to be applied to what were perceived as in some sense marginal interventions (such as tattoo removal, cosmetic breast surgery and gender reassignment), and in any case to be applied in a manner that left physicians with some leeway to decide in specific cases (Harrison and Wistow, 1992; Klein et al., 1996: 68–9). The negative news media treatment of the case of 'Child B', a leukaemia patient denied a second bone-marrow transplant on the clinical grounds that it would both be distressing for the patient and unlikely to be effective (Ham and Pickard, 1998), is unlikely to have encouraged the NHS authorities to be more explicit. The differential local availability of treatments such as *in vitro* fertilisation (IVF), dubbed 'postcode rationing' by the news media, also proved difficult to defend (Klein et al., 1996: 75–7). Just as 30 years before, policymakers of the 1990s continued to be uncomfortable with the notion of NHS rationing, a discomfort aptly represented by the alleged refusal of a Secretary of State to attend a conference with 'rationing' in its title. Whatever the abstract arguments in favour of explicitness, the various mechanisms of implicit rationing had served to keep the issue away from the political agenda (Harrison, 1988: 124). Subsequent policy on this topic has paid some attention to the need to legitimise itself more carefully.

Contemporary approaches to managing supply and demand

We have seen that recent public policy has allocated additional resources to the NHS. Of course, this is insufficient of itself to remove any further need for supply/demand management and many of the longstanding implicit rationing mechanisms described above (such as GP referral and professional autonomy) remain important (Sheaff et al., 2002). The early years of the twenty first century have, however, seen the development of three 'big ideas' for managing the supply and demand of NHS care. One of these is a supply-side policy: the aspiration that NHS efficiency can be greatly improved by the organisational separation of acute and elective care, with the latter increasingly provided by specialist organisations, often privately owned and often importing foreign medical staff, albeit at NHS expense. We deal with this in Chapter 4. The remaining two ideas are the subject of this section. The first can be seen as a more careful attempt to introduce rationing on grounds of the effectiveness (and cost-effectiveness) of medical interventions, and is centred on the work of the National Institute for Clinical Excellence (NICE). The second idea, developed in the Wanless Reports of 2001–4, is that demands for NHS care might be reduced by public health measures to encourage a healthier population.

Rationing authoritatively: the National Institute for Clinical Excellence

Prior to its general election victory in 1997, the Labour Party concentrated very much on criticising the policies of the then Conservative government, rarely making more than the most generalised pronouncements in respect of its own policy (Labour Party, 1994, 1995). The proposal for NICE was one of several new NHS institutions announced in the White Paper *The New NHS: Modern, Dependable* (Secretary of State for Health, 1997). The brief account of NICE given in the White Paper focused very much on the production and dissemination of evidence-based clinical guidelines (1997: 58). We shall examine this topic in greater detail in Chapter 3, but the relevant point for the present account is that NICE, as envisaged at this time, was to be primarily a vehicle for influencing clinical practice in line with research evidence, so-called 'evidence-based medicine'. However, when a more detailed account of NICE's functions was published in 1998, the emphasis appeared to have changed somewhat towards national appraisal of the effectiveness and cost-effectiveness of clinical interventions and subsequent authoritative advice to the NHS on what treatments should be available (NHS Executive, 1998: 14–24). Although some emphasis was also placed on standardisation as a means of ending 'postcode rationing', the clear intent was now for NICE to offer a nationally authoritative vehicle for rationing according to explicit criteria. It may be that this shift in emphasis was partly the result of a political desire to avoid repetition of the high-profile case of the drug Viagra, an apparently effective, but expensive treatment for male impotence. The Secretary of State for Health found himself in the position of pronouncing, on grounds of affordability, that only one treatment per week could be prescribed by GPs and that only for men whose condition arose from specified diseases (Dewar, 1999; Dodds-Smith, 2000; Klein, 2001: 214; McDonald, 2000: 569–72).

NICE was established in 1999 and undertakes about 20 (originally planned at between 30 and 50) evidence-based appraisals per annum of new or existing clinical interventions.

Such appraisals may result in recommendations to the Department of Health that particular treatments should not be introduced to the NHS without further trials, or in the production of 'clinical guidelines' for the management of relevant medical conditions (NHS Executive, 1998: 15–7). Appraisal is largely in the form of cost-utility analysis, that is expressed in terms of quality-adjusted life years (QALYs). Referrals to NICE take about 12 months to determine and by 2005 it had reported on 117 topics (Raftery, 2006). About half of appraisals have taken the form of qualifications about the clinical circumstances in which the treatment should be employed, with the remaining half split equally between straightforward negative and positive recommendations. Since 2003 the NHS has been legally required to implement most NICE recommendations and the government argues that the necessary funds are included in its existing allocations.

Nevertheless, it is clear that NICE's recommendations are not always regarded as authoritative by patients and patient groups. In part, this is because much of the work of NICE's appraisals committees is conducted under terms of commercial confidentiality and may therefore be seen as lacking transparency (Consumers Association, 2001; Quennell, 2003). Perhaps more importantly, the widely publicised case of Interferon beta (a drug for relapsing-remitting multiple sclerosis) has shown that it is politically extremely difficult for negative recommendations to be sustained in the face of patient and pharmaceutical company demand (Syrett, 2003). We examine this case in detail in Chapter 7. (NICE was renamed on 1 April 2005, when it took on the functions of the Health Development Agency and became the National Institute for Health and Clinical Excellence.)

'Fully-engaged' healthy behaviour: the Wanless Reports

In 2001, Derek Wanless, a former banking chief executive, was asked by the Chancellor of the Exchequer to report on 'the financial and other resources required to ensure that the NHS can provide a publicly funded, comprehensive, high quality service on the basis of clinical need and not ability to pay' (Wanless, 2001: 2). The two resulting reports (Wanless, 2001, 2002) addressed their terms of reference through a series of 'scenarios' defined in terms of the degree of assumed 'engagement' on the part of healthcare providers and patients/public respectively. Thus Wanless's 'fully-engaged' scenario assumed that providers would readily seek efficiency increases and that patients and the public would recognise and act upon the relationship between their health and their personal behaviour. Thus there would be increases in life expectancy, reductions in the proportion of life years spent in ill-health, sharp declines in obesity and smoking, better diets and more exercise (all with consequent narrowing of socioeconomic differentials in health); although very old people would make more use of hospital care, other people would make much greater use of self-care (for instance through pharmacists) with a consequent reduction in hospital usage (Wanless, 2002: 39–41). Unsurprisingly, this scenario was estimated as requiring the smallest (though still substantial) increases in future NHS resourcing. The government's 2002 budget settlement for the NHS was directly in line with this estimate (Towse, 2004: 6), implying a policy commitment to bringing about the underlying assumptions of the scenario in terms of both provider and public/patient 'engagement'.

According to the Treasury's website, the report is 'evidence-based' (www.hm-treasury.gov.uk/consultations_and_legislation/wanless/consult_wanless_final.cfm, accessed 10 August 2004) and indeed epidemiological commentators seem to agree that the report's demographic assumptions are plausible (Seshamani and Gray, 2004) and that condition-specific improvements, such as in coronary heart disease (McPherson, 2004), are achievable. Following a consultation period, the White Paper *Choosing Health* (Department of Health, 2004b) was published, promising action plans on food and health and on physical activity, along with enhanced services to encourage smoking cessation, though (unlike Scotland) initially stopping short of a legal ban on smoking in enclosed public spaces.

Wanless's 'fully-engaged' scenario seems relatively convincing in its underlying arguments that healthcare demand does not increase inexorably with an ageing population (as we noted above) and that the incidence of health problems such as heart disease can be reduced by behavioural changes in the population. However, it also important to note that there is no necessary relationship between the health status of populations and their demand for healthcare (Parkin et al., 1989); for instance, the relationship between infant mortality rates and health spending in developed countries seems virtually random, whilst the relationship between health spending and per capita GDP is very strong (Office of Health Economics, 2005: Figure 2.8), consistent with the argument that richer populations demand more healthcare. In short, it does not follow that, even if the desired population behaviour changes can be brought about and the desired health improvements occur, the reductions in patient demand will follow (Lewis et al., 2000: 510–1).

Interpreting third party payment

Since the late nineteenth century, western states have tended to become more directly involved in the financing or provision of services related to health. The logic for some such services depends on the notion of 'public consumption goods' (Laver, 1997: 29 ff). For example, measures for controlling infectious disease need to be applied to a population if they are to be effective in protecting individuals. An effective sewage disposal system for a single household will not protect its members from such disease, because they will have to mix in a world outside that household. A more comprehensive sewage system would lead to benefits for all but, since no-one could be excluded from its benefits, there would be little incentive for beneficiaries to contribute voluntarily towards the costs of its construction and maintenance. Consequently, the argument runs, the sewage system will simply not be provided unless people are compelled to contribute, either through taxation and/or legal requirements to install systems. This reasoning, which also applies to public health measures aimed at reducing other forms of environmental pollution (and, with variants, to vaccination and immunisation) provides a classic justification for state involvement in health. Yet it is health and medical *services* for individuals, rather than such public health measures, that in most developed countries constitute the most prominent elements in public policy. We have seen that third party payment for such medical services can be justified in terms of a number of rationales related to risk pooling and perhaps to equity or fairness. However, we have also seen that it presents what seems to be a somewhat intractable problem for third party payers: how to manage the demand–supply relationship. In countries where government is itself the third party payer (such as the UK) or has been heavily involved in establishing or regulating a third party payment system (as is typical in social insurance systems), this raises the question of why governments persist with such systems. Governments' real motives for supporting such systems are not necessarily related directly to the formal rationales outlined above, and there may be more pragmatic reasoning at work.

Pickstone (2000: 2–3) has suggested a public policy rationale that has changed over time. In this account, the early twentieth century was characterised by 'productionist' medicine, that is the assumption that medicine would contribute to the establishment of strong and healthy workforces and armed forces. The British school medical service, established in 1907, was famously the outcome of the discovery that almost half of volunteers to join the British army at the time of the 1899–1902 Boer War were deemed medically unfit to enlist (Baggott, 2000: 38; Perkin, 1989: 157–64). Later in the century, as we have seen, the rationale for public provision of medicine in the UK proposed by the Beveridge Report included the assumption that such provision would contribute to the return of the sick to the workforce so that health expenditure would be investment rather than consumption (Watkin, 1975: 80). By mid-century, however, the emphasis had largely shifted to what Pickstone terms 'communitarian' medicine. This notion that the wider availability of medicine, either through charitable or collectivised provision, would contribute to the development of social solidarity in the population is clearly discernible in classic British social policy texts such as *The Gift Relationship* (Titmuss, 1973). Pickstone (2000: 12–6) has noted how the productionist model of medicine as a national economic investment has been displaced by changes in technologies of war (less reliant on manpower), in the nature of paid work (towards service rather than manufacturing, to 'skill rather than brawn') and by recognition that increasing life expectancy implies continuing healthcare consumption beyond working age. We have already noted no clear relationship between countries' health expenditure and macro levels of population health such as life expectancy, and alternative explanations, such as nutrition, have been advanced to explain secular improvements in such measures (McKeown, 1980). Thus, what Pickstone terms 'consumerist' medicine has become the rule, driven by post-1960 emphases on choice in lifestyle, expectation of good health and good medical services and, by the 1970s a cult of fitness and notion of the body as a sexual commodity for individual investment. This coincides with a situation where governments have begun to redefine their role as the satisfaction of citizen demands, a contemporary policy emphasis that we shall examine in more detail in Chapter 5. Thus, 'medical care is [now] supported by western governments, not to increase the strength of populations, but to meet the demands of potential consumers in ways not so unequal as to provoke effective political resentment' (Pickstone, 2000: 16).

In the remainder of this chapter, we explore two contrasting theoretical approaches that address both the political rationale for welfare expenditure and its potential long-term consequences. Although these approaches are associated with opposite ends of the political spectrum, both posit an inherent crisis of such expenditure. One, based largely on neo-Marxist analysis, argues that state welfare services, including health services, exist to provide specific benefits to capitalism. However, unanticipated consequences in the form of rising demand have created a potentially irresolvable 'crisis of the welfare state'. The other, very much associated with the 'new right', applies economic analysis to political matters, arguing that welfare budgets rise inexorably as public service bureaucratic elites pursue their own interests and as other social groups seek gains for themselves at wider public expense.

Crisis of the welfare state? Neo–Marxist analysis

The notion that welfare states are 'in crisis' was pervasive in the 1980s and 1990s, with academic analyses forecasting such a crisis beginning as long ago as the early 1970s, though now somewhat out of fashion. In summary, the argument is that a capitalist state undertakes activities (the 'welfare state') which are against the short-term, though in the long-term, interests of capitalists; they become susceptible to pressures in the short term such that they cannot be supported in economic terms, yet are difficult to dismantle in political terms. Much of the academic writing concerning the perceived crisis employs Marxian language, but at the same time contains much that is not distinctively Marxist, employing such concepts as interest groups and public opinion. A noted example of such analysis is that of O'Connor (1973: 6–7). He distinguishes between basic types of state welfare expenditure, some of which (including health) are regarded as contributing to more than one function. 'Social investment' increases labour productivity through the provision of physical infrastructure such as roads and utilities that no single capitalist could afford. 'Social consumption' reduces the reproduction costs of labour through such programmes as education, social insurance and minimum health services. Both social investment and social consumption support capitalism materially. In contrast, 'social expenses' maintain social harmony; as a way of socialising the indirect costs of private production (including ill-health: Taylor-Gooby and Dale, 1981: 155) they are necessary to legitimate capitalism but otherwise not directly beneficial to capital (O'Connor, 1973: 150 ff). Thus, the state seeks to head off possible social unrest by a process of 'reform' (Miliband, 1977: 87), including the provision of social welfare services (Mishra, 1984: xi).

These two forms of expenditure are undertaken by the state. But other than possible surpluses from state enterprises, it has no resources of its own, being dependent upon taxation of the private economy. If economic performance declines, state institutions face a contradiction. On one hand there is pressure from capitalists to reduce taxation and on the other, pressure from the public to extend the welfare state, or at least acquiesce in rising costs of benefits. If government expenditure rises, a 'fiscal crisis' occurs; if the welfare state is cut a 'legitimacy crisis' is risked:

> *Given a low level of productivity growth and the ability of labour to protect real wages levels, it is impossible to finance this growing level of state expenditure in a way that does not worsen inflation, or growth, or both. (Gough, 1979: 126)*

The 'fiscal crisis' occurs because welfare state expenditure rises faster than taxes can be raised in a political system where interest groups, such as business lobbies and organised labour can

employ state power for their own ends (O'Connor, 1973: 9). This latter argument is more pluralist or elitist than distinctively Marxian. Indeed, in later work O'Connor specifically identifies individualism as the driving force of an 'accumulation crisis' (O'Connor, 1984). As Mishra (1984: 73) and Offe (1984: 148) note, the architects of welfare states tended to see the two functions as being complementary; for instance, the British NHS was intended to ensure a healthy workforce, thereby both helping to pay for itself and providing a legitimate response to political demands at the end of a major war (Watkin, 1975). It is only when carried beyond a certain point that accumulation and legitimation conflict with each other (Mishra, 1984: 74).

A somewhat similar analysis has been offered by Offe (1984). According to this, the origins of welfare states lie in their multi-functional character; they are politically attractive to a wide range of interests (1984: 148). Amongst these attractions are (for capital), the ability to provide services necessary for capitalism but which the system could not provide otherwise – this is equivalent to O'Connor's 'social consumption' and 'social investment'. However, the welfare state tends to grow precisely as economies decline (1984: 149) but, having set an apparently successful example of non-market relationships within society (1984: 142), cannot be cut without risk of a crisis of legitimation (1984: 138). Moreover, the economic recession has given credence to critiques that the welfare state discourages both investment and the work ethic (1984: 149). Offe stresses that whatever investors define as being the consequences of the welfare state in terms of disincentives to invest will be self-fulfilling prophecies (1984: 151). The final stage of Offe's argument is that capitalism cannot survive without the welfare state, but cannot survive with it (1984: 153). As Glennerster (1992: 27) has pointed out, the notion of the crisis of the welfare state became prominent at a time when it seemed that the welfare system of New York would bankrupt the city. Yet 30 years later, no irresolvable crisis is apparent in the UK.

On the contrary, more recent Marxist-influenced theorising about the welfare state has tended to emphasise its function in supporting capitalism, and has little to say about any legitimation function. The core of such analysis is that there has been a shift from a 'Keynesian welfare national state' to a 'Schumpeterian workfare postnational regime' (Jessop, 1999). The former of these labels refers to the welfare state as traditionally conceived, aimed at ameliorating market failures within a national economy that is managed by governments through the manipulation of demand levels, according to the economic theories of J.M. Keynes (1936). The emphasis in such a welfare state is on benefits that help to sustain both mass production and mass consumption. The latter label signifies what is said to be the contemporary situation in which the emphasis is on improving the 'supply-side' of the economy through measures aimed at promoting efficiency, worker flexibility and (now global) competitiveness, characteristics held by J.A. Schumpeter (1976 [1943]) to be endangered by modern large-scale capitalism. Contemporary social policy is thus seen as policy for promoting economic success (Evans and Cerny, 2003) through such means as removing disincentives to work at all, or to work flexibly and efficiently to meet employers' requirements.

This new emphasis on the supply side presents a theoretical lacuna in relation to health services. As our earlier discussion of resources in the early years of the NHS implies, there is no straightforward relationship between healthcare expenditure in a country and the health of its population; rather, the relationship seems to be between national prosperity and healthcare expenditure (Office of Health Economics, 2005: Fig 2.8; Parkin et al., 1989). Although the older 'crisis of the welfare state' literature allowed the possibility that in principle health services could be provided as (to continue to use O'Connor's terms) social consumption, it also saw health services as social expenses; the NHS might in principle create a healthier workforce and might in principle serve to legitimate the capitalist state. Whereas it is plausible to see social policies in sectors such as education (producing employable workers) and social security (emphasising the conditionality of benefits on availability and willingness to work) as contributing to Schumpeterian economic policy, this does not seem to be the case for health (for a contrary view, see Greener, 2004).

A number of observations can be made as to the non-appearance of a UK welfare crisis involving the NHS. First, as we have seen, the NHS has been a major beneficiary of reallocations of resources *within* the welfare state. Table 1.3 shows the dramatic growth of the NHS as a proportion of UK expenditure, largely at the expense of defence (Office of Health Economics, 2005) and, through charging policies, the social care sector. Second, and in spite of some short-term difficulties, the long-run performance of the UK economy has not given rise to any enduring crisis. The annual growth of GDP since the creation of the NHS has been positive except for brief falls in the mid-1970s (following the oil price crisis, as noted above), the early 1980s and the early 1990s, with average annual growth of 2.6 percent for the period 1948–2001 (*Social Trends 33*: 113). Third, as we have also noted above, the structure of centralised control, including the 'cash limits' system, permits tight control over expenditure. Taken together, these two points have enabled governments to manage the growth of welfare expenditure without the need for radical cuts (Klein, 2000: 161–2). Fourth, and perhaps most importantly for Marxist theory, the relationship implied by authors such as O'Connor between expenditure and legitimacy may not be straightforward. The assertion that the welfare state embodies an irreconcilable contradiction assumes that the expenditure in question does perform the stated functions, and that less expenditure would fail to do so (Alford and Friedland, 1985: 321–2; Mishra, 1984: 69). But there may not be a linear relationship between the cost of a welfare state and the degree of legitimacy which it provides, so that government promises to improve NHS efficiency may themselves contribute to legitimacy (Harrison, 1994: 139–40). Although it is difficult to show conclusively that the NHS actually does furnish the state with legitimacy, it is clear (from the public opinion figures cited earlier in this chapter) that the NHS remains a highly legitimate institution in itself. Moreover, the importance that is given to it by all major political parties is at least suggestive that politicians themselves see their treatment of the NHS as a source of legitimacy. Despite the occasional occurrence of suggestions for changes in funding arrangements all major parties continue to espouse continued tax financing, an arrangement most recently reiterated by Wanless (2002) and accepted by the government. All this suggests the continued importance for the NHS as a significant contributor to state legitimation despite the virtual disappearance of this strand of analysis from much recent Marxist theorising about the welfare state.

Empire building? Public choice theory

Public choice theory is one element of an intellectual movement, beginning in the late 1950s but gathering momentum from the early 1970s, that applies the concepts and assumptions of economics to the analysis of politics and related phenomena. For instance, Downs (1957) argued that, just as businesses are assumed to be profit maximisers, politicians are vote maximisers. In this account, party political manifestos and programmes are developed in order to win office for the party rather than being an expression of party beliefs on which the electorate is invited to pronounce. Other theorists in the same tradition have argued that voters pursue self-interest in their electoral choices, so that there is a tendency for them to support parties that offer greater quantities of publicly provided goods and services (Brittan, 1975; see also Tullock, 1976 and the concept of 'moral hazard' introduced above).

However, the work from the public choice tradition that has perhaps had the greatest impact on thinking about public services is Niskanen's *Bureaucracy and Representative Government* (1971). Niskanen sees politicians and bureaucrats as a kind of bilateral monopoly; politicians, he argues, seek to maximise the votes they receive, whilst bureaucrats seek to maximise the size of their agency's budget. Thus, in common with the basic assumptions of economic analysis of human behaviour, he takes public sector bureaucrats to be rational maximisers of their own utility, arguing that their primary means for achieving this is through increasing the size of their agency. The logic of this assumption is that such matters as salary, pension, promotion prospects, 'perks' of office, prestige, reputation for power and patronage are largely a function of agency size (1971: 38). Crucially for policy implications, the non-marketed situation of public bureaucracies means that there is no competitive context to provide a counterweight to these expansive tendencies. Taken together, the vote-maximising desire of politicians and the budget-maximising desire of bureaucrats lead to a general tendency for public sector programmes to supply a larger quantity of goods and services than would be provided in a market situation, a quantity that, from an economic perspective, would be regarded as an inefficient oversupply (Dunleavy, 1991: 159–62). Moreover, their privileged access to information about the costs and benefits of public sector programmes allows bureaucrats selectively to implement policy in a manner consistent with their own interests.

Although a good deal of this analysis has been criticised as taking too simplistic a view of the nature of agency budgets and of making unrealistic assumptions about the ability of agencies to behave as unitary entities (Dunleavy, 1991: 162 ff), it is easy to see that Niskanen's views are politically attractive to 'New Right' thinkers and politicians hostile to the state provision of health and welfare services. From such a perspective, the pattern of growth of NHS resources that we have observed earlier in this chapter is both explicable and unwelcome. Niskanen advocated reduction in the number of public sector monopolies and the creation of internal competition within them (1971: 37–8).

Many of the organisational innovations introduced to the UK public sector over the last 20 years can be seen as based on the assumed superiority of markets and as consistent with Niskanen's recommendations. Although the outright privatisation of the whole of previously public sector organisations (such as British Telecom) has not occurred in the UK health sector, we can note here that contemporary developments in NHS organisation described in Chapter 5 can be seen as moving in this direction, including contracting-out of work previously performed 'in-house', the PFI/PPP capital schemes described above, the NHS quasi-market introduced by the Conservative governments of the 1990s, and New Labour's own preference for competition. Many other organisational arrangements in the NHS can be seen as intended to mimic in various ways the operation of markets without actually creating them (Pollitt, 1993). They include the development of 'agencies' (such as NHS Estates, NHS Purchasing and Supply, and the Medicines and Healthcare Products Regulatory Agency) operating at 'arm's length' from their parent government departments (Pollitt et al., 2001), the development of sets of 'performance indicators' as the means by which organisational performance might be evaluated (Carter et al., 1992; Pollitt, 1985) and the development within public sector organisations of various forms of decentralised, workload-related budgetary systems.

Concluding remarks

The two theoretical approaches discussed in the previous section have clear affinities with opposite ends of the political spectrum: neo-Marxist crisis literature with the left, and public choice theory with the right. Yet, as Klein (2000: 160) has noted, they both contain the notion of crisis in relation to publicly funded welfare states, though neither of these approaches on their own seem to offer much direct explanatory power of a situation in which NHS resources have continued to increase in the manner described in this chapter. However, as Klein also notes (2000: 159), both have made substantial contributions to changing the dominant political discourse about welfare state and NHS expenditure from one in which it is self-evidently good to one in which it is the object of some suspicion. This is clearest in the case of public choice theory where, as outlined above, contemporary organisational arrangements very much derive from its prescriptions in terms of creating markets and breaking down monopolies. But, though more speculative, it is possible that neo-Marxist analyses of legitimation have contributed to the evident concern of UK governments to present their policy towards the NHS in the most favourable light.

Further reading

Donaldson and Gerard (2004) give a broad overview of both finance and health economics. Glennerster (2003) describes all aspects of the NHS in detail, though inevitably may soon become dated in some details. The mid-1990s saw an explosion of writing about NHS rationing, and analyses have not changed much to the present day; Hunter (1997) provides a good book-length introduction to the topic. Klein et al. (1996) present findings from an empirical study and Coulter and Ham's (2000) edited collection provides an international perspective on the subject.

Chapter 2

The Politics of Health Professionalism

Summary of chapter contents

- Professionalism: key concepts
- The history of professionalism
- Challenges to professionalism
- Ways of interpreting challenges to professionalism

The evaluative overtones of the term 'professional' are ambiguous. Some usage associates professionalism with competence. We admire the 'real pro', purchase do-it-yourself products that offer a 'professional finish' and deplore 'unprofessional' behaviour. In this usage, the opposite of 'professional' is negative; we mock the 'shambling amateur' and their 'amateur-ish' efforts. But professionalism has negative connotations too. The footballer's 'professional foul' is cynically calculated, and a professional is someone who only performs for money, as opposed to the amateur who (literally) does it for love. These contradictory usages are nei-ther new nor confined to everyday usage, having been carried over into social scientific the-orising over the last 70 years. The first section of this chapter summarises these theories and their development. The second section provides an historical sketch of how some of the health professions acquired their status. The third section summarises changes over the last 20 years that might be regarded as challenging professionalism in various ways. The final sec-tion reviews a range of alternative theoretical interpretations of such challenges.

Key concepts in professionalism

In the medieval period, the term 'profession' carried the religious connotations of making (professing) a vow, a notion that for centuries afterwards informed the view that there existed three 'learned professions', the clergy, lawyers and physicians, who saw their occupation 'not simply as a way of making a living, but as a vocation from God to be cheerfully and diligently fulfilled ... to serve the common weal' (O'Day, 2000: 11, 16). However, this usage did not preclude others, for instance referring to teachers and soldiers, or even as synonymous with a trade. Nor did it imply the uncritical acceptance of these claims to service and altruism. Since the seventeenth century, the professions have been criticised as monopolies, and professionals as failing to live up to the ideals of their vocation and as 'mystifying' their knowledge (O'Day, 2000: 15) in order to make it inaccessible to others. These pejorative associations were famously summed up in the candid remark by medical characters in Shaw's play *The Doctor's Dilemma* that 'all professions are conspiracies against the laity' (Shaw, 1932: 106).

Early theories

Early social scientific analyses sought to list the characteristics ('traits') of occupations that were deemed to define them as professions. Although such analysts did not always agree on their precise content, their lists typically included: skill based on theoretical knowledge, acquired through formal education and training, and formally assessed by examination; the existence of a code of professional conduct and a professional organisation; and service for the public good (Millerson, 1964: 4). Such approaches to professionalism are generally uncritical (the defining traits are all socially desirable) and ahistorical, lacking any explanation of how occupations come to be labelled as 'professions'. Such an uncritical approach is also evident in the theorising of professions from a functionalist perspective, which specify traits but argue further that they are in some way functional for society. The central concern of such theories with the problem of how social order is maintained provides a conservative focus that is illustrated in Carr-Saunders and Wilson's famous remark that professions:

> ... *inherit, preserve and pass on a tradition ... engender modes of life, habits of thought and standards of judgement which render them centres of resistance to crude forces which threaten steady and peaceful evolution ... The family, the church and the universities, certain associations of intellectuals, and above all the great professions stand like rocks against which the waves raised by these forces beat in vain. (Carr-Saunders and Wilson, 1933: 497)*

By the 1960s, sociologists had begun to examine the process by which occupations came to be regarded as professions, thus drawing attention to the political efforts required for professional status to be successfully achieved. Yet the general tone of such accounts remained broadly favourable to the professions, or at least some of them:

> *Some associations deserve the designation 'professional', others do not ... Much abuse of the system has produced a battery of useless, unnecessary, badly managed [professional] associations.*

Nevertheless, the total effect has been beneficial. The range and depth of improvement throughout society is beyond dispute. (Millerson, 1964: ix–x)

This particular author goes on to distinguish the 'primary functions' of professional organisation (such as qualifying and registering practitioners, furthering study of the subject and promoting high standards of conduct) from 'secondary functions' such as raising professional status, protecting professionals and encouraging co-operation between them (Millerson, 1964: 28–32). The evaluative implications are obvious; from this perspective, professionalism is only secondarily concerned with self-interest. Of course it might also be argued that skill based on theoretical (or 'esoteric') knowledge leads inevitably to professional *self-regulation* since, although clients need to be assured that professionals are properly qualified, the esoteric nature of professional knowledge means that a profession can only be regulated by its own members. One important operationalisation of this insight is the work of Jamous and Peloille (1970) which introduces the concept of the 'indetermination/technicality [I/T] ratio' as the means of characterising occupations:

The I/T ratio expresses the possibility of transmitting, by means of apprenticeship, the mastery of intellectual or material instruments used to achieve a given result … [that is] the part played in the production process by 'means' that can be mastered and communicated in the form of rules (T), in proportion to the 'means' that … are attributed to the virtualities [sic] of producers (I). (Jamous and Peloille, 1970: 112)

In other words, some elements of work can be clearly specified, whilst others must be left to the judgement of the worker. Jamous and Peloille go on to argue that professions are occupations that display a high I/T ratio, that is rely heavily on workers' own judgement (1970: 113). This insight is central to the contemporary politics of medical knowledge that are the subject of Chapter 3. Jamous and Peloille also note that such indeterminacy provides a basis for professions to claim dominance over other occupations (1970: 139), an observation that provides a link to the more critical theorisations of professionalism that arose in the 1970s.

Critical theories

By the early 1970s, sociologists in the US and UK had adopted a more thoroughly critical approach, clearly signalled by the titles of volumes such as *Professional Dominance* (Freidson, 1970a) and *Professions and Power* (Johnson, 1972). Such analyses began to apply to occupations the notion of 'social closure' based on Weberian sociology of how status groups restrict access to rewards and privileges (Murphy, 1988; Parkin, 1982: 100–3). Their main focus was on the politics of obtaining and maintaining professional status ('occupational closure'), and specifically on autonomy for practitioners and the exercise of power over other occupations. In Freidson's account, a profession is an occupation that has achieved autonomy as a result of society's acceptance of its claims both to exercise an important and esoteric knowledge-based skill and to be exceptionally trustworthy:

It is useful to think of a profession as an occupation which has assumed a dominant position in a division of labour, so that it gains control over the substance of its own work ... The occupation sustains this special status by its persuasive profession of the extraordinary trustworthiness of its members. The trustworthiness it professes naturally includes ethicality and also knowledgeable skill ... The profession claims to be the most reliable authority on the nature of the reality it deals with. (Freidson, 1970a: xvii)

Freidson's argument here is not really concerned with whether or not professional claims about the importance of their skills and the extraordinary nature of their ethics are justified. Rather, the successful recognition of an occupation as a profession hinges upon whether or not such claims are *believed* by governments and other influential social groups; it thus depends heavily on the extent to which the occupation is able to muster political support, and on the wider economic and social climate in which it does so. Light and Levine (1988) have argued that the medical profession in the US largely *created* its own dominance in the early twentieth century by organising and campaigning against physicians entering into contracts to work for industrial companies or friendly societies. Stone (1980: 39–40) has reached similar conclusions in respect of German medicine in the mid-1930s. In the UK, the provisions of the 1911 National Insurance Act allowed GPs to escape from the tight control of the friendly societies with whom they were previously under contract (Eckstein, 1958: 128; Lewis, 1992: 326–7). Along with successful acceptance, according to Freidson, come a set of institutions that legally establish the profession's autonomy and protect it from competition. The form of such institutions provides for the *self-regulation* of the profession; that is, within a broad legal framework it is regulated by its own members according to its own criteria, rather than by outsiders. Amongst the matters subject to self-regulation are accreditation of training standards and qualifications, the licensing of individuals as fit and competent practitioners, and the disciplining of individuals who have failed to adhere to professional rules or standards. Despite Freidson's central concern with how occupations become professions, he also has an evaluative position. He suggests that professions may deceive themselves into believing that they are truly acting in the public and client interest, consequently abusing their autonomy by failing properly to regulate themselves (1970a: 370).

Johnson's account has much that is consonant with Freidson's, but places greater emphasis on the market conditions that allow successful professionalisation. His argument (1972: 41–5) may be summarised as follows. First, the development of specialised skills in society creates a potential asymmetry between producer and consumer. The social class of clients may have an impact on the occupation's ability to professionalise; the higher the socioeconomic groups to whom services are provided, the easier for the occupation to obtain official recognition. An occupation may be able to exploit this by 'mystifying' its specialist knowledge. This is not solely a result of the complexity of the knowledge; 'uncertainty is not ... entirely cognitive in origin but may be deliberately increased to serve manipulative ends' (Johnson, 1972: 42). Second, the ability of an occupation to impose its own definition of the situation (for instance in terms of client needs) will be greater where the clientele is heterogeneous and fragmented, as opposed to where the clients are few (such as large organisations). Third, successful imposition of its knowledge base enables an occupation to secure autonomy both for its individual practitioners and for practitioner associations which regulate the profession. For Johnson, profession is not an occupation, but a specific means of controlling an occupation. Practitioner associations sustain professional culture; they

> *bestow status and identity, and attempt to sustain uniform interests among the members and pro-*
> *mote uniform policies by imposing a monopoly on practice in the field and regulating entry to it … *
> *Equal status and the continuous occupational career are important mechanisms for maintaining*
> *a sense of identity, colleague-loyalty and shared values. Also, the myth of a community of equal*
> *competence is effective in generating public trust … (Johnson, 1972: 54, 55)*

An important element in Freidson's argument about professional autonomy not so far mentioned is that any one field of endeavour is likely to feature a single occupation that has acquired the authority to 'direct and evaluate' others in the field. Although other occupations in a given field may possess important skills and exceptional ethics, and are perhaps termed 'professions', they are nevertheless subordinate to a single 'dominant' profession (1970b: 137). The historical notion of medicine as one of the three 'learned professions' has already been mentioned, and it is easy to see how this is consonant with the application of Freidson's analysis to the field of healthcare. Freidson and other analysts typically see the profession of medicine (that is, physicians) as dominant, and professions (or as some analysts insist 'semi-professions': see Etzioni, 1969) such as nursing, midwifery and physiotherapy as subordinate. Subordination may take a variety of forms, ranging from individual physicians giving instructions to individual nurses, through medical domination of training and licensing criteria for other health professions, to a broader conceptual domination of the field through what is variously termed the 'medical' or 'biomedical' model of health and care, which sees ill-health as a breakdown in the functioning of an individual's body, to be tackled individually by means of medical interventions (Gabe et al., 2004; Lawrence, 1994), rather than (say) as economically, socially and politically caused and hence to be tackled collectively at a more macro-level. The idea that much of the social power of medicine is derived from its access to expertise in a body of knowledge that conceptualises disease in this way has also been emphasised by contemporary sociologists working on the lines established by Foucault (Armstrong, 1983; Foucault, 1976). The political prominence of this view of illness is discussed in Chapter 3.

Collegiality, autonomy and dominance

Notions of collegiality, autonomy and dominance are central to Freidson's and Johnson's conception of professionalism. A dominant profession such as medicine maintains the appearance of collegiality, or equal status of its members. This serves the twin purposes of socialising members into an attitude of loyalty to colleagues, and of presenting to the outside world an image of an occupation all of whose members are competent and trustworthy. This internal collegiality contrasts sharply with relations with more subordinate professions, whose activities are bounded by the dominant profession in various ways. At the level of clinical care, for instance, hospital in-patients are 'owned' by a named consultant physician, who makes treatment decisions and approves the various contributions to the patient's care made by other professionals, whilst in primary care patients are 'owned' by a GP. Dominant professions operate at an organisational level too. We shall see below that, until recently, the professional regulatory institutions of nursing and other health professions in the UK have been shaped in disputes with the medical profession. An implication of internal collegiality for dominant occupations such as medicine is that, once fully qualified, practitioners have a considerable degree of professional autonomy, though such autonomy could not be absolute, since absolute autonomy would imply both unlimited resources and the paradoxical ability of autonomous physicians to violate each others' autonomy.

The dimensions of this concept and its application to medicine have been examined by several analysts (Elston, 1991; Schulz and Harrison, 1986; Tolliday, 1978), whose classificatory schemes are broadly consonant. Perhaps the most basic dimension of professional autonomy relates directly to the *micro level* clinical situation, comprising control over diagnosis and treatment (decisions about what tests and examinations to order, what drugs and procedures to prescribe, to whom to refer), control over evaluation of care (judgements about the appropriateness of the care of particular patients), and control over the nature and volume of medical tasks (the ability of doctors to determine their own movements, priorities, times and workloads). A second dimension of autonomy, perhaps logically entailed by the first, is a meso level of institutionalised relationships between the medical profession and the state. As we shall see in more detail in the next section, the legal basis of state licensure and self-regulation is part of this, along with the various corporatist arrangements through which medical interests are mediated, including joint government/professional committees and official recognition of 'peak associations'. These relationships have at times resulted in a degree of contractual independence greater than that enjoyed by ordinary employees, such as physicians' unilateral rights for example to engage in private medical practice, to publicly criticise their NHS employers, and to appeal directly to the government in the event of dismissal. The third dimension of autonomy is the macro-level phenomenon of the 'biomedical model' as noted above, the pervasive, taken-for-granted assumption that ill-health equals individual pathology, and that healthcare therefore consists of individual medical interventions. This is a macro-level concept in the sense that it not only underpins the individual clinical decisions that doctors make about patients, but also legitimises medical expertise in the design of health services and facilities more generally. This need not imply that these assumptions go entirely unchallenged. Esland (1980a: 216–7) has noted that professions may contain counter-groups who espouse critical perspectives and advocate alternative approaches to professional practice; the 'anti-psychiatry' movement of the 1960s provides a good example (Laing, 1969; Szasz, 1970; for a discussion, see Porter, 1997: 522–3).

Autonomy and illusion

Some sociologists (for instance Starr, 1982) have been less certain of the apparent strength and durability of professional autonomy. In particular, there is an important group of Marxist-influenced writers who have argued that professional autonomy as discussed above is largely illusory. The argument runs roughly as follows. First, and in contrast to the 'professional dominance' argument, it was the social elite who established the dominant role of professions, rather than the professions having actively secured elite approval for their work (Navarro, 1988: 61). Second, 'elite' in this context really means the capitalist state, which has sanctioned ostensible professional dominance for its own purposes, specifically to help the state control society; as one analyst has put it:

> the professions ... can be seen as having been co-opted into governmental decision making and in some cases as having been allowed to develop as agents of control for a powerful state. (Esland, 1980a: 214)

For example, the profession of occupational psychology can be seen as supporting capitalist employers in selecting the most suitable job applicants (Esland, 1980b: 252), whilst the profession of medicine issues various kinds of certificate (of sickness, disability or mental incapacity) which legitimate absence from work or school, or allow an offender to be treated as 'mad' rather than culpable for their criminal acts. Professions thus act as 'reality definers' on important social issues (Esland, 1980a: 213), a role that includes the delimitation of potential solutions of social problems to ones that do not threaten capitalism. Thus a physician may diagnose and treat a case of lung cancer, but cannot issue a prescription to ban the sale of tobacco. Third, specifically in relation to the health professions, the form of medicine that is dominant today has achieved this status at the expense of alternative models. As noted above, the contemporary notion of medicine addresses a 'biomedical' model of ill-health or disease, in which individuals experience problems mainly as a result of disease processes within their own bodies; such problems are properly addressed by means of therapeutic interventions (such as drugs or surgery) that aim to arrest, retard or reverse the disease in individual patients. This notion is so dominant (Navarro, 1988: 62) that it can be difficult to remember that there are alternatives. The famous nineteenth century pathologist and Prussian politician Rudolf Virchow saw disease as the result of the oppressive nature of society, to be ameliorated primarily by social, political and economic interventions rather than by clinical medicine; indeed he famously remarked that 'medicine is a social science and politics nothing but medicine on a large scale' (quoted in Porter, 1997: 643). It is clear that this perspective on the relationship between the medical profession and the state is closely related to some of the arguments summarised in Chapter 1 about governments choosing to socialise healthcare and other welfare services as a means of securing political legitimacy and avoiding political unrest. Despite starting from a theoretical position very different from that of Marxists, analyses based on Foucault's concept of 'governmentality' (Foucault, 1991) share the notion that professions and the state are integrally related, and that the independence of the former both enhances the legitimacy of the latter and buttresses its capacity to control society (Flynn, 2002; Johnson, 1995)

Professions as jurisdictions in flux

Despite their considerable differences, the theories considered above all focus mainly on what is assumed to be the dominant profession in any sector, and on the national-level processes by which this dominant status (the 'golden age' identified by McKinlay and Marceau, 2002) is obtained, maintained and, more recently, challenged. In contrast, Abbott's theory of 'jurisdictions' sees interprofessional competition as an enduring situation, resulting in the decline and occasional disappearance of occupations, and their replacement by others (1988: 3, 18). He places more emphasis than most other theorists on what occurs in the workplace:

> *The professions ... make up an interdependent system. In this system, each profession has its activities under various kinds of jurisdiction. Sometimes it has full control, sometimes control subordinate to another group. Jurisdictional boundaries are perpetually in dispute, both in local practice and in national claims ... It is control of work that brings the professions into conflict with each other and makes their histories interdependent. (Abbott, 1988: 2, 19)*

For Abbott, a profession is an occupation that has secured substantial (though not necessarily total) control over the theoretical basis of its work (1988: 8,16), a definition that is more inclusive than many of the theories outlined above. Abbott observes that what he terms 'jurisdictional claims' by an occupation tend to be made to three 'audiences', that is the legal system, the 'public arena' and the workplace (1988: 59). The types of jurisdictional claim that can be successfully pursued within the legal system may involve a monopoly of certain work procedures, exclusive use of particular titles or technical terms, or the exclusive right to receive particular types of 'third party' payment (see Chapter 1). In the UK health field, successful pursuit of this type of claim has typically resulted in a national licensing body, legally recognised as able both to judge the competence of practitioners (placing them on an approved register) and to discipline practitioners, including removing them from the register. Jurisdictional claims made in the 'public arena' include advice columns in newspapers and magazines, advice booklets intended for public consumption and dramatic portrayals of professionals on television and radio (Abbott, 1988: 60). (The last of these has become somewhat double-edged as dramatists have increasingly chosen to represent professionals in a less than wholly positive manner. Some readers will be able to compare the doctors in the 1960s television programme *Dr Finlay's Casebook* with those in *Holby City.*) In a comment that is consonant with the myth of professional 'collegiality', Abbott notes that these public images

> *must concern homogeneous groups. All doctors are equivalent, all nurses are equivalent ... differences ... are differences between archetypes. (1988: 61)*

Abbott's third 'audience' is the workplace. He argues that, in real-world organisations, divisions of labour between occupations do not correspond to what is formally expected. If there is a shortage in one profession, some of its work is done by others, perhaps employing a pragmatic 'craft' version of the original profession's knowledge that is devoid of the original theoretical content (1988: 66). Such departure from the formalities is rarely publicly acknowledged, since to do so would undermine the validity of the original jurisdictional claims (1988: 66). Instead, the formal position is often re-emphasised in the workplace by symbolic means such as dress codes, modes of address and an emphasis on theory in technical presentations or lectures (1988: 67–8).

Abbott's approach to defining an occupation as a profession centres on its ability to control the abstract or theoretical knowledge that underpins its practice. It follows that any substantial threat to the abstract nature of this knowledge presents a threat to jurisdiction. One such threat is the reduction of abstract knowledge to more concrete rules for professional practice (Abbott, 1988: 55, 98), which (as we shall see in Chapter 3) may paradoxically derive from the efforts of academic members of the professional community to clarify the components of effective practice. The production of clinical guidelines, whilst based on academic research, has the effect of concretising and routinising the application of abstract knowledge. This vulnerability to routinisation may be increased by two other factors. One is the tendency of professionals to delegate unwanted routine or 'dirty' work (Hughes, 1958) to subordinate occupations whilst retaining overall control. Yet the revelation that the work can be successfully undertaken without abstract knowledge undermines the assumptions on which professionalism is based (Abbott, 1988: 126). Another factor is pressure from the organisations by which professionals are employed (1988: 117). If it becomes evident that routinisation is possible, this both enhances the ability of managers to undertake surveillance of professional work and offers the opportunity for staff economies.

An historical sketch of health professionalism in the UK

The foregoing discussion has stressed a need to think of professions in terms of the processes by which they are created, maintained and modified. In this section, we examine the dynamics of health professionalism in the UK, focusing primarily on the last two centuries. A key element in this examination is the *institutions* of professionalism. Since the nineteenth century, the health professions in the UK and elsewhere have been closely involved with the state, most obviously through the licensure of self-regulating monopolies. Although, as we have seen, this involvement can be explained from a number of theoretical standpoints, and although the institutional arrangements for such modes of regulation differ in important ways between countries (Moran, 1999), they can be seen as embodying an implicit compact in which an occupational monopoly and substantial operational autonomy for practitioners are granted in return for the occupation regulating itself and disciplining its members. In practice, two kinds of institution are important in the development and operation of this implied compact. First, there are independent organisations that directly represent professional interests, whose functions include various amalgams of the development of the profession, qualification of members, and pursuit of members' economic interests. Second, there are the statutory organisations of 'state registration', whose function is to maintain registers of practitioners legally entitled to practise a particular profession. Of course, formal institutions are not the whole of the story. New members must undergo a process of socialisation into professional culture (Becker et al., 1960; Melia, 1987; Sinclair, 1997; Watkins, 1987), there are internal status hierarchies and various means by which members seek advancement within the profession and, as noted above, internal divisions and dissensions (Alford, 1975; Eckstein, 1960).

The roots of self-regulation

The professional institutions of medicine are the oldest in the health field. From the sixteenth century, medicine was notionally divided into three branches, physicians, surgeons and apothecaries, each of which was to some extent organised and regulated. The College (later Royal College) of Physicians was founded in 1518 as a regulatory rather than educational body, consisting mainly of university-educated physicians and claiming the right to license practitioners of medicine as well as a right to practise surgery (O'Day, 2000: 193). Around 1563, the College established a set of requirements for its members which, although they may well not have been enforced, express ideas that are discernible in the sociological accounts summarised above. Members were not to criticise one another, were to relate fees to the amount of time expended on the patient (rather than take advantage of the patient's situation of need), were not to reveal medical remedies or skills to persons outside the profession, were to refuse to work with unlicensed physicians or with apothecaries who also practised medicine, and were to undertake long training and rigorous qualifying examinations (O'Day, 2000: 198). The United Company of Barber-Surgeons was formed in 1540 to regulate and train for surgery. Surgeons were required to be literate and a distinction between surgeons and barbers was maintained, the latter being forbidden to perform surgery other than tooth extraction (O'Day, 2000: 195); it became the College (later Royal College) of Surgeons in 1800.

Apothecaries were initially dispensers of drugs, not supposed to take fees for diagnosis or advice to clients. Notionally, a physician would pass the task of dispensing to the apothecary. Until 1617, when the Society of Apothecaries obtained its own Royal Charter, they were subject to inspection by the Royal College of Physicians (Allsop, 2002: 81; O'Day, 2000: 197–8.) In practice, however, there was a good deal of overlap between physicians, surgeons and apothecaries and the 'official' division of these occupations does not seem to have matched reality. This was partly the result of a shortage of qualified physicians, making the law impossible to enforce, partly that of practitioners seeking to make a living by performing more than one role, and partly that the appearance of opiate drugs in the seventeenth century increased reliance on apothecaries (O'Day, 2000: 198–9). Although most healing efforts were undertaken by women in domestic or neighbourly settings, helping with childbirth, making lotions and potions and comforting the sick (Stacey, 1992: 15), the overlapping practices of apothecaries dispensing directly for the patient, of physicians dispensing drugs, and of surgeons practising medicine as an adjunct to their cutting can be seen as constituting a sort of general practice from the beginning of the seventeenth century (Loudon, 1992: 219; O'Day, 2000: 205, 229, 249–51).

Despite these roots, the processes of developing the profession of medicine as we now recognise it date from the nineteenth century, which is also when the concept of the hospital as a place for the care of the physically sick, largely dormant since the dissolution of the monasteries in the mid-sixteenth century, was revived (Stacey, 1992: 15), resulting in the foundation of numerous new hospitals between the late eighteenth and mid-nineteenth centuries (Cherry, 1996: 45; Granshaw, 1992: 200–2). In 1815, the apothecaries (or 'general practitioners' as they were increasingly termed) became the first UK health occupation to be subjected to statutory licensing; it became illegal to prescribe drugs without possession of the Licentiate of the Society of Apothecaries, though prosecutions were at the Society's own expense, and therefore relatively infrequent (Loudon, 1992: 235–6). The Apothecaries Act of 1815, from which these provisions derived, was largely the product of political pressure from physicians whose incomes were falling and practices threatened by the expansion of 'druggists', shopkeepers selling drugs directly to patients, without the advice of a physician (Loudon, 1992: 230–1). Due to the College of Surgeons' insistence on retaining its monopoly of (and hence income from) surgical qualifications the apothecaries were unable to secure their desired reforms to the content of professional training, which remained very narrowly based round the dispensing of drugs (Loudon, 1992: 235). The wider system of state registration of medical practitioners that subsequently developed also owed much to the discontents of medical practitioners, in this case ordinary (non-specialist) physicians in the 1830s and 1840s (Stacey, 1992: 16; 2000: 28). Such practitioners resented both the privileged elite of largely London-based medical grandees, able to secure high fees from wealthy clients, and fierce competition from a range of unqualified practitioners for the business of poorer patients (Porter, 1997: 354). The Provincial Medical and Surgical Society was formed in 1832, becoming the British Medical Association (BMA) in 1855. Political pressure for reform eventually culminated in the Medical Act of 1858, which established a General Council of Medical Education and Registration, abbreviated to 'General Medical Council' (GMC) in 1951.

The new Council epitomised the principle of professional self-regulation introduced above; three-quarters of its initial members all represented the medical royal colleges and universities. Despite their role in securing the Act, no general practitioners (GPs) were able to obtain Council membership until a number of elective seats were later introduced. The Council's function was to maintain a statutory register of 'registered medical practitioners'. It was not (and is still not) illegal to engage in unregistered practice, but it became illegal to falsely represent oneself as registered. Government medical employment (including the armed forces), and the right to certify official documents (such as death certificates), were reserved for the registered (Porter, 1997: 356; Stacey, 1992: 18–9). This monopoly of state medical employment was subsequently extended to receipt of fees under the National Insurance Act of 1911 and to employment in the NHS from 1948 (Stacey, 1992: 19). The Council had the power to inspect medical schools and to recognise specific medical qualifications as enabling their holders to be registered. In 1886, it began to specify the content of medical training, when it required the inclusion of medical, surgical and obstetric subject matter (Allsop, 2002: 80; Stacey, 1992: 21–3). From its beginning, the Council also had the power to remove individuals from the register as a penalty for 'serious professional misconduct' (Gladstone, 2000: 3), though such offences were usually sexual in nature, and until the 1980s the Council took a very narrow view of its role, being generally reluctant to pursue allegations of professional incompetence (Allsop, 2002: 80; Stacey, 2000: 29).

The expansion of state regulation

The medical profession was not the first to obtain state licensure. The Pharmacy Act of 1852 had established the distinction between qualified and unqualified practitioners without banning unqualified practice, a model that, as we have seen, was followed by the 1858 Medical Act. However, this was modified in 1868 to prohibit unqualified dispensing (Donnison, 1988: 70, 94). Other demands followed. Dentistry was within the remit of the GMC from 1878 (Stacey, 1992: 23). Demands for the licensure of midwifery and nursing took much longer to satisfy. In the case of midwifery, some form of regulation was undertaken by the church from the thirteenth century onwards, though had broken down by the early nineteenth century, a period by which, for the first time, substantial numbers of men had begun to practise (Donnison, 1988: 14–8, 35). The breakdown of licensing and competition from men, and later from surgeons claiming obstetrics as a branch of medicine, provided a double threat to the livelihoods of midwives. Any increase in the formal status of midwives would also threaten the incomes of GPs, the poorest section of the medical profession. At the same time, however, the availability of formal midwifery training had increased. The last 30 years of nineteenth century saw numerous attempts to legislate for the licensure of midwives, all failing as a result of various combinations of opposition by sections of the medical profession and of associations seeking the state licensure of nurses, disagreements between midwives' organisations, lack of public interest and anti-feminism (Donnison, 1988: 86–156). However, by the turn of the century, public and political interest had increased, partly as a result of some highly publicised maternal deaths and partly from fears that British difficulties in the Boer War implied a physically deteriorating national population which might be addressed by better maternal and neonatal care (an example of the 'productionist medicine' introduced in Chapter 1). A 'severe and public humiliation' followed for the GMC and BMA (Donnison, 1988: 173), which had failed to muster sufficient parliamentary opposition to the proposals. The 1902 Midwives Act provided for a Central Midwives Board (CMB) to register practitioners and banned the unqualified practice of midwifery after a period of grace expiring in 1910. Midwives could be erased from the register for personal or professional misconduct, and were also required to be supervised by local government Medical Officers of Health (Donnison, 1988: 174–8). Although the GMC was to have no role, the majority of CMB members were physicians (Donnison, 1988: 169), so that the state licensure of midwives cannot be seen as self-regulation of the kind enjoyed by the medical profession. Nevertheless, midwives were regarded as independent practitioners in relation to 'natural labour', required to refer women to physicians only in cases of complications.

Improvements in the training of nurses had also taken place from the mid-nineteenth century (Abel-Smith, 1960: 17–35), and efforts to obtain state licensure had been deployed in parallel with that for midwives. Indeed, some nurse leaders had opposed midwives' registration on the grounds that midwifery should be regarded as a branch of nursing (Donnison, 1988: 134). The nurses' organisations seeking regulation were split over the length of training required and the desirability of recruiting only from the higher social classes, whilst some leading figures in nursing opposed registration altogether (Abel-Smith, 1960: 61–71; Rafferty, 2000: 522–3). The BMA and hospital doctors generally supported registration, whilst GPs feared that nurses would compete with doctors for the care of patients at home (Abel-Smith, 1960: 75, 78). As with midwifery, numerous bills for registration were presented to Parliament but none received government support (Abel-Smith, 1960: 81–2). However, the 1914–18 war changed the political climate (Abel-Smith, 1960: 86, 92–3). First, women generally and nurses in particular had been seen to contribute to the war effort. Second, women's demands for the right to vote (with which some nursing leaders had been associated) had been met. Third, nurses who had trained in civilian institutions were concerned that volunteers rapidly trained for wartime duties might subsequently be able to present themselves as nurses. Fourth, there was concern that failure to grant recognition to nurses might drive them into the arms of the trade union movement. The postwar government therefore accepted nurse registration in principle. Continuing divisions within the pro-registration movement led to a government decision to draft its own Bill, which became the Nurses Registration Act of 1919 (Abel-Smith, 1960: 96; Dingwall et al., 1988: 85). This provided for the establishment of a General Nursing Council (GNC) of 16 nurses and nine other members, and the maintenance of a nursing register with supplementary sections for males, mental health nurses and children's nurses. Admission to the register was initially to depend on having three years of bona fide practice by 1919, and subsequently upon passing an examination. The GNC, which also had power to recognise training schools, came into existence in 1920 and the first examinations were held in 1925 (Abel-Smith, 1960: 101, 113). Registration conferred protection of the title 'registered nurse' rather than reserving any specified duties for registrants (Dingwall et al., 1988: 88); the model therefore resembled that of medicine rather than of midwifery.

The process of obtaining state licensure for other healthcare occupations was no less protracted than the cases of midwifery and nursing. The opticians had first sought registration in 1906 (Donnison, 1988: 178) and others, including physiotherapists and chiropodists (Larkin, 1983), were inspired to do so in the inter-war period by the midwives' and nurses' success. However, although the dentists were awarded a legal monopoly over the repair and removal of teeth in 1921, their registration body, the Dental Board, remained under the supervision of the GMC until 1957 (Thorogood, 2002: 109). The medical profession, operating through the GMC and the BMA, was able to persuade governments to refuse licensure to others, even where the occupation in question had sought to accommodate medical demands (Larkin, 1983: 131–8). A wide range of arguments was deployed in order to do so, but fears of loss of work by GPs (whose incomes were often rather low until the creation of the NHS) played some part, as did the claim that only a medical practitioner could exclude serious illness before referring for the treatment of minor conditions. By the mid-1930s, the medical profession had come to recognise that straightforward opposition to the aspirations of other occupations would be seen as crude protectionism, and its efforts shifted to controlling the terms upon which the latter might operate. In 1936 it established its own licensing arrangements, the Board of Registration of Medical Auxiliaries (BRMA), through which it both controlled training requirements and insisted that occupations covered worked only under medical direction (Larkin, 1983: 19–20). Physiotherapists, radiographers, opticians, orthoptists, dieticians, speech therapists and chiropodists were amongst those who joined this voluntary arrangement (Armstrong, 1976; Larkin, 1983: 157–8).

The creation of the NHS in 1948 provided the occasion for many of these claims to be re-opened, and the period 1957 to 1960 was one of considerable activity in relation to the state licensure of other occupations. In 1957 dental registration was removed from the purview of the GMC by the creation of a General Dental Council, and opticians obtained their own licensure through the creation in 1958 of a General Optical Council. Medical attempts to recreate regulatory arrangements similar to those of the BRMA were unsuccessful, and the government instead created in 1960 a Council for the Professions Supplementary to Medicine (CPSM) to oversee the licensure of chiropodists, physiotherapists, remedial gymnasts, occupational therapists, radiographers, dieticians, medical laboratory technicians and later, orthoptists (Armstrong, 1976: 157–8; Larkin, 1983: 160–79). Within this arrangement, each profession had its own specific board, dominated by professional members and in practice responsible for establishing standards of training and conduct, and sometimes the supply of trainees (Harrison, 1981; Larkin, 2002: 125). Further regulatory changes took place in 1983 when the functions of the CMB and GNC were subsumed into a UK Central Council for Nursing, Midwifery and Health Visiting with a majority of nursing members (and associated boards) for each of the four countries of the UK (Davies, 2002: 98; Davies and Beach, 2000; Dingwall et al., 1988: 207). Yet in 1997 some health professions, including clinical scientists, osteopaths, chiropractors and herbalists, remained unregulated by the state.

A number of points emerge from this account. First, the politics of obtaining state licensure were complex. Economic self-interest has been central for all the professional groups, with qualified practitioners seeing licensure as the means of resisting competition for the unqualified, and the less prestigious elements of the medical profession concerned at potential competition from the qualified, even in clinical areas where there was little contemporary medical interest. However, professions and governments were sometimes concerned to improve standards and to improve access to care across social groups. Other elements in the professionalisation process included identity politics, such as the role of feminism in the promotion of female occupational groups, and medicine's self-image as disinterested guardian of overarching knowledge of illness, diagnosis and treatment, a view to which governments generally deferred. These complexities were also the source of divisions over strategy amongst proponents of state licensure, and within a medical profession that was rarely wholly unified against licensure of others. Second, state licensure for those groups that obtained it had different endpoints. In most cases, what was secured was 'protection of title' and some control over training and codes of practice. Some registration bodies, such as the CMB, did not have majorities of their own profession, but midwives, dentists, ophthalmic opticians and pharmacists were able to obtain legal monopolies for their activities. Despite all of this, analysts have generally concluded that the relative status of occupations cannot simply be read off from these formalities and overall assessments have generally concluded that these occupations did not obtain anything like the degree of self-regulation enjoyed by medicine (Davies, 2002: 97; Dingwall et al., 1988: 97; Larkin, 1983: 186).

The high plateau of medical self-regulation

Although neither the 1815 nor 1858 Acts had anywhere near met the contemporary demands of practitioners (Loudon, 1992), the hundred years following the establishment of the GMC saw the medical profession obtaining much of what it sought from government, especially through the efforts of the BMA. It forced up doctors' fee levels during the negotiations over the post-1911 health insurance scheme (Eckstein, 1958: 127; Perkin, 1989: 346), played an important role in shaping policy ideas about the future organisation of health services (Perkin, 1989: 345; Watkin, 1975), and secured major concessions on the inception of the new NHS in 1948:

> ... no salaried [GP] service, no local government control, modified powers of [ministerial] direction, the removal of all hospitals from local government ... special treatment for teaching hospitals, seats [for doctors] on the administrative bodies, no disciplinary machinery. (Willcocks, 1967: 105; see also Eckstein, 1960)

Although the three decades after the Second World War saw the beginning of the critical analyses of medicine outlined above, they were memorably characterised by Klein (1990) as the 'politics of the double bed', shared by government and medical profession, though other health professions also benefited in terms of state registration, expansion of numbers and improved education. This period can be examined in relation to the macro, meso and micro levels of professional autonomy introduced above.

At the macro level, the creation in 1948 of an NHS based on the 'biomedical model' described above rather than a broader public health approach (Colwill, 1998), was perhaps a crucial underpinning for professional autonomy; if illness is individual, so must be its treatment, and so must be the clinical decisions of medical professionals. At the meso level, professional institutions had increased in number and status with the postwar formation of further medical Royal Colleges, including the Anaesthetists and Ophthalmologists, with General Practitioners, Pathologists, Psychiatrists and Radiologists following in the 1960s and 1970s. Within the profession, the culture was very much one of mutual trust, perhaps typified by the fact that the GMC had virtually ceased to carry out inspections of universities (Committee of Inquiry, 1975). Even within the Department of Health (and Social Security, as it was from 1968 to 1988), there were parallel hierarchies of administrators and health professionals, the latter responsible to the Chief Medical Officer rather than to the Permanent Secretary (Webster, 1996: 381). The 1960s and 1970s exemplify corporatism, a situation in which the absence of challenges to professional autonomy and dominance was as much the result of government's *acceptance* of the role of medical institutions as of any negotiated settlement between the two (Cawson, 1982; Schmitter, 1974). Such corporatism was also reflected in formal management structures. As we shall see in greater detail in Chapter 5, until 1974 the local statutory bodies which ran the NHS had large numbers of doctors in membership (Ham, 1981) and from 1974 until 1982 were dominated by management teams, half the places on which were occupied by doctors, each effectively with a power of veto (Harrison, 1982). Consultants' contracts of employment were insulated from managerial discretion by being held at the regional, rather than hospital level, and a proportion of consultants was able to receive substantial 'distinction awards' in addition to salary; these awards were unilaterally, and secretly determined within the profession. Although a substantial programme of new hospital building began in the 1960s (Allen, 1979; Mohan,

2002), consultants were for many years able to maintain themselves in relatively short supply (Harrison et al., 1990: 109–13). GPs were self-employed contractors, somewhat insulated from the remainder of the NHS with duties specified in only the vaguest terms (Ellis and Chisholm, 1993: 12).

At the micro level, the key symbolic manifestation of medical autonomy was an official promise of autonomy in clinical decisions, a promise reiterated on numerous occasions by both Conservative and Labour governments up to 1979 (Harrison, 1988: 24–6). The following quotations, from almost 30 years apart, are illustrative:

> *Whatever the organisation [of the future NHS] the doctors taking part must remain free to direct their clinical knowledge and personal skill for the benefit of their patients in the way in which they feel to be best. (Ministry of Health, 1944: 26)*

> *Professional workers' … clinical freedom … is cherished by the professions and accepted by the Government. It is the safeguard for patients today and an insurance for future improvements. (DHSS, 1972: vii)*

Thus GPs were able to refer their patients freely to any specialist in any hospital anywhere in the UK, the financial consequences of such decisions falling upon the hospitals. Subject to administrative intervention only in extreme cases, they could prescribe from the NHS pharmacopoeia in whatever quantities they chose. Hospital consultants (specialists) had unilateral right to undertake private practice. Research from this period makes it clear that this autonomy was real. A review of some 25 empirical studies conducted up to 1983 (Harrison, 1988) concluded that doctors at large, rather than managers, were the most influential actors in the NHS. The overall shape of services was created interactively as an aggregate of individual clinical decisions, leaving managers and planners weak in the face of medical opposition. Managers were reluctant to question the value of existing patterns of service or to propose major changes. Both planning and actual change were incremental, with little of the officially intended redistribution of resources from hospitals to community services. There was a general absence of evaluation, and managerial conflict with doctors was generally avoided. Finally, managers behaved as if doctors, rather than the public, were the clients of the NHS and managerial agendas were dominated by issues raised by 'insider' groups. In summary,

> *Managers neither were, nor were supposed to be, influential with respect to doctors … Managers in general worked to solve problems and to maintain their organisations rather than to secure major change. (Harrison, 1988: 51)*

Contemporary challenges to professionalism

Within a few years of the appearance of theories of medical dominance, analysts, especially in the United States, began to consider whether medical autonomy and dominance might be under challenge from either (or both) healthcare consumers, and from managers acting on behalf of government and commercial interests in the field. Haug (1973) described the possibility of a trend towards 'deprofessionalisation', in which professional legitimacy and monopolies of knowledge might be eroded by (amongst other factors) the growth of a more educated and less deferential public, and of the development of patient or consumer pressure groups. However, neither Haug (1988) herself, nor commentators such as Alford (1975), Freidson (1984) or Navarro (1988) were confident that significant changes along these lines had occurred by the mid-1980s. In contrast, social scientists had begun to agree that medical dominance and autonomy in the US, UK and elsewhere were under challenge from policy makers and from hospital and health services managers though, as we shall see below, they disagreed about how this should be interpreted in theoretical terms. These challenges occurred at both meso and micro levels, though it should be noted that there is no necessary relationship between the two since changes in professional institutions or national policies do not automatically impact on day-to-day professional work (Annandale, 1989; Harrison et al., 1990: 113–4). This section summarises the main challenges, whilst the final section of the chapter examines alternative interpretations of these events.

Challenges to medical self-regulation and dominance: the meso level

In the late 1960s the apparent internal unity of the medical profession had been dented by a major dispute over doctors' GMC registration fees, which resulted in a Royal Commission report that left the GMC with a majority of elected members and university and royal college representatives in a minority (Committee of Inquiry, 1975; Stacey, 2000: 32). However, it was in the 1980s that medicine's dominance over health policy was dented by two very public defeats over the form of NHS organisation. Further details of the contexts of both of these situations are given in Chapter 4, but we can note here that the BMA strongly objected to both the introduction of 'general managers' after the Griffiths Report of 1983, and later to the NHS quasi-market that followed the 1989 White Paper *Working for Patients* (Harrison, 2001). On the first of these issues, the BMA wrote to the Secretary of State in the following terms:

> *It could be interpreted from the report that a somewhat autocratic 'executive' manager would be appointed with significant delegated powers, who would – in the interests of 'good management' – be able to make major decisions against the advice of the profession ... it should be clearly understood that the profession would neither accept nor cooperate with any such arrangement – particularly where the interests of patients are concerned ...* (quoted in British Medical Journal, *288, 14 January 1984: 165*)

This virtual declaration of independence was accompanied by demands for modifications to Griffiths' scheme and a trial period. Despite all this and some diffidence by the Secretary of State, the new arrangements were accepted by the government in 1984 when it became clear that they had the Prime Minister's support (Harrison, 1994: 90–1). On the second issue, the government also faced a good deal of BMA opposition:

> *[BMA Council] is convinced that many of the proposals would cause serious damage to NHS patient care, lead to a fragmented service and destroy the comprehensive nature of the existing service. The Government's main proposals would appear to be to contain and reduce the level of public expenditure devoted to health care. The proposals would undoubtedly increase substantially the administrative and accountancy costs of the service, and they ignore the rising costs of providing services for the elderly and of medical advances. In the absence of any additional funding the proposals would inevitably reduce the standards of NHS patient care. (British Medical Association, 1989: 2)*

By mid-1989 there was a widespread perception that the government was losing political ground on the issue, evidence for which continued to be apparent in opinion polls throughout 1990 and 1991. However, the government persisted with the necessary legislation, and in June 1992 the BMA formally ended its campaign against the changes, more than a year after they had been implemented. Indeed, many individual doctors were prepared to break ranks in such matters as opting for the 'GP fundholding' arrangements contained within the proposals. As a result, it became practice during the 1990s for consultants to be employed by the NHS institutions in which they worked, and the numbers of both salaried GPs and of GPs who have been induced to adopt more specific contacts for services increased. By this time, the governing bodies of almost all NHS institutions were modelled on commercial organisations' boards of directors with doctors in a very small minority. By the late 1990s, the Chief Executives (few of whom are qualified health professionals) of NHS service delivery organisations had become legally and organisationally responsible for the quality of clinical services delivered. This innovation also introduced the notion of 'clinical governance', despite its anodyne official definition (NHS Executive, 1998: 33), a mechanism for controlling the health professions.

This period was also one in which issues of the professional competence of doctors began to surface, compelling the GMC to reconsider its criteria and procedures for dealing with 'professional misconduct'. In 1980, it introduced a procedure for cases where a doctor's illness (which, though drug or alcohol misuse may be involved could only with difficulty be regarded as 'misconduct') affected clinical performance (Allsop and Mulcahy, 1996: 87–8). Over the next few years, in the wake of prominent cases of apparent clinical neglect or incompetence, ministers began to press the GMC to review its misconduct procedures so as to be able to deal more firmly with cases of poor clinical performance, in some of which doctors had been unwilling to expose medical colleagues (Allsop, 2002: 86; Allsop and Mulcahy, 1996: 85; Salter, 2000: 14; Stacey, 2000: 33). A new procedure was eventually introduced in 1995 (Allsop and Mulcahy, 1996: 90–1; Stacey, 2000: 35).

Perhaps the most widely and lengthily publicised such case was that of two paediatric cardiac surgeons at Bristol Royal Infirmary whose high surgical mortality rates had not led to local action, despite the fact that the hospital chief executive was himself a doctor, and where staff attempts to report matters had been repeatedly ignored (Klein, 1998). The doctors were disciplined by the GMC after parents had reported them, eventually triggering an independent inquiry (Dyer, 1998; Klein, 1998; Public Inquiry, 2001; Salter, 2001) which also led to a further independent inquiry at Alder Hey Hospital, where organs of children who had died after surgery had been retained for research purposes without proper parental consent (Redfern, 2001). These events, along with a number of other high-profile cases of incompetence (Department of Health, 2000a; Dyer, 2000), and the conviction of a Manchester GP for multiple murder (www.the-shipman-inquiry.org.uk/firstreport.asp, accessed 25 January 2005), contributed to a policy trend of increasing government control of doctors. From 2002 onwards the GMC agreed to introduce compulsory five-yearly revalidation of each registrant's fitness to practise medicine (Allsop, 2002: 89; Salter, 2001: 874), though in 2006 it emerged that this was considered by the government to be insufficiently rigorous, and proposals have now been made for the GMC to lose a number of its functions, including the determination of individual fitness to practise cases, control over the curriculum for undergraduate medical training and recognition of medical schools (Cole, 2006). A new overarching Council for Healthcare Regulatory Excellence, able to supervise not just the GMC but the state regulatory bodies of all other health professions, has been introduced. The new council is able to require subordinate regulatory bodies to modify their procedures, and to refer their disciplinary decisions for review by the high court (Dewar and Finlayson, 2002), which has already begun to overrule GMC judgements (Pritchard, 2004: 2).

More generally, new institutions of *surveillance* have appeared. The Commission for Health Improvement was established in 1999 to inspect and report on all NHS institutions at four yearly intervals and to conduct non-routine investigations into specific allegations of service inadequacy. The Audit Commission also conducts topic-based 'value for money' audits in both health and social care. Surveillance, monitoring and evaluation are facilitated by the annual collation of 'performance indicators' within a national performance assessment framework for healthcare (Secretary of State for Health, 2000). Performance indicator data, inspection results and other information have been summarised in a shifting series of assessment regimes for service provider organisations. It is important to note that, although it is managers who are primarily liable to sanctions, their existence provides an obvious imperative for them to seek greater control and surveillance over doctors. From 2004, a new Commission for Healthcare Audit and Inspection (subsequently renamed the Healthcare Commission) incorporates many of these functions.

These institutions of surveillance apply to healthcare provision more generally and not just to medical work. Other health professions were also affected by a further glut of regulatory activity in the early twenty-first century. Nursing, midwifery and health visitor regulation was deemed to be inadequate to deal with poor professional practice and the UKCC was replaced in 2002 by a Nursing and Midwifery Council (Davies, 2002: 104) with a narrow majority of professional members. The task of attending a woman in childbirth remains a monopoly for registered midwives. At the same time, the CPSM was replaced by a new Health Professions Council with a narrow lay majority, responsible for the licensure of 13 professions, but currently considering extending its ambit to over 60 further healthcare occupations, including psychologists, dance therapists, acupuncturists, operating department practitioners and surgical care practitioners (www.hpc-uk.org, accessed 27 December 2006). Taken together, these changes can be seen as representing a significant shift away from self-regulation; as Salter (2001: 874) has put it 'self-regulation remains, at least in name, but is situated within a state-administered apparatus of accountability'.

Finally, there is evidence that the ability of the medical profession to shape the roles of other health workers has diminished somewhat. A substantial thrust of NHS human resources policy is represented as increasing the flexibility of the workforce, breaking down occupational barriers and opening up new opportunities for training and the development of new constellations of skills to fill perceived shortages (Secretary of State for Health, 2000, 2005). This has led to important role extensions for some professions other than medicine, such as the ability of appropriately trained nurses and pharmacists to prescribe virtually the entire pharmacopoeia (Day, 2005) and the creation of cadres of nurse specialists in such areas as heart failure care. New occupations are also being developed, some of which, such as non-medically qualified 'surgical care practitioners' and 'physician assistants', are controversial (*BMA News,* 20 May 2006: 14; Kneebone and Darzi, 2005) and there has been considerable growth in non-professional support occupations (Saks and Allsop, 2007).

Challenges to clinical freedom

The meso-level challenges described above have been accompanied by micro-level challenges of three related types. First, the UK is now prominent amongst the many countries that have been working on methods to *formalise and codify medical knowledge.* So-called 'casemix' measures, most famously 'diagnosis-related groups' (DRGs; in the UK Healthcare Resource Groups, or HRGs), have been developed as a means of providing standardised descriptors of medical workloads in both hospital and (later) ambulatory care (Bardsley et al., 1987; Benton et al., 1998). Such codification, which provides a means by which medical work can be systematically measured and controlled, is scheduled to become the 'currency' of financial relationships between NHS funding bodies and the actual providers of NHS care (Department of Health, 2002c); we shall consider this further in Chapter 4. Second, the former prominent official statements about clinical autonomy have been replaced by a strong emphasis on the need for clinicians to adhere to *rules and criteria* (*BMA News Review,* March 1999: 16; Harrison, 2002), which are increasingly available in forms such as 'clinical guidelines' or 'clinical protocols', which codify and to some extent standardise the treatment for particular patients (Berg, 1997a). (Guidelines are examined in greater detail in Chapter 3.) In addition, National Service Frameworks (NSFs) have been developed as official specifications of services for particular patient groups (for instance, Department of Health, 2000a). The two basic approaches of codification and guidelines, often combined with micro-economic analyses, have been used as the basis of more complex systems of 'managed care' 'disease management' and 'patient pathways' (Robinson and Steiner, 1998).

We shall examine some of the empirical research evidence in more detail in Chapter 4, but we can summarise here by noting that the above developments have occurred towards the end of 20 years in which medical autonomy has been steadily, if gradually, eroded by management (Harrison and Ahmad, 2000). A review of 24 empirical studies conducted between 1983 and 1990 (Harrison et al., 1992: 54–92) concluded that this era had led to only modest changes in the medical/managerial power balance, but to significant changes both in perceptions of managerial legitimacy and in government/management relationships. A consistent picture is provided by a review of post-1990 research into medical–managerial relationships (Harrison and Lim, 2003). NHS managers were by the early 1990s more ready than before to 'take on' doctors resulting in decisions where managerial interventions were decisive, most notably in the pursuit of NHS 'Trust' status (see Chapter 6) against medical opposition. Doctors were sometimes drawn into co-operative networks with managers, though this was not always the case, and managers were unable to control the acute medical sector or to make other than incremental adjustments to services. Radical organisational change in hospitals, for instance via 'business process re-engineering', proved extremely difficult to secure. Yet as in the earlier period, there was little indication of any desire to return to the earlier organisation arrangements. Published empirical evidence in respect of the period since 1997 seems to relate wholly to primary care. Whilst managers still perceive GPs as enjoying substantial autonomy (Marshall et al., 2002), there are indications that, in primary care at least, initial medical resistance to management and regulation (Harrison and Lim, 2000) gave way to unenthusiastic compliance (Harrison and Dowswell, 2002), followed (as we shall see in Chapter 4) by more active compliance as the result of a new contract that provides financial rewards for compliance.

Survival of the biomedical model

Despite the meso- and micro-level challenges discussed in the preceding subsections, the macro-level biomedical model of health and illness has received little serious challenge. From one point of view, this is perhaps surprising in a context where public and patient interest in 'complementary and alternative therapies' has burgeoned (Saks, 2003: 107–17). Yet some such therapies have effectively been co-opted by mainstream medicine. Since the mid-1990s, chiropractors and osteopaths have obtained state licensure and protection of title through a General Chiropractic Council and General Osteopathic Council, each with majorities of professional members. Moreover, some formerly 'alternative' therapies, such as acupuncture, have been adopted by mainstream practitioners. It may also be noted that the individualism of the biomedical model is in many ways consistent with prevailing models of management (Harrison and Ahmad, 2000). It allows 'cases' to be defined, counted and traded as quasi-commodities (Harrison, 2006), an important requirement for the NHS organisational developments that we shall examine in Chapter 4.

Interpreting the challenges to professionalism

In thinking about challenges to medical autonomy and dominance, we must enter some qualifications. First, challenges are not always successful, and governments do not always achieve the outcomes they desire (Bovens et al., 2001: 606–17). Second, as already noted, it is possible in principle to obtain desired results in one sphere without impacting on others; Annandale (1989), for instance, recognises that states may indeed co-opt elites at meso level (in the manner described by Coburn: see below), but shows that this does not necessarily lead to changes in the micro-level medical labour process. Third, analysts need to be wary of exaggerating challenges by conflating projections of the future with developments that have already occurred, and assuming that changes in organisational formalities necessarily lead to changes in power relationships (Freidson, 1994: 34). Fourth, the state and its managers are not the sole source of challenges to medicine. The systematisation of medical knowledge may make it more easily usable by patients, a possibility much enhanced by the growth of Internet usage (Coeira, 1996). Evidence of 'challenges' to medicine can be interpreted in a variety of ways, of which we review five.

The Marxian perspective

Perhaps the starkest account (from medicine's point of view) draws on Marxist analyses (see for instance Braverman, 1974) of the ways in which labour processes have become ever more tightly specified and controlled as a means of maximising capitalists' profits. The best-known analysis in this tradition is that of McKinlay and various colleagues, who have seen reduction in medical autonomy as an example of 'proletarianisation' in which medicine

> is divested of control over certain prerogatives relating to the location, content and essentiality of its task activities, thereby subordinating it to the broader requirements of production under advanced capitalism. (McKinlay and Stoeckle, 1988: 200; see also McKinlay and Arches, 1985)

In later work McKinlay accounts for 'the end of the golden age of doctoring' in terms of these economic factors, but adds some social and political factors such as the erosion of patients' trust in physicians and splits in medical interest groups (McKinlay and Marceau, 2002). Other Marxist analysts have taken a different view; the view (outlined above) that medical autonomy and dominance is largely illusory implies that there is no reason to expect the profession not to be subjected to the same kind of controls that are applied to other groups of workers. Moreover, McKinlay's account seems exaggerated; physicians' autonomy may have declined but they are certainly not subjected to the level of control experienced by industrial manual workers, or (to employ a more contemporary example) call centre operatives:

> While the medical profession has never been the dominant force in medicine, it has nevertheless been a major force. Its power... has been declining for some time now. But this loss of power cannot be equated with ... proletarianisation ... Proletarians do not have supervision over others, do not have some space for decision making, do not realise mental rather than manual work, and do not have skills that need to be credentialed by the state. (Navarro, 1988: 69–70)

McKinlay's analysis is very much oriented towards the US system in which over half of all healthcare is funded, and most provided, by private enterprise. However, roughly parallel reasoning has been applied to health systems that are substantially publicly funded (such as Canada) or publicly both funded and provided (such as the UK). The argument is consistent with the Marxian theoretical analysis, introduced in Chapter 1, that the state's motive in financing healthcare is somewhat in tension with the tendency for demand to increase. As a result, it may be argued that the state will eventually experience just as much necessity as any private medical corporation to restrict medical autonomy in order to control expenditure (Coburn et al., 1997; Harrison et al., 1990). The term 'eventually' in this formulation means that there is scope for analysts to make judgements about how far the balance of power between physicians and managers may have shifted in particular places at particular points in time. Alford's (1975) analysis of the healthcare sector in New York City in the 1950s and 1960s defined 'structural interests' in terms of the extent to which their 'interests [are] served or not served by the way in which they "fit" into the basic logic and principles by which the institutions of society operate'. In that specific context, medicine remained the *dominant* structural interest, 'served by the [current] structure of social, economic and political institutions'. This dominance existed in spite of *challenging* interests including hospital administrators and government health planners 'created by changing technology and division of labour in healthcare production and distribution', sharing an interest in 'breaking the monopoly of physicians over the production and distribution of healthcare' (Alford, 1975: 14–15). In contrast, a much more recent analysis of the UK, employing Alford's theory, concluded that NHS managers could reasonably be argued to have displaced physicians as the dominant structural interest (Harrison and Ahmad, 2000; see also Foster and Wilding, 2000), whilst similar findings are evident in Robinson's more descriptive (1999) account of corporate medicine in the USA.

Restratification

A more optimistic (from medicine's point of view) interpretation of contemporary challenges is the neo-Weberian view that they represent a new form of stratification *within* medicine rather than overall decline (Freidson, 1988; Reed, 1994). Despite the public image of collegiality within medicine referred to above, there have always been differences of status within the profession, especially between its various specialties, between academic physicians and rank-and-file, and in terms of earnings (Freidson, 1984: 141, 144). However, a number of developments have led to further breakdown in professional collegiality and to a new form of stratification, sometimes referred to as 're-stratification'. First, legislative and organisational changes have left physicians openly competing with other, and making explicit evaluative judgements about each others' clinical practice via clinical audit and peer review systems (Freidson, 1984: 140, 142). Second, more physicians are now to be found in roles which are both individually and collectively responsible for supervising other fully qualified doctors. What Freidson calls the 'administrative elite' 'serve in executive management and supervisory roles ... clearly delineated by their formal rank [and possess] authority ... distinct from that of their rank-and-file colleagues' (1984: 142). Third, Freidson notes that professional work is increasingly bureaucratised in the sense of becoming increasingly determined by 'formats' (1984: 139), that is by detailed rules ('clinical guidelines' and 'protocols' are obvious examples) about how work is to be done. These 'formats' are largely produced by what Freidson terms a 'knowledge elite', that is an 'elite segment of the profession, composed of those who devote themselves on a full-time basis to research' in university departments 'devoted to research, experimental practice and theorising', and who also provide professional advice on public policy issues (1984: 143). Both elites may be in conflict with rank-and-file practitioners, since the 'administrative elite' creates a 'less collegial and more superordinate relationship' with rank-and-file professionals (1984: 142), whilst the 'knowledge elite' may produce rules that are impractical for everyday clinical situations (1984: 143). These changes constitute a breakdown of the profession as a community that shares common experience and identity, and maintains a degree of solidarity:

> *the magnification and formalisation of these relationships into a considerably more overt ... system of stratification within the profession which can no longer be protected by the face-saving norms of traditional professional etiquette. (Freidson, 1984: 144)*

However, Freidson concludes that, contrary to the Marxist views summarised above, professional restratification is a means of *maintaining* medical power, since both the administrative and knowledge elites remain within the profession, and sees little evidence that the overall social or intellectual place of medicine has been eroded:

> *So long as the formulation, direction and execution of the control of professional work remains in the hands of members of the profession, it is not intellectually useful to employ ... the concept of proletarianisation. (Freidson, 1994: 144; see also Mechanic, 1991: 495)*

Freidson's analysis has been criticised from Coburn's (1992: 509; Coburn et al., 1997: 19) perspective, according to which restratification implies the *weakening* of professional power through state co-optation of medical elites. Writing about the Canadian context from 1978 to 1993, Coburn et al. note that government has become very involved in managing the *content* of medical care and not just in its financing (1997: 5). In reaction to this, the authors argue

> *Medical elites ... are trying to preserve medical power with new strategies for what they perceive as a radically new political and economic context. While seeking to preserve power for medicine as a whole, medical elites and representative and self-regulatory organisations are being drawn into controlling practitioners. (1997: 5)*

In this process, Coburn et al. argue, medical elites become socialised into a less professionally dominant view of health and healthcare as a result of contact with other health professions, the state and regulatory agencies (1997: 18). The effect is to distance the medical elite from identifying with rank-and-file physicians. In summary, 'medical institutions are being used, co-opted by external forces into constraining their own members' (1997: 18). Drawing an explicit parallel with the NHS, Coburn et al. conclude that their analysis

> *emphasises the clearly contingent nature of medical power. The influence of the state, and of those forces determining or shaping state health policy, are clearly part of the explanation of the changing power dynamics within healthcare. (1997: 19–20)*

Countervailing powers

A third interpretation of contemporary challenges to medicine is that they are a natural prod-uct of the ebb and flow of politics; no political actor can expect to be dominant for an indef-inite period since a reaction from other actors will eventually occur, though such reactions may take decades to develop. This view has been labelled as a theory of 'countervailing powers' (Light, 1995; see also Mechanic, 1991). In Light's formulation,

> *Dominance slowly produces imbalances, excesses and neglects that anger other ... latent powers and alienate the larger public. These imbalances include (1) internal elaboration and expansion that weaken the dominant institution from within; (2) a subsequent tendency to consume more and more of the nation's wealth; (3) a self-regarding importance that ignores the concerns of clients and institutional partners; and (4) an expansion of control that exacerbates the impact of the other three. (Light, 1995: 27)*

It is easy to see how this interpretation may be applied to medicine in the late twentieth cen-tury. Medical activities have indeed come to consume an ever-increasing proportion of national wealth of many countries (including, as Chapter 1 has shown, the UK) and, as we saw above, tighter regulation of UK medicine has occurred partly in response to a number of 'scandals' that have been interpreted by government precisely as symptoms of 'self-regarding importance' on the part of the profession. It is less clear whether the general public perceive matters in the same way; an opinion poll conducted shortly after some of the scandals found that 89 percent of respondents trusted their doctor (Hall, 2001: 751). It is certainly true however that professional collegiality and cohesion have become difficult to maintain, and this has provided the opportunity for UK governments to employ 'divide and rule' strategies in relation to medicine, as will become evident in Chapter 6.

Governmentality

A fourth and relatively recent interpretation of challenges to medicine is to be found in Johnson's later (1995) work, which employ's Foucault's (1991) notion of 'governmentality'. The essence of Johnson's position is that the state and the professions are symbiotic, so that it makes little sense to think in terms of one challenging the other:

> *The independence of the professions depends on the interventions of the state, but ... the state is dependent on the independence of the professions in securing the capacity to govern as well as legit-imating its governance ... We must develop ways of talking about the state and profession that conceive of the relationship not as a struggle for autonomy and control but as the interplay of integrally related structures ... (Johnson, 1995: 16)*

On this view, the professions play a part in shaping the conduct of individuals so that it does not challenge the state (Hindess, 2001: 44). The idea of governmentality has been more recently employed by Flynn (2002) to analyse the situation of medicine in the UK. An important strand in Foucauldian thought is that of *surveillance* as a means by which society is regulated. The professions, including medicine, are part of the apparatus by which people are regulated but, paradoxically, are also themselves increasingly regulated by governmental agencies and systems of audit (some of which we shall examine in Chapter 4). The solution to the paradox, in Flynn's view, is the socialisation or co-optation of medicine into alignment with managerial views of the world, so that they come to accept the need for regulation. We shall see in Chapter 6 that there have been continuous attempts since the mid-1980s to co-opt doctors into roles that support government policy. Flynn goes on to argue that contemporary regulation of medicine is a form of 'soft bureaucracy' where 'processes of flexibility and decentralisation co-exist with more rigid constraints and structures of domination' (Courpasson, 2000: 157). In this context, it is worth noting that there are already strong consonances between the 'biomedical model' described above and the ways in which managers tend to think about production generally; individual patients and treatments can be counted, costed and treated as production outputs (Harrison and Ahmad, 2000).

The decline of 'club' government

Each of the four theoretical interpretations outlined above is specific to medicine, though we have seen that each also draws on elements of broader social theory. In contrast, none is specific to the UK or any other country. (Even though Freidson has tended to write only about the US, his analysis has been adopted more widely; see, for instance, Mahmood, 2002.) In contrast, our fifth theoretical interpretation is UK-specific, but not medicine-specific, preferring to see the challenges to medicine merely as a specific manifestation of more general changes in the character of state regulation in the UK. This analysis begins with Marquand's famous observation that British government in the twentieth century had

> the atmosphere ... of a club, whose members trusted each other to observe the spirit of the club rules; the notion that the principles underlying the rules should be clearly defined and publicly proclaimed was profoundly alien. (Marquand, 1988: 178)

Moran (2003: 31–6) has explained the origins of this situation as follows. The character of the British state as it existed for most of the twentieth century was shaped in the nineteenth century, when only a small proportion of the population was permitted to vote and when government was essentially a London-based oligarchy that feared any extension of democracy. However, government administrative capacity was weak, and detailed regulatory and administrative questions were considered as mundane technicalities that could appropriately be delegated to 'insiders' as a matter of informal co-operation rather than formal legal determination. This situation was underpinned by a belief that 'outsiders' lacked the necessary (and largely tacit) knowledge to regulate a field effectively. For Moran, therefore, the system of medical self-regulation described in this chapter was simply one example of a more general British approach to regulation, also typified in such institutions as the City of London and the higher civil service (2003: 33). Moran further argues that the decline in medical self-regulation over the last 20 years mirrors the decline in 'club government' more generally (2004: 28), with the same two root causes. First, economic pressures meant that governments sought to reorganise the economy and to make it more efficient, a strategy that inevitably extended to the reorganisation of the welfare state. Since (as we saw above) the decisions of doctors largely define the NHS and determine its expenditure, such reorganisation necessarily extended to the medical profession (2004: 33, 36). Second, and separately, a growingly assertive public made it less practicable to conceal medical (or other professional) scandals within an effectively private system of regulation (2004: 32).

Concluding remarks

We have seen that most theories of professions and professionalisation give a degree of importance to the idea that professionals enjoy a greater degree of autonomy, either collectively, individually or both, than do members of other occupations. Although theoretical explanations vary, medicine has usually been treated as one of the archetypical modern professions, manifesting high degrees of both autonomy and dominance over other occupations. It seems clear, however, that medicine in the UK has been experiencing a series of challenges over the last 20 years that have led to a steady but real decline in autonomy. We can discern quite direct evidence for Light's 'countervailing powers' thesis in the form of political reactions to the various medical 'scandals' discussed above. The creation of new health professions and role extensions for occupations historically subordinate to medicine provide direct evidence for Abbott's conceptions of professional jurisdictions as always in flux. Although the medical profession has not been 'proletarianised' in any literal sense, the role of the state in challenging medical autonomy and dominance is clear. Moran's thesis of the decline of 'club government' aptly reminds us that developments in the health field have parallels in other aspects of state activity. However, each of the major interpretations of the governmental and managerial challenge to medical autonomy and dominance rests on a different basic set of assumptions about how the state and society interact. As a consequence, each takes a slightly different angle on essentially the same set of facts and we cannot make straightforward comparisons between them. Whereas analysts such as McKinlay and Coburn are interested in the autonomy of the individual medical practitioner, Freidson maintains that it is the autonomy of medicine as a corporate entity that matters (Hafferty, 1988: 206–7). McKinlay, Coburn and Moran are all interested in the relationship between state, society and medicine, whereas Freidson and Light focus much more on politics between the medical profession and other social actors, and Johnson and Flynn tend to discount the significance of treating state and profession as discrete actors.

Further reading

From the voluminous literature on the professions, an accessible overview of concepts and issues can be obtained from Abbott (1988). For an overarching history of medicine from ancient times, see Porter (1997). For a history of modern scientific medicine and its techniques, see Marks (1997) and Daly (2005). Allsop and Saks (2002) examine professional self-regulation and the implications of regulatory change for the future of healthcare.

Chapter 3

The Politics of Clinical Knowledge

Summary of chapter contents

- Knowledge and evidence: key concepts
- Evidence-based practice: history and contemporary developments
- Interpreting scientific–bureaucratic medicine

As we saw in Chapter 2, the connection between medicine and the universities goes back several centuries and the notion of a 'profession' entails an element of esoteric knowledge. The belief that the practice of medicine, and subsequently of other clinical professions, ought to take account of some kind of 'evidence' has also been held and acted upon by some individuals over several centuries. However, widespread acceptance of the explicit claim that daily clinical practice should be based on *systematic* research evidence about the effectiveness of the interventions employed has grown only over the last 50 years and has been an active component of UK health policy only since the early 1990s. This chapter focuses on the way in which this policy of 'evidence-based medicine' (EBM) has developed and on EBM as a political, rather than exclusively scientific, phenomenon.

At its simplest, EBM is the doctrine that clinical medical practice ought to be based upon sound research evidence about the effectiveness of each diagnostic or therapeutic procedure ('intervention' hereafter). The same principle has been extended to other clinical professions, including nursing, midwifery, dentistry, physiotherapy and others, so that more generic expressions such as 'evidence-based practice' (EBP, the term we use hereafter) and 'evidence-based healthcare' are now current. As we shall see in the final section, similar reasoning has been employed in sectors other than health, especially in education, criminal justice and social work. EBP is usually presented by its proponents in the language of science, and there is clearly some justification for this; currently dominant ideas about EBP are indeed very much based on the notion of applying scientific research findings to clinical practice. But EBP is also a political phenomenon, in at least two senses. First, there is more than one conception of what constitutes EBP, so that the contemporary orthodoxy described below represents the domination of one set of ideas, and their exponents, over another. Second, this orthodoxy has become a core element of UK public policy.

The first section of this chapter discusses some alternative ways of thinking about 'evidence' and about its implementation in clinical practice. From these, we generate and discuss four alternative models of EBP, the last of which has come increasingly to characterise the approach adopted in the NHS. The second section provides an account of what we have termed the 'pre-history' of EBP, focusing in particular on the development of ideas about experimentation as the key to generating valid research evidence. The third section provides an account of more recent history, focusing in particular on the way in which EBP has become institutionalised as an element of UK health policy and on contemporary critiques of it. The final section sketches out two rather different theoretical approaches to explaining the rise of EBP, one based on theories of public policy agenda formation, the other on broader contemporary social theory.

Key concepts in knowledge and evidence

As noted above, to speak of EBP entails having some notion of what constitutes valid (or 'good' or 'sound') evidence upon which practice can be based. Although such notions of validity reflect scientific thinking, it does not follow that there is complete agreement about them. Hence, differences of view about what constitutes valid evidence of clinical effectiveness provide one dimension along which concepts of EBP may be analysed. The fact that (as we examine in greater detail below) EBP has become public policy in the UK points to a second dimension of analysis, relating to organisational implications. If EBP is policy, how is that policy implemented? These analytical dimensions provide the subject matter for the next subsection. In the following subsection, we combine the two dimensions into a matrix that illustrates four alternative models of EBP.

Defining and implementing valid evidence

We begin by considering the character of valid knowledge about cause and effect, and where it is to be found. A simple way of presenting alternative possibilities is to present them as poles of a spectrum. One pole represents the primacy of the participants' own experience, reflection upon it and peer discussion as the source of valid knowledge about the effectiveness of healthcare. In this model, evidence is internal to the clinician.

The opposite pole represents the primacy of accumulated externally generated published research findings. This represents a view that has become increasingly dominant since the early 1990s, and is crystallised in the so-called 'hierarchy of evidence', widely cited as an authoritative definition of the soundness of scientific research purporting to demonstrate

Table 3.1   The 'hierarchy of evidence'

Level of validity of findings	Type of research
I	Strong evidence from at least one systematic review (including meta-analysis) of multiple well-designed randomised controlled trials
II	Strong evidence from at least one properly designed randomised controlled trial of appropriate size
III	Evidence from well-designed experimental but non-randomised studies, e.g. single group pre-post, cohort, time series or matched case-controlled studies
IV	Evidence from well-designed non-experimental studies from more than one centre or research group
V	Opinions of respected authorities, based on clinical evidence, descriptive studies or reports of expert committees

Source: adapted from Department of Health (1996)

the effectiveness of clinical interventions. A brief account of the development of this model is given later in this chapter, and it has now become quite complex (for a full description, see Sackett et al., 2000: 173–7), but its essentials may be more simply represented, as in Table 3.1.

The principle which underpins this hierarchy is *validity*, that is the elimination from research findings of bias arising from any differences between patients treated by means of the intervention being researched and patients treated with other interventions or simply not treated. The pinnacle of the hierarchy is occupied by the randomised controlled trial (RCT), an experiment in which patients are conscientiously allocated randomly (and with their consent) between the group which will receive the intervention under investigation and whatever group(s) with whom they will be compared: 'control' groups receiving perhaps placebos, or no treatment, and/or existing conventional treatment, as the case may be. Ideally, it is held, RCTs should be 'double blind', that is neither the treating clinician nor the patient should know which intervention they are receiving. This ideal cannot of course always be met; for instance it is difficult to conceal whether or not surgery is occurring or ethically to perform a dummy operation. (For a detailed account of this method, see Elwood, 1988: 96–101; Gomm, 2000.) Special quantitative methods, described as 'meta-analysis', have been developed in order to aggregate the results of several RCTs (Mulrow, 1994). Other research methods are ranked lower in the hierarchy, with other types of *controlled* study second to the RCT and uncontrolled methods a poor third; in practice, advocates of RCTs tend to regard uncontrolled (non-experimental) methods, and indeed qualitative research, as suitable only for feasibility testing and/or hypothesis-building with a view to an eventual controlled study. (For a summary of the content of methods listed for each level, see Gray, 1997: 72–91.)

Alternative ways of thinking about how knowledge should be implemented can also be rather simplistically represented by two poles of a spectrum. One pole implies that it is largely individual clinicians who internalise and apply knowledge, so that the application of EBP is mainly a matter of the internal motivation of professionals, perhaps supported by information systems that provide easy access to colleagues' advice or to published research

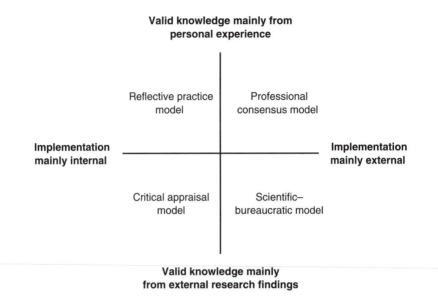

Figure 3.1   Four models of 'evidence-based practice'
Source: Harrison (2002)

evidence. On this view, clinical professionals can largely be relied upon to integrate valid evidence into their daily practice, with few or no organisational implications; EBP is therefore little more than an extension of proper professional conduct. The other pole implies that managerial and/or organisational effort is required in order to implement EBP. Such external means of distillation and promulgation of knowledge might take the form of rules such as 'clinical guidelines' or 'protocols' (Berg, 1997a), perhaps accompanied by incentives and/or sanctions for clinicians to adhere to them. The logic of guidelines is essentially algorithmic, that is, they guide their user to courses of (diagnostic or therapeutic) action, dependent upon stated prior conditions: 'if ... then' logic. The logic is also normative, that is it tells the clinician what *ought* to be done, though guidelines do not always claim to determine clinical action completely, and degrees of discretion are left.

Four models of evidence-based practice

These two spectrums, respectively denoting locus of evidence and locus of clinicians' motivations, can be combined to produce the two-by-two matrix shown as Figure 3.1.

Each of the four resultant cells of the matrix provides a different model of EBP, which might be summarised as follows (Harrison, 2002). The first model is what may be called 'reflective practice' – it centres on the notions that an individual clinician should be constantly self-critical of his or her own practice, that such a critical stance can be facilitated by regular audit of the outcomes of that practice, and that both the audit itself and remedial action based on it are best facilitated by an open and non-defensive collegiate approach involving other clinicians as peers. Although this model may imply a somewhat idealised perspective on professions, there are examples of its successful implementation in the UK (Gruer et al., 1986; Simpson, 2004). Perhaps the best theoretical statement underpinning this approach is provided by Argyris and Schon's *Theory in Practice*, subtitled *Increasing Professional Effectiveness*:

> *Maximising valid information about oneself and others requires speaking in directly observable categories ... encouraging independent interpretations ... (T)his is likely to make the actor seem less threatening, which is again likely to lead other people to offer valid information ... This creates a predisposition towards inquiry and learning. (Argyris and Schon, 1977: 90–1; see also Schon, 1983)*

A second model of medical care is built on the generation of professional consensus initially by bringing together professional elites to 'consensus conferences' to discuss published evidence but mainly personal experience of a particular clinical topic with the aim of producing a 'consensus statement' to guide the behaviour of the professional rank and file. The key feature of such a model is precisely the generation of consensus; the participants may be carefully selected to this end, and the resultant statement may evade controversy by means of a certain strategic vagueness (*Lancet* editorial, 339: 1197–8, 1992) and the absence of sufficient scientific data (Woolf, 1992).

The third model of medical care may be called critical appraisal after its preferred approach to the interrogation of published research findings. It rejects one of the central assumptions of the above models, that personal experience, even if critically examined, is the main source of valid knowledge. It substitutes the view (expressed in the 'hierarchy of evidence') that only randomised controlled trials (RCTs) provide the most clearly valid inferences about the effects of clinical interventions, and that the appropriate means of aggregating the findings of several trials is meta-analysis or other forms of systematic review. Indeed, much of the development of the hierarchy of evidence has come from proponents of critical appraisal. Its preference for the formal aggregation of published research evidence therefore implicitly downgrades the type of personal experience upon which the first two models are based. Nevertheless, critical appraisal assumes that neither academic research nor clinical guidelines can be applied unproblematically and hence practitioners should be prepared to invest the time to read research and assess its validity and applicability for themselves; the approach has been described by proponents as 'the integration of best research evidence with clinical expertise and patient values' (Sackett et al., 2000: 1). Since practitioners may not have the necessary skills to make such critical appraisals of the literature, the model entails a programme of appropriate training (Guyatt and Rennie, 1993).

Scientific–bureaucratic medicine (Harrison, 2002) is the fourth model. Like critical appraisal, it centres on the assumption that valid and reliable knowledge is mainly to be obtained from the accumulation of research conducted by experts according to the scientific criteria expressed in the 'hierarchy of evidence'. It further assumes that working clinicians are likely to be both too busy and insufficiently skilled to interpret and apply such knowledge for themselves, and therefore holds that professional practice should be influenced through the systematic aggregation by experts of research findings on a particular topic, and the distillation of such findings into protocols or guidelines which may then be communicated to practitioners with the expectation that practice will be influenced accordingly (Field and Lohe, 1992; NHS Executive, 1996a, 1996b). In general, guidelines do not claim either to be applicable to all patients or to determine clinical action completely, and degrees of discretion are left. Albeit in the highly professionalised context of healthcare organisations, such guidelines are a species of bureaucratic rule, hence the chosen label. As we shall see in the third section of this chapter, scientific–bureaucratic medicine seems to be on its way to becoming the dominant model of EBP in the UK.

Although critical appraisal and scientific–bureaucratic medicine share the same concept of evidence, and although the concepts of critical appraisal are often cited in justification of guideline adherence, these models differ in respect of their attitudes to guidelines. As Sackett, one of the leading exponents of critical appraisal in the 1990s, has put it:

> *Evidence based medicine is not 'cookbook' medicine. Because it requires a bottom up approach that integrates the best external evidence with individual clinical expertise and patients' choice, it cannot result in slavish, cookbook approaches to individual patient care. External clinical evidence can inform, but can never replace, individual clinical expertise, and it is this expertise that decides whether the external evidence applies to the individual patient at all and, if so, how it should be integrated into a clinical decision. Similarly, any external guideline must be integrated with individual clinical expertise in deciding whether and how it matches the patient's clinical state, predicament, and preferences, and thus whether it should be applied. (Sackett et al., 1996: 72)*

An historical sketch of evidence-based practice

As we shall see below, the contemporary 'evidence-based' practice movement dates from the early 1990s. However, we begin by summarising the long history of the ideas that underpin the 'hierarchy of evidence' outlined above, specifically that valid knowledge about causal relationships is dependent upon the adoption of research methods that aim to minimise bias. Although the United States has long possessed institutions aimed at promoting EBP (Marks, 1997: 22; see also Harrison et al., 2002c), it was not until the early 1990s that such institutions (other than those concerned with the safety of drugs; Rivett, 1998: 140–1) began to be established by the UK state. The second subsection provides an account of these developments.

An outline history of clinical experimentation

This history is rather varied but may be characterised with reference to four themes. First, proponents of what is now called EBP were often challenging an existing epistemological orthodoxy, that is prevailing views about the nature of causal knowledge and its relationship to clinical practice. A second theme in this pre-history is the view of EBP proponents that such knowledge needed to be formally and systematically acquired through what would now be seen as scientific investigation, rather than derived from unsystematic experience and 'clinical instinct'. Third, and following partly from that, is the notion that only quantitative data about a multiplicity of cases could provide the necessary confidence about causation. Finally, also related to the second theme, is the importance of methodological considerations in research, and particularly the importance of establishing validity through comparison ('controls' in contemporary jargon) and of avoiding bias through the careful allocation of research subjects to intervention and control groups. The account that follows provides a number of 'snapshots' that might be seen as sketching out the intellectual pre-history of EBP. (For general accounts and critical discussion of these elements from contrasting standpoints, see Brown et al., 2003: Chaps 5–6; Oakley, 2000: Chaps 4–5).

The notion of establishing validity of causal inferences in healthcare through clinical comparison evidently dates back more that 450 years, to about 1545, when Pare tested the efficacy of onions as dressing by applying them only to sections of wounds, leaving other sections untreated or treated by other means (Brown et al., 2003: 123; Oakley, 2000: 146). A 100 years later, the French mathematician and scientist Pascal had effectively introduced the notion of 'control' in his research into atmospheric pressure (Oakley, 2000: 145). A further 100 years afterwards, the now-famous experiment of citrus fruit as treatment for the debilitating disease of scurvy, frequently suffered by sailors, was conducted by James Lind, a naval surgeon on HMS Salisbury. In 1747, Lind identified 12 similarly diseased sailors whom he divided into six groups, each of which received a different treatment, including cider, oil of vitriol, sea water, vinegar, a concoction of garlic, radish, myrrh and Peruvian balsam, and oranges and lemons. The pair who received the citrus fruits regained their fitness in six days, whereas the other ten did not (Currie, 2003; Porter, 1997: 295). Lind is now regarded as probably having conducted the world's first controlled clinical trial, though it is worth noting both that Lind's theory about why citrus fruits were effective was mistaken, and that it was another 50 years before his findings were generally adopted on British ships (Porter, 1997: 295–6). Perhaps the most systematic attempts to employ such approaches were those of the Parisian school of physicians of the early nineteenth century, and in particular of P.C.A. Louis. In the 1830s, Louis employed the 'numerical method' to evaluate whether the outcome for what we now assume to be pneumonia was better if blindly selected groups of patients were 'bled' early or late in the course of their disease, and if large or small amounts of blood were removed (Lilienfield and Lilienfield, 1979; Porter, 1997: 312–3). This approach was also strongly advocated, and indeed applied in some of her own writings on public health, by Florence Nightingale after her return from the Crimea in 1856 (Oakley, 2000: 117).

The preceding examples are all of deliberately engineered comparisons, but our pre-history also includes examples of what would now be termed 'naturally occurring experiments' in order to draw valid causal conclusions. The Hungarian physician Semmelweiss discovered that fatal fevers could be transmitted from cadavers to obstetric patients via the unwashed hands of medical students. The male medical students were accustomed to go straight from the post-mortem room to obstetric clinics, whereas female midwifery students were not expected to examine the dead. Semmelweiss noticed that the clinics staffed by the medical students had a mortality rate three times that of the clinics staffed by midwifery students. In 1847, Semmelweiss introduced hand-washing in chloride of lime, as a result of which the mortality equalised (Oakley, 2000: 146–7). As in Lind's case, it was some time before Semelweiss's findings had any wider effect, partly because although 'germs' had been hypothesised, bacteria had not then been discovered, so that the method of disease transmission remained mysterious (Oakley, 2000: 147; Porter, 1997: 369).

By the late nineteenth century, concern that the inappropriate allocation of research subjects to control and intervention groups might lead to groups that were systematically different and so bias the findings had led to methodological development. The idea that the problem could be solved by randomising research subjects to the various study groups seems initially to have been proposed, though not actually employed, by van Helmont, a Flemish physician, in 1662 (Brown et al., 2003: 126, 144–5) but not applied until the end of the nineteenth century. In a non-medical context, the American psychologist and philosopher C.S. Pierce employed the technique in his psychological experiments, randomising by the selection of playing cards, whilst at about the same time the Society for Psychical Research used it in investigations of telepathy (Brown et al., 2003: 146; Oakley, 2000: 144). In medicine, the Danish medical researcher Fibiger was employing 'alternation' (that is, the first patient to one group, the second to another, and so on) in the 1890s as a method of allocating patients to treatment and comparison groups when studying an anti-diphtheria serum (Brown et al., 2003: 123; Dollery, 1993: 14; Oakley, 2000: 146). It was still being employed in clinical trials 50 years later (Chalmers, 2002; Patulin Clinical Trials Committee, 1944). The subsequent history of EBP is intimately associated with the development of inferential statistics in the early twentieth century, initially outside the field of medicine. The statistician R.A. Fisher was employed in agricultural research from 1919 onwards, where he was faced with the methodological problem of distinguishing between differences in crop yields that resulted from the crop varieties planted and those that resulted from differences in environmental conditions, such as soil and weather. In the course of addressing this problem, he drew on his historical knowledge of experimentation to develop designs such as the 'Latin square' (Fisher, 1935; Oakley, 2000: 144–5), which are still sometimes employed in the healthcare field (see, for instance, Wright et al., 2003). The core of Fisher's advocacy of randomised controls lay partly in his theoretical position that valid inferences about causality could only be drawn where experimental subjects had an equal chance of being selected for each of the treatment and control groups in the study, and partly in the ability of randomisation to equalise the distribution of 'confounders' (factors that, though unknown to the researcher, might affect experimental results) between the above groups (Marks, 1997: 144).

However, subsequent advocates of randomisation tended to rely more on pragmatic considerations such as the known variability of human disease (implying that individual case reports are not a valid basis for generalisation) and the possibility that clinicians' optimism about new treatments might bias allocation to study groups or bias the interpretation of results (Marks, 1997: 145). This was the justification for the approach adopted in the UK Medical Research Council's trial of the then new antibiotic streptomycin for pulmonary tuberculosis (TB). This was apparently to be the world's first randomised controlled trial of a medical intervention and was paralleled by a US RCT of streptomycin (Marks, 1997: 121–5). The UK streptomycin trial was designed by A.B. Hill, a protégé of one of Fisher's students, and imitated the approach employed by Fisher in his agricultural experiments (Oakley, 2000: 154; Porter, 1997: 529). The allocation method was originally planned as alternation, but was modified to randomisation as the means of avoiding special pleading by clinicians in the difficult ethical context of an almost certainly fatal disease and a drug in short supply. The streptomycin trial has come to be regarded as a pivotal moment in the history of contemporary medical science; the *British Medical Journal* devoted an entire issue to celebrating its 50th anniversary. (For a detailed account of randomisation in the context of this trial, see Yoshioka, 1998.)

However, the popularisation in the UK of the notion that randomisation between comparison groups is a crucial means of avoiding bias in biomedical outcomes research dates from A.L. Cochrane's seminal Rock Carling Lecture of 1971, published the following year as *Effectiveness and Efficiency: Random Reflections on Health Services* (Cochrane, 1972). Cochrane's experience as an ill-equipped medical officer in a number of German prisoner-of-war camps between 1941 and 1945 had convinced him that the relationship between medical therapy and health outcomes was often tenuous. He later took the view that much NHS activity was ineffective, a view neatly illustrated in the following (perhaps apocryphal) story retailed in his lecture:

> *I once asked a worker at a crematorium, who had a curiously contented look on his face, what he found so satisfying about his work. He replied that what fascinated him was the way in which so much went in and so little came out. I thought of advising him to get a job in the NHS, it might have increased his job satisfaction ... (Cochrane, 1972: 12)*

The institutions of EBP in the UK

The term 'random' in Cochrane's title is of course a reference to the desirability of more rigorous evaluations of medical interventions; he was the great proselytiser for RCTs, and his name still carries great symbolic significance for contemporary medical researchers, being preserved in the 'Cochrane Centre' established in 1992 at the University of Oxford (www.cochrane.co.uk), and its numerous international collaborations that aim both to set methodological standards for judging clinical research and to aggregate the findings of such research through techniques of systematic review. Before his death in 1988, Cochrane and his sympathisers had expressed support for the concept of systematically reviewing RCTs on a particular clinical topic so as to provide an up-to-date statement of contemporary knowledge on that topic.

However, some of the intellectual and institutional developments behind EBP as it was to become institutionalised in the UK in the 1990s seem to have largely developed in Canada, and especially at McMaster University in Ontario, the site of the 'invention' of the techniques of both clinical epidemiology and of healthcare microeconomics (Daly, 2005). Clinical epidemiology seems to have developed in the belief that the systematic examination of clinical outcomes, and its necessary statistical techniques, would only be credible if pursued in close collaboration with physicians in the clinical specialties, rather than from a traditional public health perspective. Microeconomic analysis developed as a means of comparing the costs and outcomes of clinical interventions. Such studies both require data about the effectiveness of treatments and, when completed, have implications for decisions about healthcare priorities, and the technique of cost-utility analysis that we encountered in Chapter 1 also originated at McMaster. The origins of the 'hierarchy of evidence' are sometimes traced to a review of the research evidence about the value of periodic health examinations for children (Canadian Taskforce, 1979) which, faced with the need to make judgements about the relative validity of the findings of numerous studies, explicitly gave most weight to randomised studies, less weight to studies controlled but without randomisation, and least weight to uncontrolled studies. By the 1990s, these ideas and techniques had gelled into the notion of 'evidence-based medicine' itself, apparently initially conceived, again at McMaster University, as a method of teaching medical students based on research evidence rather than the perceived prejudices of professors. The prestigious journal *JAMA* carried an article entitled 'Evidence-Based Medicine; a new approach to teaching the practice of medicine'; authorship was listed as by the Evidence-Based Medicine Working Group (1992: 2420–5). By 1993 however, it was being promoted as a philosophy of clinical practice (Greco and Eisenberg, 1993; Guyatt and Rennie, 1993) involving the critical appraisal of published research evidence and such statistical concepts as risk ratios, relative and absolute risk reductions, and 'numbers-needed-to-treat'. All these ideas were to prove influential in UK contexts such as the 'quasi-market' of the 1990s (discussed in Chapter 4) and NICE (see Chapters 1 and 7).

It may also be that the subsequent development of NICE owes something to the example of the US federal Agency for Health Care Policy and Research (AHCPR), established in 1989 as a key policy tool in the battle against what was perceived as an unacceptably high level of healthcare expenditure and to the wide variations in the rates of particular treatments undertaken by physicians, and the inference drawn that the high end of this distribution represented so-called 'unnecessary care'. AHCPR's mandate was

> to enhance the quality, appropriateness and effectiveness of healthcare services … through the establishment of a broad base of scientific research and through the promotion of improvements in clinical practice. (Gray, 1992; AHCPR, 1993)

AHCPR sought to modify physician behaviour by bringing it into line with published evidence of effectiveness. It therefore undertook literature review and synthesis, and developed outcome measurement tools in order to define good clinical practice, and in 1992 began to publish and disseminate guidelines based on these (Gardner, 1992). The Agency also figured prominently in the failed Clinton healthcare reform plan (Skocpol, 1996), which led to some loss of cross-party political support and, from 1997, a modified role more concerned with the development of scientific capacity and scientific methods than the direct production of guidelines (Kahn, 1998).

The concepts and techniques which underpin scientific–bureaucratic medicine were current in the UK long before the election of New Labour in 1997. Following recommendations from a House of Lords Committee on Science and Technology (House of Lords, 1988), the Conservative government created a national research and development (R and D) strategy for the NHS in 1991, involving the creation of national and regional directors of R and D, the establishment of national and local research budgets to be the object of competitive bidding, and reorganisation of the flow of research funds through NHS hospitals (Baker and Kirk, 1996). A central objective of this programme became the disaggregation of the large proportion of health interventions stated never to have been the subject of proper evaluation into two categories: the effective and the ineffective. Second, a range of specialist institutions was publicly funded as the means of reviewing, collating and disseminating the findings of effectiveness research to the NHS; these include the Cochrane Centre, mentioned above, and the NHS Centre for Reviews and Dissemination at the University of York (NHS Executive, 1996b). Throughout the early and mid-1990s, it steadily became the conventional academic and policy wisdom that valid evidence of the effectiveness of clinical interventions should be defined by the 'hierarchy of evidence'. The dominance of this approach to evaluating evidence is illustrated by the treatment of the Centre for Reviews and Dissemination's published rules for undertaking systematic reviews (Centre for Reviews and Dissemination, 1996) as authoritative, and the difficulty for researchers in obtaining NHS national R and D funds for health technology studies based on other methodological assumptions.

The notion that research could guide NHS resource allocation decisions eventually found its way into a formal Conservative government policy statement:

> The overall purpose of the NHS is to secure, through the resources available, the greatest possible improvement in the physical and mental health of the people ... In order to achieve this, we need to ensure that decisions about the provision and delivery of clinical services are driven increasingly by evidence of clinical and cost-effectiveness, coupled with the systematic assessment of actual health outcomes. (NHS Executive, 1996b: 6)

It is possible to assemble a number of quotations from the White Paper *The New NHS: Modern, Dependable*, published some months after New Labour's 1997 general election victory to obtain a parallel statement:

> What counts is what works ... We are proposing ... to shift the focus onto quality of care ... in its broadest sense: doing the right things, at the right time, for the right people, and doing them right ... Nationally, there will be new evidence-based national service frameworks [which will] bring together the best evidence of clinical and cost-effectiveness ... (Secretary of State for Health, 1997: 10, 11, 17, 18)

Contemporary evidence-based practice

We suggested in the first section of this chapter that EBP in the UK was moving in the direction of what we termed 'scientific–bureaucratic medicine'. This has occurred over the period of slightly more than a decade and we might summarise the process by saying that the

Conservative governments of the early and mid-1990s legitimised the 'scientific' element of scientific–bureaucratic medicine, and their New Labour successors have institutionalised the bureaucratic element. This institutionalisation has occurred through three main routes. First, clinical guidelines have become ubiquitous, alongside increasing managerial and organisational pressures to ensure that they are implemented. At national level, NICE (see also Chapter 1) commissions the production of evidence-based guidelines on specific topics by groups of experts (www.nice.org.uk/pdf/CG013NICEguideline.pdf, accessed 22 January 2005). It is expected that such NICE-approved guidelines will normally be adhered to, and the Chair of NICE has publicly advised clinicians to record the reasons for any non-compliance in patient case notes (*BMA News Review*, March 1999: 16). In addition to such national guidelines, the NHS has numerous local guidelines and guideline implementation programmes, sometimes including local performance incentives.

Second, and in addition to the central specification of *clinical* models, central specification of *service* models has been developed through the creation of National Service Frameworks (NSFs) for such topics as coronary heart disease, mental health, cancer, services for older people, services for children, and diabetes. NSFs are significantly evidence-based, though the breadth of their subject matter and their concern with service organisation mean that this does not apply to the totality of their content. Although developed in consultation with experts and consumers, both NICE guidelines and NSFs are nationally promulgated by the Department of Health, and compliance is a dimension of NHS performance management (NHS Executive, 1998: 25–8), having been an element of the rolling programme of reviews of NHS Trusts and PCTs conducted by the Commission for Health Improvement (NHS Executive, 1998: 55) and has been continued by its successor the Healthcare Commission.

Third, the new (2004) GP contract and the associated Quality and Outcomes Framework (QOF) offer general medical practices the prospect of additional financial rewards of up to 20 percent of present income in return for meeting specified performance requirements in relation to the management of chronic diseases in their patients. Most of the 'quality markers' that attract such payments are in some way 'evidence-based' (Marshall and Roland, 2002; Roland, 2004).

All these institutions are manifestations of 'scientific–bureaucratic medicine' in that they combine evidence-based treatment guidelines with incentives for implementation. Of course this is not to imply that treatment decisions are entirely bureaucratised, in part because the existence of 'adequate' research evidence and of guidelines is not uniform across all areas of healthcare. For instance, the treatment of chronic disease in primary care and the treatment of cancer are very much guideline-governed, whereas treatment of acute illness in primary care, musculo-skeletal conditions and mental health problems is currently much less so. Some studies of guideline construction have suggested that it is as much a negotiated process as the straightforward application of scientific evidence (McDonald and Harrison, 2004). Moreover, there is considerable empirical evidence that organisational measures to enhance physicians' adherence to clinical guidelines are only variably effective (Effective Health Care, 1994, 1999; Grimshaw and Russell, 1993; Oxman et al., 1995; Wensing et al., 1998). As we saw in Chapter 2, the general idea of guidelines is increasingly accepted by GPs (Harrison and Dowswell, 2002) and apparently more enthusiastically by practice nurses (Harrison et al., 2002a).

EBP is very much a commonsense aspiration for a healthcare system such as the NHS; after all, the alternatives (random practice, prejudice-based practice, ignorance-based practice) are hardly tolerable, and what patient wants to be the object of ineffective interventions? In practice, however, advocates tend to present EBP as the potential solution to one or more of a series of perceived problems in relation to clinical practice. One group of such perceived problems relates to the finite time and cognitive abilities of clinicians (Berg, 1997b: 32) in a context of ever-expanding technological possibilities (Dowie and Elstein, 1988: 1) so that it is impractical for clinicians routinely to read and understand how to apply every scientific publication relating to their clinical area (Sackett and Straus, 1998). On the latter point some analysts calculated that in order to keep fully abreast of relevant publications a practitioner of general medicine would need to read 19 learned papers a day, 365 days per year (Davidoff et al., 1995). A second group of perceived problems relates to the observed differences with which clinicians treat ostensibly similar patient cases: so-called 'medical practice variations' (Andersen and Mooney, 1990). Much of the drive for standardisation of medical treatment in the US derives from empirical studies that have failed to identify systematic reasons for such variations (Brook, 1991; Wennberg, 1984). Some UK advocates have seen EBP in the same way (Needham, 2000) whilst for others NICE's existence is an answer to so-called 'postcode rationing', the differential availability of therapies between different geographical areas of England. A third perceived problem is that of waste of healthcare resources; we noted above that Cochrane (1972) was a vehement critic of what he saw as well-meaning but ineffective NHS treatment. A final group of perceived problems is that of vested interests; Marks (1997: 3,7) notes that many advocates of EBP have been inspired by mistrust of the motives of pharmaceutical and medical equipment producers, examplars of the 'supplier-induced demand' in Chapter 1 above.

There is therefore a multiplicity of overlapping rationales for EBM. But there are also critiques, six of which are briefly summarised below. The first three can be seen as primarily targeted at the 'scientific' aspects of scientific–bureaucratic medicine, whilst the remainder are critiques of its bureaucratic aspects. In examining these critiques, it should be noted that none are constituted as crude attacks on science or bureaucracy. 'Science' as perceived in some quarters seems to have become increasingly the focus of public mistrust in recent years, a phenomenon well illustrated by recent controversy, further discussed in Chapter 7, over whether the measles-mumps-rubella vaccine is associated with autism (Heller et al., 2001), and that has led to innovations such as university chairs in the 'public understanding of science'. In contrast, 'bureaucracy' has received a bad press for many years by virtue of having entered everyday language as a pejorative term to signify presumed unnecessary paperwork and formality ('red tape'), usually in the context of government agencies. As an organisational form, bureaucracy has specific consequences, not all of which are necessarily negative. Indeed, one sociologist has recently written at some length 'in praise of bureaucracy' (Du Gay, 2000), correctly noting its potential for securing greater fairness, due process and transparency in public resource distribution. But bureaucracy has other consequences, most

Table 3.2 Alternative epistemological positions in medicine and research

Traditional biomedical/laboratory research	Outcomes research/randomised controlled trials
Reveals cause-effect mechanisms (via aetiology, pathology, etc.)	Demonstrates statistical relationships from past experience
Provides knowledge of what *ought to be* effective, and why	Provides knowledge of what is *likely* to work, irrespective of why
Based on deterministic models	Based on probabilistic models
Underpinned by realist/naturalist epistemology	Underpinned by empiricist/positivist epistemology
Espoused by working clinicians	Espoused by epidemiologists and health services researchers

Source: adapted from Tanenbaum, 1994

of which have been the subject of sociological knowledge for many years, yet have somehow disappeared from contemporary discourses of public service organisation and management.

Rival epistemological positions

The epistemological underpinnings of randomised controlled trials and meta-analyses which, as we have seen above, form the basis of the EBM movement are in fact not necessarily identical with the way working clinicians think about evidence of effectiveness. Indeed, it may be that neither pole of the vertical axis of Figure 3.1 (see page 58) adequately characterises the manner in which working clinicians think. This question has been examined in a small-scale, but important, American study of clinicians (Tanenbaum, 1994). In her study, Tanenbaum contrasts the traditional biomedical model of research, which is based in laboratory methods, with that entailed by RCTs. The contrast is summarised in Table 3.2.

For the sake of contrast Table 3.2 presents the two epistemologies (theories of knowledge) as ideal types, though in the real world it seems unlikely that many clinicians are not influenced by elements of both. The point, however, is that *in the last analysis* it is the traditional model that predominates in medical decision making. (In contrast, as Table 3.1 above makes clear, the health services research model places clinical observations at the bottom of the hierarchy of evidence.) The traditional model, taught to and espoused by clinicians, relies on the discovery of cause-effect mechanisms by the observation of the way in which disease processes develop over time and impact upon normal physiological processes. Treatment is therefore very much a *logical* process of intervening in the aetiology (natural history) of a disease so as to arrest, reverse or retard it. Expressed in more philosophical/technical terms, the model is *deterministic* (that is, it assumes that clinical events necessarily have causes which can be identified and, in principle, modified) and *realist* or *naturalist* (that is, it entails a belief in a world of objectively real entities whose nature can be observed).

The outcomes/RCT model is the foundation of epidemiology and the relatively new discipline of health services research. It consists primarily of the *inference* of cause-effect relationships from past statistical relationships between treatment and outcomes. It is therefore less concerned with disease processes than with establishing what interventions are *likely to be effective, irrespective of why.* In technical philosophical language, the model is therefore *probabilistic* (that is, one where the cause-effect relationships are inherently uncertain) and *empiricist* (that is, one where knowledge can only justifiably be derived from past experience).

A very practical consequence of these apparently rather abstruse observations is that clinical doctors may be more likely to be influenced in their practice by their own (and close colleagues') experience with similar types of patient, and by their own reasoning about treatment logic, than by the publication of meta-analyses of large numbers of cases. This, of course, is highly consonant with the individualistic ethic of the practice of medicine and to the habit of doctors of being influenced by their own experience of single cases, a habit that used to be reflected by the occasional column in the *British Medical Journal* entitled 'A Memorable Patient'.

Effectiveness in populations and individuals

Much of the point of the RCT design is to establish valid knowledge about the effects of treatments in classes of patient, defined by diagnosis and perhaps by other characteristics such as disease severity and age. As we noted above, properly conducted randomisation processes are intended both to minimise the opportunity for clinicians to allocate patients to treatment and control groups in a manner consciously or unconsciously calculated to confirm existing prejudices (selection bias) and to randomly allocate 'confounders' between treatment and control groups. The resulting research findings should in principle be valid in aggregate for a population similar to the one studied, even though it is widely accepted that there may well be difficulties in generalising to slightly different populations and indeed to treatment settings and clinicians different from those involved in trials. However, there is a further difficulty; clinicians treat individuals, not populations, and as Byrne (2004: 84–7) has pointed out there is no logical means of moving from knowledge of a treatment's effectiveness in a population to knowledge of its probable effectiveness in an individual. The consequence seems to be that if clinicians simply apply population probabilities to individuals without further thought, they are implicitly applying utilitarian criteria (Harrison, 2004: 182). This is well-understood by the critical appraisal school of evidence-based practice, with its emphasis on integrating research evidence with other considerations related to the individual patient. But it is less clearly comprehended by the scientific–bureaucratic school, whose assumption seems to be very much that clinical guideline compliance should be the norm, and departures from guidelines wholly exceptional. Some legal commentators take the view that adherence to evidence-based guidelines may eventually become a legal expectation of clinicians (Harpwood, 2001; Tingle and Foster, 2002).

Effectiveness and political legitimacy: rival criteria for rationing

Rationing interventions on grounds of probable effectiveness is sometimes justified (or even argued not to constitute rationing at all) by the assertion that consumers do not want healthcare for its own sake but only for the improvement that it will bring to health. Such views can be described as 'instrumental' and lead logically to the provision of healthcare on grounds such as effectiveness, cost-utility or certain concepts of equity (Harrison and Hunter, 1994).

A neat expression of this instrumental view has been put forward by one of the McMaster health economists referred to above:

> *Patients seek care in order to be relieved of some actual or perceived, present or potential, 'disease'. The care itself is not directly of value; it is generally inconvenient, often painful or frightening. As a thought experiment, one could ask a representative patient (or oneself) whether he/she would prefer to have ... a condition perceived as requiring care plus the best conceivable care for that condition, completely free of all ... costs, or would prefer simply not to have the condition ... [C]are is not a good in the usual sense, but a 'bad' or 'regrettable' made 'necessary' by the even more regrettable circumstances of 'dis-ease'. It follows that patients want to receive* **effective** *healthcare, i.e. care [in respect of which] there is a reasonable expectation [of] a positive impact on their health! (Evans, 1990: 118–19, emphasis original)*

This formulation is inadequate in two ways. First, it is a matter of fact that people sometimes do value care for its own sake, irrespective of its effectiveness. Any GP has the story of a patient who demands a prescription for antibiotics despite being assured that it will do no good, and the public often value heroic but obviously vain rescue attempts. Second, Evans's reasoning rests entirely on the ability of the relevant social actors to agree upon what constitutes a 'reasonable' expectation of a positive outcome from treatment. It is easy to see that, in fact, such agreement is not always forthcoming, as was graphically demonstrated in the 1990s by the much-publicised case of 'Child B' who was denied a second bone marrow transplant by her local health authority – NHS haematologists and a private consultant differed over the probable effectiveness of such treatment whilst her family felt that any positive probability was acceptable. (For details of this case, see Ham and Pickard, 1998 and for a similar example Freemantle and Harrison, 1993.) Nor does the addition of cost criteria seem to make it any easier to agree, again as graphically illustrated in the case of the drug Interferon beta for multiple sclerosis, discussed in Chapter 7 (see also Quennell, 2003).

It is thus difficult to avoid the conclusion that, just as beauty is proverbially in the eye of the beholder, 'goodness' in healthcare, as in other areas of economic activity, is in the eye of the demander. Yet, as we saw in Chapter 1, not all demands can be met and a policy of effectiveness implemented through EBP not only promises authoritative answers to such disputes but also allows the rationing process to be defended with the authority of science. But there remain other, non-instrumental, rationing criteria which have their attractions too.

The term 'rescue principle' was coined by the philosopher Dworkin to refer to the belief that the moral imperative of medicine is to attempt to help those who are acutely ill or whose lives are threatened (Dworkin, 1994; see also Boyd, 1979). The moral content of such action is in the process (hence 'attempt') rather than in the outcome. Although the application of such a principle clearly implies potentially significant opportunity costs (since others may suffer whilst resources are expended on hopeless cases) it is one which seems to receive wide support in public policy generally, underpinning as it does such services as air/sea rescue and mountain rescue. We once saw a cartoon in which a coastguard is answering a distress call with the words 'Stay with your boat sir, whilst the Secretary of State decides how important you are.' It is far from obvious that such an outrageous suggestion would become any less outrageous by the substitution of 'Stay with your boat madam, whilst the coastguard calculates whether the probability of getting to you in time is high enough to make it worth bothering.' Whatever its internal incoherence or unsought consequences, the rescue principle is one to which many people subscribe. It is also the ostensible moral basis of medicine; and as the BMA 2004 *Handbook of Medical Ethics* advises, any attempts to depart from this principle by concealing information from patients threatens the doctor–patient relationship.

> *It is important to provide the highest degree of transparency possible concerning NHS decisions about rationing ... In cases where the treatment cannot be funded, patients should have access to information about the factors leading to the rationing decision ... Although it could be argued that patients should be protected from the distress of receiving information about treatment options that are not publicly funded, this undermines the increasingly accepted concept of partnership in decision making between patients and health professionals. (BMA, 2004: 39)*

An alternative non-instrumental view might be termed 'entitlement': strictly speaking (and in contrast to the detailed statutory provision for social security) UK citizens have no rights to specific elements of publicly financed healthcare, except where NICE recommendations are operative. However, this does not mean that people do not see themselves as having rights to treatment irrespective of calculations of effectiveness. Denied arterial surgery on the ground that his continued smoking increased the risks of treatment and reduced the probability of benefit, a 62 year old Wakefield man was quoted as saying

> *I have worked since I was 14 up until recently and paid a hell of a lot in taxes to the government both in income taxes and on the 40 cigarettes a day I smoked. Surely it is not too much for me to ask to have an operation that might ease my pain in my old age and make me live a little longer. (Yorkshire Evening Post, 26 August 1993: 1)*

Litigation in pursuit of treatment has typically taken the form of an action against the Secretary of State for breach of statutory duty to provide a comprehensive health service, or against health authorities or Trusts for reaching rationing decisions on 'irrational' grounds.

The technical capacity of rules

The technical incapacity of bureaucracy and rules has been analysed in detail by a number of authors. One example is the work of Dunsire (1978), who conceptualised organisations as 'Towers of Babel' in which vertical and horizontal differences in knowledge, language and culture make top-down detailed command-and-control literally unachievable, requiring instead either that organisational superiors give only generalised instructions, or check with subordinates that proposed detailed instructions are actually reasonable ones. A more famous example is Polanyi's (1967: 34) concept of 'tacit knowledge' by which (for instance) knowing how to perform some task entails losing sight of its individual components; paying attention to the components loses sight of the task as a whole. This notion that we can know more than we can tell is perhaps all the more telling for its origin in the work of an author who had trained as physician, and later held university chairs in both physical chemistry and social science. Thus Majone (1986) has argued that collegiality may be more appropriate than bureaucracy for dealing with cognitively complex issues.

The political capacity of rules

Guidelines, protocols, casemix measures and other systematisations of medical practice into bureaucratic rules can be seen as an attempt to substitute a form of 'blackboxing', that is the condensation of a set of political criteria into a set of ostensibly technical or scientific rules, whose perceived legitimacy suppresses contestation (Latour, 1987). Thus it is clear that front-line public service workers ('street-level bureaucrats') cannot simply follow rules but must 'invent benign modes of mass processing that more or less permit them to deal with the public fairly, appropriately and successfully' in conditions where there is always too much work to be completed (Lipsky, 1980: xii). In simple terms, as we observed in Chapter 1, professional discretion may be a necessary condition for getting the work done without the exposure of resource inadequacies. It follows that the development of explicit rules for determining clinical decisions may be perceived by patients and public as illegitimate denials of need. Public perceptions of the adequacy of state involvement in medical care finance or provision may well rest on a degree of trust being conferred on doctors, the occupation most centrally associated with such services. Part of the durability of medical self-regulation and autonomy lay in the advantages they offered to profession, government and patient. Yet the developments that challenge medical autonomy and self-regulation all imply distrust of doctors in that they seek to substitute confidence in systems (of guidelines, performance indicators and so on) for trust in individuals, hence abandoning the moral content of the client/practitioner relationship (Smith, 2001). The very creation of such systems may therefore be self-defeating in political terms; they may communicate to citizens that doctors and the care that they provide at public expense are not to be trusted (Davies, 1999; O'Neill, 2002: 51–3).

The behavioural capacity of rules

There is a long-established literature dealing with the adverse consequences of bureaucracy in terms of alienation, morale and trust. Blau's research in the late 1940s famously showed that 'goal displacement' (in which adherence to the rules becomes an end in itself: Mouzelis, 1975: 55) resulted from fear of superiors' reactions to rule breaking, especially in the context of a reward system based on compliance: for instance

> *the supervisor refused to set aside a recent order of the departmental head, although there were good reasons for doing so, because he worried about possible negative reactions from his superior, on whom his [performance] rating depended. (1975: 185)*

Scientific–bureaucratic medicine implies that the NHS is increasingly adopting systems of management based precisely on rewarding compliance. Bureaucratic rules and targets for their adherence court perverse incentives (O'Neill, 2002: 49, 55), including the deprioritisation of that which is not measured and rewarded, along with a range of 'gaming' strategies

to maximise apparent performance. There is also a long-established literature, derived from a variety of theoretical and political perspectives (Fox, 1974; Fukuyama, 1995; Power, 1997), suggesting that the existence of performance measurements based on rule adherence results in a mutual lack of trust between managers and other organisational actors. Such mistrust may well result in a spiral of reciprocal mistrust and consequent adversarial intra-organisational relationships, including narrowly calculative employee behaviour, inflexibility and an inability to respond to crises (Fox, 1974: 43–4, 55; Fukuyama, 1995: 225; Gouldner, 1954: 78ff), and increasing transaction costs as further bureaucracy is introduced to counter such problems (Fukuyama, 1995: 151–2).

Interpreting scientific–bureaucratic medicine

As we noted in Chapter 1 in connection with the adoption of systems of 'third party payment', the ostensible rationales for governments' adoption of particular policies do not necessarily constitute complete explanations. In the final section of this chapter, we shall consider two contrasting theoretical approaches to explaining the rise of scientific–bureaucratic medicine. The first of these employs contemporary theory, largely based on the work of Kingdon (1984) about how government 'policy agendas' are formed. The second theoretical approach is much broader, drawing on contemporary sociological theorising about macro-level phenomena such as risk, and the transfer to 'management' of the deference formerly accorded to 'science'.

The theory of policy agendas

The literature which directly addresses the question of what *specific* issues reach the policy agendas of governments (as opposed to general ones such as 'the economy') is not extensive, but contains some important consonances (Hall et al., 1975: 475ff; Solesbury, 1976). Amongst these are the extent to which a government believes that the issue in question is one where political party ideology allows involvement, the perception of crisis and, crucially, the absence of any necessity for logical or sequential occurrence or consideration of issues:

> There may be nothing distinct or sequential about the search for attention, legitimacy and action. They may equally well proceed in together or in parallel. Rather, they should be regarded as three tests which the nascent issue must pass in order to remain on the agenda for debate and discussion. Only a failure to pass all three tests would remove the issue from the agenda completely. (Solesbury, 1976: 395)

This rejection of the need for policy making to take place in a rational or sequential fashion is now commonplace in policy analysis and has been theorised in that context by Kingdon (1984). The intellectual roots of Kingdon's approach are to be found especially in the work of non-rationalist 'garbage can' theorists such as Cohen et al. (1972); governments are seen as 'organised anarchies', that is as possessing the following characteristics. First, their goals are multiple, vague and inconsistent; the organisation discovers preferences through action more than it acts on the basis of preferences. Second, processes within the organisation operate more on a trial-and-error basis than according to explicit theory. Third, participation in the organisation is fluid; participants' interests and involvement vary over time and across issues. Consequently, what is conventionally labelled a 'decision' is seen as an outcome of several, largely independent, 'streams' rather than a rational sequential approach to an objective or problem (1972: 3). Cohen et al's rejection of a straightforward logical relationship between problems, policy objectives and policy solutions can be summarised in their own words:

> *An organisation is a collection of choices looking for problems, issues and feelings looking for decision situations in which they might be aired, solutions looking for issues to which they might be an answer, and decision makers looking for work. (1972: 2)*

Kingdon adapts the notion of streams in his own theory, which is derived from his empirical studies of US public policy; he posits three, as follows. First, *problem recognition* refers to the way in which one matter rather than another captures the attention of actors in and around government. The perception of crisis, or change in a perceived key economic or social indicator, are ways in which this might occur. Second, there are *political processes*, the normal stuff of micropolitics, such as public opinion, changes of office holder and pressure group activity. Third, there are *policy proposals*: these are not necessarily developed in response to specific issues or problems and may well have their origins in 'policy communities', often in, or on the fringes of, academia. Hence

> *Much as molecules floated around in what biologists call the 'primeval soup' before life came into being, so ideas float round in these policy communities. (Kingdon, 1984: 122–3)*

The core of Kingdon's theory (1984: 188–9) is that an issue is only likely to reach a government decision (that is, where a decision is likely rather than being left to float around in the 'policy primeval soup') where the three streams of (to use shorthand labels) problems, policies and politics are in some way 'coupled' [*sic*]. Such coupling is likely to occur during the possibly brief existence of a 'policy window' created by the combination of problem recognition and political processes, and may be assisted by a 'policy entrepreneur', a member of a policy community who utilises the window of opportunity to press for the adoption of a favoured policy; as one of Kingdon's respondents put it

> *Government does not come to conclusions. It stumbles into paradoxical situations that force it to move one way or another. There are social forces that you can identify, but what comes out of them is just an accident. (quoted in Kingdon, 1984: 199)*

An illustrative application of Kingdon's theory to EBP in the NHS might proceed as follows. We might take the *problem stream* to be represented by the increasingly pressing issue of healthcare rationing in the early 1990s. We saw in our discussion of demand and rationing in Chapter 1 that for much of its history the NHS achieved such rationing by largely implicit means: a combination of waiting lists, 'gatekeeping' by GPs and the clinical autonomy of physicians. But by the 1990s, this tacit arrangement was beginning to break down under several pressures. First, waiting lists were increasingly seen by government and (perhaps as a result) by the public as a mark of NHS inadequacy; the *Patient's Charter* set minimum standards and NHS institutions were penalised for failing to meet them. Second, resources were becoming tighter and managerial reforms had begun to make modest incursions into the scope of clinical autonomy (Harrison, 1999) as a result of which consultants and perhaps also GPs were less willing to 'play the game'. Third, the level of academic and media comment on the topic of rationing may well have entailed a sort of 'loss of innocence'. Fourth, the logic of the so-called 'purchaser/provider split' introduced in 1991 was that the purchasing bodies should prioritise expenditure from their finite budget (Harrison, 1991; see Chapters 1 and 4 for discussion of these organisational arrangements). In 1993 health authorities were asked to begin to identify interventions of which they would in future purchase more and less, on grounds of effectiveness and ineffectiveness respectively (NHS Management Executive, 1993). Some authorities chose the insertion of grommets (a treatment for children with otitis media – 'glue ear') and dilatation and curettage ('D and C': a treatment for dysfunctional uterine bleeding) for women under the age of 40 as their candidates for the 'purchase less' category (see also Klein et al., 1996). Both procedures had been the subject of well-publicised academic reviews questioning their value (Effective Health Care, 1992, 1995).

If implicit approaches to rationing were looking less tenable, the only alternative was explicit rationing. But this in turn raises further questions; *who* should make rationing decisions? and *what criteria* should such decisions be based upon? It can be suggested that, from the point of view of politicians and other policymakers, there was considerable attraction in leaving the decisions to doctors; their legitimacy for such a role as perceived by the public, the controversy which has accompanied managerial attempts to fulfil the role, and the perception that a politician's involvement can only be a vote-loser are highly persuasive factors. Yet it remained necessary to persuade doctors to co-operate in circumstances where, as noted above, there has been increasing reluctance to do so. The adoption by the government of the notion of EBP can be seen as having provided both a potential means for securing the involvement of doctors and an answer to the question of 'what criteria?'

As we saw above, the *policy stream* seems to have had both transatlantic and domestic origins, involving separate influences from Canada and perhaps the US as well as the UK government's decision to establish an NHS R and D programme, whose first Director can perhaps be seen as a 'policy entrepreneur', making the link between Canadian ideas and the UK research programme. The *politics stream* can be seen as the material interests in EBP of several groups of actors. One such group was the medical Royal Colleges, who for some years prior to the passage of EBP into formal policy had received Department of Health funds to support the production of clinical guidelines, though such guidelines tended to be based more on professional consensus than upon direct interrogation of research evidence. It is therefore possible that support for EBP (perhaps most notably by the Royal College of Physicians, which established a dedicated unit) was a route by which such bodies sought to protect this income stream. Another obvious interest group is academia; the policy has supported substantial expenditure upon research grants, academic chairs and indeed several whole new university units and departments. Several new academic journals were founded to focus upon the topic.

There is little evidence, however, that pressure groups were responsible for placing scientific–bureaucratic medicine on the government policy agenda. The 'policy window' that finally allowed it to become policy occurred during the 1992 general election campaign. The early years of the NHS quasi-market were marked by widespread academic and media criticisms of the new organisational arrangements and their apparently perverse effects in such terms as non-co-operation between institutions, 'adverse selection' of patients, and a perverse 'efficiency formula' which rewarded patient throughput without reference to quality or outcomes. These criticisms were linked with the rationing problem described above through public and media concern at 'rationing by postcode' and more specifically by the so-called 'war of Jennifer's ear'. In this latter episode, electoral capital was made from the apparent refusal of the NHS to perform a grommet insertion for a girl with 'glue ear'. As the 1990s progressed, this critique grew in volume and cogency and by 1993 the speeches of the then Secretary of State for Health were marked by references to the R and D Programme apparently as a defence against such criticisms.

Some connections to contemporary social theory

An alternative, though not necessarily incompatible, way of explaining the rise of EBP is as a reaction to dilemmas resulting from trends identified by contemporary social theorists in their analyses of the macro-social changes variously labelled as postmodernity or late modernity (for a general overview of which see Lyon, 1999). We identify dilemmas resulting from two aspects of the contemporary social world: incredulity towards metanarratives, and the development of new discourses about risk.

The philosopher Lyotard famously coined the phrase 'incredulity towards metanarratives' (Lyotard, 1984: xxiv) to signify that overarching patterns of meaning, explanation and direction in the ways in which people think and act (Browning, 2000: 31) are nowadays met with scepticism. For Lyotard, science is a prominent example. His argument seems to be both philosophical and empirical and can be seen as a further contribution to the thread of scepticism towards overarching scientific explanation developed by writers such as Kuhn (1962) and Feyerabend (1993) and now a prevalent stance amongst social theorists (Browning, 2000: 39; for examples, see Barnes et al., 1996; Fuller, 1997). This raises the question of whether 'management', apparently itself a metanarrative, can plausibly be seen as displacing the metanarrative of science. Lyotard, however, identifies a contemporary emphasis on 'performativity', that is the appraisal of thought and action in terms of their capacity to increase operational efficiency, which has come to prevail in public services (Browning, 2000: 24). He sees the ubiquity of performativity as what remains after the dissolution of metanarratives (rather than as itself a metanarrative) because it has the potential to serve as an *internal* mode of legitimation for an activity (Browning, 2000: 29; Lyotard, 1984: 46). The process of justifying a practice by the efficiency of its performance allows for a process of legitimation whereby evaluation is not conducted by external criteria but by examination of the internal efficiency of a social practice (Browning, 2000: 29; Lyotard, 1984: 54; see also Ritzer, 2000: 178). Thus, there is a tendency for the deference traditionally accorded to scientific medical knowledge to be eroded and to be subordinated to managerialism. Thus, apparently paradoxically, 'whilst the macro environment of society becomes more uncertain and irregular, the micro world ... is ... subject to processes of standardisation and regularisation' (Turner, 1996: 16). We might therefore sum up by saying that there is a tendency for the authority of medical science to be replaced by the authority of managerial rules for the application of medical science; this is of course a characterisation of scientific–bureaucratic medicine.

Second, there seems to be a consensus amongst contemporary social theorists that late modern society is a 'risk society' (Beck, 1992; see also Giddens, 1990; Reddy, 1996) in which heightened perceptions (and perhaps decreasing tolerance) of risks are an important feature of the social world. Medicine's capacity for iatrogenesis and other unsought consequences, such as population increase, is an obvious example and is treated as such by Beck (1992: 204–12; for other examples, see Fox, 2000: 412–16). Fox (2000: 412) has suggested that, given that modern societies are safer and healthier than ever, contemporary anxieties about health reflect an expectations gap. As we saw in Chapter 2, medical professional power has often been associated with physicians' ability to cope with uncertainty (Jamous and Peloille, 1970), but 'incredulity towards metanarratives' of scientific expertise implies that individual experts are no longer trusted (Giddens, 1990: 88–92, 124–30) by either government or the public to make judgements about risk and how to deal with it. For the state, there is thus a paradox of simultaneous demand for certainty and denial of its possibility; professionals cannot provide certainty and are in any case not trusted to do so. Their means of side-stepping this paradox is to substitute *confidence* in systems for *trust* in individuals (Smith, 2001); to introduce systematisation and bureaucratisation as the means of legitimising a body of expert knowledge by the language of management, and by the mechanics of dull routine. It may be that uncertainties cannot be managed by such means, implying that scientific–bureaucratic medicine may, like the wider phenomenon of public sector audit, be a 'ritual of verification' (Power, 1997). Theorists have suggested that mistrust is counterproductive in situations of crisis (Webb, 1996), at work (Fox, 1974) and in social relations more generally (Fukuyama, 1995). Nevertheless, confidence in systems offers reassurance, so that the risk society produces the audit society (Power, 1997: 138).

Concluding remarks

The two theoretical approaches that we have reviewed in this chapter are very different, and neither offers a complete explanation of the rise of EBP. Policy agenda theory looks specifically at a particular policy field and captures the randomness and non-linearity of the policy process very well. In this particular case however, it seems unable to easily explain the fact that policy promotion of EBP is confined neither to the health sector nor to the UK. Within the UK, similar ideas have achieved policy status in education, social work, probation services and elsewhere (for reviews, see Davies et al., 2000; Trinder and Reynolds, 2000). And the international coincidence of the general approach means that the spread of policy is perhaps somewhat less random than Kingdon's theory suggests (Harrison et al., 2002c) and perhaps affected by the wider social forces to which Kingdon's respondent (quoted above) refers. In contrast, the suggested explanation based on contemporary social theory is precisely concerned with such larger social forces. However, the very breadth of this explanatory approach means that it is perhaps better seen less as an explanation for the specific phenomenon of EBP and more as giving an indication of how it can flourish as policy in a social world where science is increasingly questioned and consumerism is dominant.

Further reading

A broader account of medicine alongside other social interventions is contained in Oakley (2000). Accounts of the application of EBM to the NHS are Dopson and Fitzgerald (2005) and Greenhalgh et al. (2005). Valuable resources on almost anything related to contemporary medicine are the edited volumes by Cooter and Pickstone (2000) and Albrecht et al. (2000).

Chapter 4

The Politics of Organisation and Management

```
Summary of chapter contents

•  Markets, bureaucracy, clans and networks
•  NHS organisation: history and contemporary developments
•  Interpreting the third way
```

When we describe some activity as 'organised', we signify that it has in some way been planned, the necessary resources assembled and the activity performed in a focused manner with a degree of application. In this sense, an activity may be described as 'organised' even if it involves only a single actor; indeed we may even use the term 'organised' as a label for an individual who habitually conducts their activity in the above manner. In the context of studying politics or the phenomena that we term 'organisations' however, we are usually referring to the performance of tasks that require collective, rather than individual, effort. Organisation in these contexts therefore implies *social co-ordination*, that is processes for seeking to align the efforts of multiple individuals involved in the task; 'co-ordination implies the bringing into a relationship [of] otherwise disparate activities' (Frances, 1991: 3). It is obvious that many of the tasks upon which the contemporary world relies can only be performed by organised groups. Moreover many tasks that could be performed by individuals become much more efficient when performed by groups; the early economist Adam Smith's famous example of pin manufacture offers the classic justification for the 'division of labour' that underpins the social organisation of work:

> A workman.... could scarce, with his utmost industry, make one pin in a day ... But in the way in which this business is now carried on ... it is divided into a number of branches ... One man draws out the wire, another straights it, a third cuts it, a fourth points it, a fifth grinds it at the top to receive the head ... The important business of making a pin is ... divided into

about eighteen distinct operations … Ten persons [organised in this way] could make among them upwards of 48,000 pins in a day … (Smith, 1979: 109–10; originally published 1776)

Strictly speaking, 'organisation' in the sense employed above is an abstract noun, denoting a quality of being organised. Yet the term has become widely understood as an ostensibly concrete noun, referring to companies, government departments, military entities and so on. In this sense, organisations have formal, usually legal, 'corporate' identities; the University of Manchester, the Department of Health, J Sainsbury plc, Bradford Teaching Hospitals NHS Foundation Trust, and so on. We shall examine some of the consequences of this usage below, but for the moment we can retain the more abstract definition. If we do so we can readily see the main options for the co-ordination of pin making as described by Smith.

One way in which such co-ordination might occur is simply to leave the outcome to the interactions between the actors. The worker who draws the wire could sell it to the worker who cuts it, and so on. If the wiredrawer charges more than the wirecutter wishes to pay, the latter might purchase wire elsewhere. Each acts in accordance with his or her own interests, but is constrained by the self-interested actions of others. Another approach is for someone to be 'in charge' of the group, instructing them what to do. Such an approach implies either that the group members are simply willing to obey (perhaps because they agree about the basic nature of, and necessity for, the task) or that the person in charge can deploy incentives and/or sanctions in order to secure co-operation. A third approach is for the various actors simply to agree about what needs to be done and how; perhaps they share a particular social or familial background and are generally socialised to see things in the same way. Finally, small groups of like-minded individuals might contact other similar groups and so build a network sufficient to accomplish the task. This somewhat folksy account serves to introduce respectively the four main modes of social co-ordination: market, bureaucracy, clan and network, which we shall examine in more detail in the first section of this chapter. The second section of the chapter examines the changing mix of approaches to the organisation of the NHS employed between its foundation in 1948 and 1997, whilst the third section provides a thematic treatment of contemporary NHS organisation. The final section addresses interpretations of recent NHS organisational changes.

Key concepts in social co-ordination

We have already introduced the four core approaches to organisation: market, bureaucracy, clan and network. We should note that these approaches are 'ideal types' and that (as we shall see) real world organisation usually displays elements of all of them though to different degrees. Thus most markets are populated by competing bureaucracies, many networks are networks of bureaucracies or of actors embedded within bureaucracies, networks and clans may formalise themselves into bureaucracies (for instance an informal network may become a formal association) and clans may nest within bureaucracy (Mintzberg, 1991). These four approaches can be arranged in the kind of matrix shown in Figure 4.1. The vertical axis suggests that markets and bureaucracies operate on the assumption that their participants'

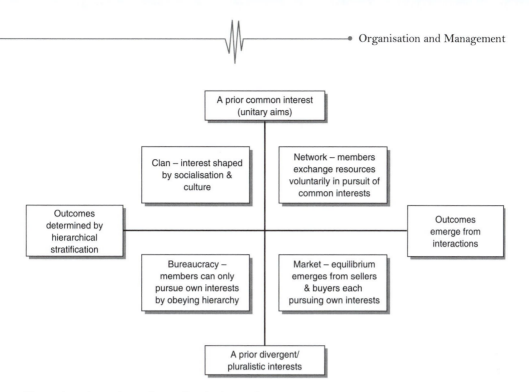

Figure 4.1   A typology of co-ordination/control

interests are primarily divergent, whereas clans and networks assume that such interests are mainly congruent. The horizontal axis suggests that the outcomes of markets and networks emerge from interactions between the parties, whereas the outcomes of clans and bureaucracies are mainly determined by the use of hierarchical authority. Each of our four approaches is further discussed below.

Markets

The central characteristic of markets is that they consist of actors more-or-less freely pursuing their own interests, exchanging resources where they see fit, but each constrained by the terms on which others are willing to exchange. For example a series of decisions not to purchase may lead to price reductions; a series of decisions to purchase may lead to increases in the production of the good in question. Consequently, the outcome of a market is not determined by any single actor, but rather is an 'interactive' outcome. The economic textbook's graph of how 'equilibrium' prices are determined by the interaction of demand and supply curves is the classic illustration of such a process (see, for instance, Lipsey, 1966: 100). A market which is 'perfectly' competitive will result in an allocation of goods and services across society in which total utility, or satisfaction of consumers, and total profits of producers are maximised. However, the conditions which together define perfect competition are numerous and are actually met by few real markets; the most important of these conditions are as follows:

> In the theory of perfect competition, it is assumed that all producers seek to maximise their profits. Each producer is so small, and one of many, that individually they cannot exercise control over any aspect of the market except for their own costs of production. Without the possibility of

collusion with others, producers are forced to compete with each other on the basis of price. Another assumption of this 'classical' model of economic behaviour is that consumers are fully informed and knowledgeable, and will therefore possess the ability to seek out the producer with the lowest prices. This situation results in producers having an incentive to operate at minimum cost so as to be able to set prices low enough to attract as many consumers as possible ... High-cost producers will go out of business. Those remaining in business will be technically efficient in their production, either by maximising output for a given cost or by minimising costs for a given level of output. (Donaldson and Gerard, 1993: 14–15)

It is easy to see that markets in healthcare are unlikely to meet any of these conditions. First, many hospitals in many countries are non-profitmaking, whether as a result of public ownership, or of charitable or similar status. Perhaps oddly, this may be the least important of the ways in which healthcare markets diverge from the perfect market. This is because the profit-making status of the organisation does not necessarily determine the motives of the most influential actors in the organisation; for instance if the managers of a public or charitable hospital can use surpluses to increase their own salaries and fringe benefits, their behaviour may not differ from that in a commercial hospital. Second, healthcare producers tend to be large rather than small organisations, and enormous capital investment would be required by any new entrant to the market, though of course this would be less so for producers interested only in the less high-technological sectors of the market, such as community care. It is not surprising that ownership is highly concentrated, and large producers may well be able to exert control over what is offered in the market, and at what price, since consumers will be more dependent the fewer the sources of supply. Expressed in another way, the monopolist (the sole supplier) is likely to be powerful.

Third, producers do collude with each other in order to avoid competition or to blunt its effects. Fourth, given the complexity of health professional expert knowledge and of medical technology, it is hard to imagine buyers ever achieving 'information symmetry' with sellers; this factor allows the supplier-induced demand discussed in Chapter 1. It is easy to see that third party payment further confounds the assumption that there is a straightforward link between demand, willingness to pay and supply. Finally, the theory of the perfectly competitive market seems to be based on the assumption that commodities are to be bought and sold on a 'one-off' basis, in the short term. This is often not the case with healthcare, and indeed for other services too, where what is being purchased is often a long-term supply. This is particularly likely to be the case where the purchaser is an organisation rather than an individual, as is so in third party payment for healthcare. The consequence is that the operation of the market is not costless in the way assumed by the theory. There are, for instance, costs in negotiating and writing contracts and costs in monitoring them. This is even more the case if administrative measures, such as regulations about quality, information about products, performance league tables and so on are introduced in order to try to deal with the other divergences of the real market from the perfect one. These can be termed 'transaction costs'. It is also difficult to exclude non-payers from some health services; we all benefit from vaccination, even if we are ourselves unvaccinated, because it lowers the probability of any individual passing on the relevant infection to us. (For discussions of such 'public goods' see Laver, 1986; Levacic, 1991: 37–40; Lipsey, 1966: 295–6.)

A good deal of political rhetoric appears to make the assumptions that it is self-evidently desirable for real-world markets to approximate as closely as possible to the 'classical' model and that co-ordination by the market is somehow a natural and desirable state of affairs, from which public policy should only depart when absolutely necessary. In reality, especially in the modern world, all markets are political in the sense that their form is shaped by powerful political and economic actors rather than occurring as a fact of nature (Polanyi, 1944). We might say that market talk has become widely 'naturalised', that the use of such language has

> the capacity to impose and maintain a particular structuring of some domain or other – a particular way of dividing it into parts, of keeping the parts demarcated from each other, and a particular ordering of those parts in terms of hierarchical relationships of domination and subordination. (Fairclough, 1989: 13)

One response to the impracticality of markets in healthcare is the 'quasi-market', generally defined along the following lines. In common with other markets, there are independent competitive producers on the provider side but, unlike classical markets, some or all of the following characteristics may be present (LeGrand, 1991: 1259–60). First, producers cannot be assumed to be profit maximisers. Second, consumer purchasing power is confined to a specific range of goods or services, so that the purchaser cannot decide to spend the resources thus 'earmarked' on anything else (in effect, the purchasing power is a 'voucher', whether or not so labelled). Third, purchasing decisions are made by an agent rather than by the prospective consumer of the goods or services. Finally, payment for the goods or services is made by a 'third party payer' (see Chapter 1) rather than by the prospective consumer. As we shall see later in this chapter, quasi-markets have in the 1990s been influential as a means of organising the NHS, and are currently enjoying a resurgence of policy popularity.

Another response to shortcomings of the market involves the development of hierarchy. Organisational mergers to create 'horizontal' or 'vertical' integration (i.e. merging with competitors or suppliers/customers respectively) result in larger organisations, characterised by hierarchy as an organisational form. This drive to hierarchy is the focus of 'transaction cost economics' (Williamson, 1975, 1996) which argues that markets frequently impose substantial costs on participants as a result of the necessity to guard against being cheated. Thus it is simply not possible to write a contract that is not subject to several interpretations and it is naïve to assume that actors will always fulfil their promises. Hence participation in markets incurs costs for dispute settlement and for checking mechanisms (Williamson, 1996: 56–7). Such costs may be less within a hierarchy because its authority structures are a more flexible means of settling or avoiding disputes than are formal legalities such as lawsuits (Williamson, 1975: 71ff).

Bureaucracy

The predominant form adopted in many countries for large formal organisations of most kinds is 'bureaucracy' (Mouzelis, 1967; Weber, 1947). This term is used here in a technical sense, rather than in the pejorative 'red tape' sense of everyday conversation. One key element of bureaucracy is *authority deriving from actors' formal positions in the organisation*. In other words, it is hoped that participants will accept formal hierarchical relationships as legitimate, and therefore obey instructions given to them by actors who are defined as hierarchically superior; the hierarchy legitimately directs and monitors their work. The key feature of hierarchy for our purpose is that subordinates can best secure their own interests by conformity with the instructions of superiors (Douglas, 1985: 93–4). Such formal authority may or may not bring actual power with it, but authority structures are created with the intention that they should do so. Another way of looking at this is to say that organisations try to make *formal* roles take precedence over other roles. The formal hierarchy is the ubiquitous mode of portraying specific organisations; for many people, the hierarchy of authority (or 'line management'), drawn as a sort of family tree diagram with the chief executive at the top, virtually defines the organisation. Such hierarchies may be of various shapes or 'configurations'. A 'tall' hierarchy has a high ratio of tiers or levels of management to the total workforce. The average 'span of control', that is the number of subordinates directly responsible to a single superior, is low in relation to the total workforce. In contrast, a 'flat' hierarchy has a low ratio of tiers of management, and a large average span of control, to the total workforce. As we shall see later in this chapter, the NHS (like many large UK organisations) has moved from the tall towards the flatter model, shedding many tiers of management and therefore many middle managers. This is one obvious example of how such formalities can affect people. Another example pertains to the nature of promotion in these configurations; in a tall hierarchy, individual promotions will tend to be modest, but there will be good promotion opportunities, whereas in a flatter hierarchy individual promotions will be more dramatic, but rarer. (See Child, 1984 for a fuller discussion.)

A second key element of bureaucracy is *formalisation*. We have already discussed the hierarchy, itself one aspect of this, but formalisation is also manifest in the many written documents which pervade large organisations: rules, procedure manuals, job descriptions, standard operating procedures, standing financial instructions, explicit performance targets and so on. (We discussed 'clinical guidelines' as an example of such rules in Chapter 3.) Such formalities seek to routinise the authority of hierarchical superiors, to ensure that matters are dealt with in a way of which they approve even when they are not immediately involved. A good deal of managerial writing and discussion employs the notions of centralisation and decentralisation, the latter being currently fashionable. These terms refer to the level in the hierarchy at which decisions are made. But this may not tell us very much about an organisation; an individual may hold a delegated budget but actually have little discretion within the virement rules. Decentralisation cannot therefore be equated with high levels of discretion. Moreover, the point in the organisation at which a decision is made is not simply determined (though it may be affected) by the number of tiers in the hierarchy, so that decentralisation cannot be equated with a flat configuration. The massive international comparative study by Hickson and McMillan (1981) showed an inverse relationship between the number of hierarchical levels and the extent of formalisation in organisations, the implication being that flatter hierarchies and wider spans of control are more reliant on rules and formal procedures. Bureaucracy therefore involves both hierarchy and rules, though (as we shall see below in the case of the NHS) the relative emphasis given to each may vary.

A third key element of bureaucracy is the division of labour. In addition to the division of labour between individuals, that is job specialisation, an organisation of any size is usually formally subdivided into smaller units, perhaps termed 'departments' or something similar, between which also there is a kind of division of labour. Various principles can be employed, usually in combination, to effect this 'grouping' (Child, 1984). The simplest forms of organisation tend to employ 'functional' grouping, that is the aggregation into a department of employees of similar skills or professions, an arrangement which is often comfortable as it entails working alongside people similar to oneself. Other grouping possibilities are by type of client and product, by type of production process, and (in organisations which are geographically dispersed) site or area. Readers who are familiar with health service organisations will recognise all these types, in practice employed at different hierarchical levels of the same organisation.

The shift in the predominant conception of 'organisation' from abstract to concrete outlined above has given rise to a mode of speaking and writing that 'reifies' (Silverman, 1970: 9) hierarchical organisations, that is misleadingly endows them with human attributes, in such terms as 'this organisation needs x, y and z'. Perhaps the most pervasive and also problematic manifestation of reification is the treatment of organisations as 'having objectives'. This is clearly misleading; whilst it may be historically true that a particular organisation was founded by particular individuals for particular purposes at a particular point in time, it cannot be taken from this that such objectives are shared on an ongoing basis by contemporary members of the organisation. At best, such objectives are those set by the organisation's 'dominant coalition' (Lohr, 1973; see also March and Simon, 1958) at a point in time, but of course the effect of describing them as 'organisational' objectives is to seek legitimacy by implying either that they are shared by all, or that only the views of the dominant coalition count. This is another example of 'naturalisation'; organisation does not need to be conceived as hierarchy (Ouchi, 1980: 127), but it usually is.

Although public sector bureaucracy has virtues in terms of providing 'due process' and a transparent distribution of resources (Du Gay, 2000), the archetypal description of bureaucracy as we presented it above has long been the subject of criticism by both academics and those (workers and customers/clients) who have experienced it directly. The classic so-called 'dysfunctions of bureaucracy' centre on its lack of flexibility and responsiveness (Merton, 1949). Thus, emphasis on rule-adherence or 'red tape' can encourage staff to follow the rules slavishly and inappropriately, displacing any recognition of what the rules are aimed at achieving (Blau, 1955). It has also been argued that bureaucratic hierarchies tend to acquire more levels than thought to be necessary to perform the work, in order to multiply promotion opportunities for members (Parkinson, 1957). Such organisations have also been criticised for their inability to respond to a changing environment (Burns and Stalker, 1961). In addition, and despite the advantages of hierarchy identified by transaction cost economics, it is of course impossible to create a comprehensive set of rules to cover all eventualities. In the UK public sector, responses to perceptions of hierarchical inflexibility have taken two forms. First, there has been something of a shift to what might be called 'regulatory bureaucracy' or 'neo-bureaucracy' (Harrison and Smith, 2003), in which organisations are ostensibly freed from direct control from Whitehall departments and instead subjected to various forms of *regulation* by organisations located outside the hierarchy (Hood et al., 2000).

Contemporary NHS examples of such bodies include the Healthcare Commission, the National Institute for Health and Clinical Excellence and 'Monitor', the Regulator of Foundation Trusts. (For a review in the context of healthcare, see Walshe, 2003.) These arrangements seem to attenuate hierarchy but to strengthen rules. Concerns about inflexibility have also led to advocacy that NHS organisations should be managed through manipulation of their 'organisational cultures' and that various forms of multi-organisational and multi-professional networks should be established.

Clans

Compared to our other three approaches to social co-ordination, relatively little has been written about clans. A clan is an association of individuals that resembles a kinship network, but is not confined to blood relations (Ouchi, 1980: 133) and is 'tied together through a variety of bonds' (Ouchi, 1981: 83). Over time, clan members are socialised through their membership into the position of recognising 'that their interests are best served by the dedication of each individual to the interests of the whole' (Bourn and Ezzamel, 1986: 206). Socialisation is made possible by a period of 'apprenticeship' during which the neophyte internalises what is expected of them, perhaps reinforced by various symbols and ceremonies (Bourn and Ezzamel, 1986: 206). The performance of clan members is reciprocally monitored by fellow members (Alvesson and Lindkvist, 1993: 431) and, rather than being based on explicit rules and standards (as in bureaucracy), 'relies on a subtle reading of signals' (Ouchi, 1980: 136) of approval and disapproval. Because members identify with clan interests and have learned to respond to such signals, precise specification of expectation of their performance is unnecessary.

Thus clans are largely held together and differentiated from 'outsiders' through their *culture*, their shared beliefs and frames of reference (Alvesson and Lindkvist, 1993: 430). Whilst they may be employed within hierarchies, they may nevertheless exhibit greater loyalty and attachment to the clan than to the hierarchy. Nevertheless, clans are in a sense hierarchical; more senior members are guardians of their culture. But the form of authority is more akin to 'traditional' authority than to the more formal 'rational-legal' authority which characterises bureaucracy (Ouchi, 1980: 137; Weber, 1947). We can see from Chapter 2 how professions such as medicine approximate to the clan concept (Ouchi, 1980: 136), particularly by virtue of their long period of training, self-regulating codes of conduct and the myth of collegiality.

Although the clan approach to social co-ordination is potentially subject to much of the range of critical analysis that we saw applied to professions in Chapter 2, it is perhaps ironic that the perceived virtues of clans in terms of not needing to develop precise rules or precisely defining 'performance' have been appropriated by management theorists for importation into more bureaucratic forms of co-ordination. The notion of 'organisational culture' and the accompanying assumption that this might be open to managerial manipulation were popularised in a number of best-selling books (most famously Peters and Waterman, 1982) during the 1980s as the means of avoiding some of the 'dysfunctions of bureaucracy' referred to above: if members can be inculcated with a few basic values about the role desired for the organisation, they will use these core values flexibly to make the right decisions in unpredictable circumstances and without specific guidance (Peters and Waterman, 1982: 74). Though

it is far from clear either that bureaucratic organisations can meaningfully be said to have an overall organisational culture, or that such cultures are readily manipulable, interest in this topic has led to numerous attempts to measure culture quantitatively and to relate such measurements to organisational performance (Cameron and Freeman, 1991; Mannion et al., 2005).

Networks

In contrast to the literature on clans, there is a voluminous and varied literature on networks. In part, this is because the latter concept is capable of very wide interpretation, to the point that markets and hierarchies can be seen as forms of network (Thompson, 1993: 51). As John (2001: 141) has pointed out, analyses of networks differ both in terms of whether they conceive network participants to be individuals or formal organisations, and of what is perceived to be exchanged within them: for instance, 'epistemic communities' (Haas, 1992) exchange ideas and information, whilst 'policy networks' (see below) negotiate resources such as finance or legal approval in order to obtain desired outcomes. There is also an influential tradition in network analysis that is primarily concerned to map networks of individuals by measuring the level of contacts between network members and relating it to levels of performance defined in various ways (Coleman et al., 1966; John, 2001: 146–8; Knoke and Kuklinski, 1982; Milward and Provan, 1998). In our usage, network relationships are primarily informal, though they may have formal elements. The actors in a network discover that they have significant common interests and perhaps shared 'world views' and accordingly develop what tend to become long-term relationships in which trust and reciprocity are developed and short-term gain may be sacrificed in order to maintain the network itself and for the sake of longer-term benefits (Thompson, 1993: 51–60). Bargains between members of a network will often be implicit rather than explicit and if there are formal relationships such as contracts or places in a consultative mechanism, these will tend to be *outcomes* of the network's activities rather than drivers of that activity. Sometimes, relationships which are ostensibly of the market type can be better viewed as networks; for instance many organisations habitually deal with the same suppliers over many years, developing a 'give and take' relationship which is not reflected in any formal agreements or contracts that may result (Flynn et al., 1996). Indeed, networks may develop over years into what might be called a 'regime' (the term is taken from studies of the relationships between sovereign states), that is a complex of rules, norms, informal understandings and procedures that regularise the behaviour of network members towards each other and to others (Keohane, 1984). Networks and regimes can be as important, or indeed more important, in their social, economic and political effects than formal organisations. They may endure as institutions over similar, or longer periods. Contemporary interest in the concept of *social capital* as a resource that contributes to community well-being (Coleman, 1988; Putnam, 1993; see also Bourdieu, 1986) draws very much on these perceived positive features of networks.

One form of (very restricted) network that has long been recognised as having significant effects on public policy is the 'corporatist' relationship (Schmitter, 1974) between government and so-called 'peak associations' representing capital and labour. Versions of such corporatist arrangements were present in many specific sectors of the UK political economy in the 1960s and 1970s (Cawson, 1985; Grant, 1985). For example, there was a very close relationship between the Department of Health and the British Medical Association (the doctors' trade union) and the medical Royal Colleges (Lee-Potter, 1997) from the inception of the NHS until the early 1980s, supporting a range of formal joint committees between the profession and the civil service which were the sources of key decisions about such matters as medical workforce planning. (For broader accounts of corporatism in the context of the UK welfare state, see Cawson, 1982; Harrison, 1984). The corporatist analysis was also somewhat modified after Richardson and Jordan's (1979) study showed that policy was to a considerable degree influenced by elite networks of civil servants and producer groups operating within particular policy sectors, spawning two decades of research and analysis of 'policy networks' in the UK (much of which is summed up in Marsh and Rhodes, 1992; Rhodes, 1997). Critics of networks often stress the non-transparency and therefore the lack of potential accountability of networks, together with the possibility that they create and sustain social elites which are difficult for others to enter or challenge (Rhodes, 1997: 21–2). Much of the policy networks literature has, however, emphasised the notion of *governance*. It is important to note that this academic usage does not really correspond to the usage in such phrases as 'corporate governance' or 'clinical governance', which refers to primarily bureaucratic modes of control (Harrison, 2004: 180), but rather signifies a process of policy determination by networks rather than hierarchies (for an overall review, see Pierre and Peters, 2000). Depending on which actors are thought to populate such networks, governance can either be seen as a reaffirmation of the closed and elite character of policy making (Hay and Richards, 2000: 13; Rhodes, 1997) or as an opening-up in which a wider range of actors than before (including public and service user groups) have access to the policy process (Pierre and Peters, 2000: 137–59). As we shall see in Chapter 5, contemporary political rhetoric tends to stress the latter of these interpretations, emphasising the many formal initiatives taken to enhance public and service user 'involvement' in sectors such as the NHS, though of course it is not a necessary consequence of such initiatives that elite power is actually attenuated.

Finally, we can note that intra-organisational networks have been urged on UK public sector organisations as a means of breaking down the inflexibilities perceived to result from professional and formal bureaucratic boundaries, thereby enhancing 'joined-up government' (for a review of which see Peters, 1998; Pollitt, 2003b). An NHS example is 'managed cancer networks' (Expert Working Group, 1999) which attempt to link specialist cancer centres with cancer units at general hospitals with primary care in order to provide an effective and 'seamless' service, though it is far from clear whether such arrangements actually do transcend existing boundaries (Addicott et al., 2006).

An historical sketch of NHS formal organisation

Since its creation, the NHS has been the subject of successive waves of reform intended to improve its management, especially since the early 1970s. Commentators have sometimes characterised these changes initially as movement from bureaucracy to market and, following

the 1997 election, to networks as the dominant organisational form (Exworthy et al., 1999), a depiction that has also been offered by the post-1997 Labour governments. In this section, we examine NHS organisation and reorganisation up to 1997, suggesting that these developments are more accurately seen as a gradual transition (in the terms of Figure 4.1) from clan to bureaucracy as the dominant form of organisation.

1948–79: the illusion of hierarchy

The organisational form of the NHS newly created in 1948, was somewhat different from that outlined in earlier plans (Ministry of Health, 1944). Rather than establishing a partnership between voluntary and statutory sectors, the hospitals were nationalised, with clear formal lines of accountability to the Minister of Health, a situation that the founding Minister acknowledged in a speech immediately prior to the commencement of the Service:

> *The Minister of Health will be the whipping-boy for the Health Service in Parliament. Every time a maid kicks over a bucket of slops in a ward, an agonised wail will go through Whitehall …* (Aneurin Bevan, quoted in Foot, 1973: 192)

The creation of the NHS has been described as the 'transformation of an inadequate, partial and muddled patchwork of health care provision into a neat administrative structure' (Klein, 2001: 1). In fact, the structure was not so neat, but represented a political compromise between the government and various provider groups. The hospitals had indeed been nationalised under regional boards, with at least the appearance and possibility of hierarchical control, though doctors dominated many of the boards and committees (Ham, 1981). But the remaining elements of the 'tripartite' NHS (primary care and local government) had not. Even before the inception of the service, the medical profession had secured substantial government concessions on matters such as clinical autonomy (see Chapter 2), private practice and GPs' self-employment status. GPs, dentists and community pharmacists remained as independent contractors, whilst local government remained responsible for preventive services and some community health services (Webster, 1998: 21). Few early attempts at 'command-and-control' were made. Where a regulatory body (the Hospital Advisory Service) was established in the wake of reports of maltreatment of patients (Watkin, 1975: 72–80), its powers were limited (Walshe, 2003: 113–16). The pattern of resource distribution in the NHS remained similar to that prior to 1948 (Webster, 1998: 57–9) until attempts at redistribution began in the mid-1970s through the 'RAWP' formula (Resource Allocation Working Party, 1976), and no new hospitals were planned until the early 1960s (Allen, 1979). Thus, although these early days of the NHS have been interpreted by some commentators as the start of a process characterised by hierarchy and central control (Powell, 2003: 731–2), the evidence suggests that central control was weak (Haywood and Alaszewski, 1980: 45–6), a view shared by at least one cabinet minister (Crossman, 1972).

Although more systematic planning for new hospitals began in the early 1960s (Allen, 1979; Mohan, 2002: 133–57), a number of commentators trace the establishment of hierarchies and associated practices of centralised planning and strategy development to the period following the 1974 reorganisation of the NHS (Exworthy et al., 1999; Holliday, 1992). The reorganisation attempted to create an effective chain of command, by unifying the tripartite structure and transferring community health services from local government to NHS control. The 1974 reforms created a complex and highly formalised four-tiered hierarchical structure (DHSS, 1972; Harrison, 1988: 16–20), aimed at securing 'maximum delegation downward, maximum accountability upward' (Klein, 2001: 76). Managers were now more specialised, more numerous and better paid and a national planning system was introduced. Nevertheless, GPs continued to operate as independent contractors, and the reforms did nothing to curb the influence of doctors, rather recognising it by placing executive power at local level in the hands of multidisciplinary consensus management teams, with half the places occupied by doctors, each effectively with a power of veto (Harrison, 1982). As we saw in Chapter 2, empirical research conducted in this period demonstrated that the NHS managers still possessed little influence relative to doctors and were still reluctant to question the value of existing patterns of service or to propose major changes. Planning and service change were mainly incremental, with (for example) little of the officially intended redistribution of resources from hospitals to community services (Harrison, 1988: 30–55). Thus the 1974 organisational arrangements might be better described as 'professional bureaucracy' (Mintzberg, 1991), a hybrid organisational form in which routine housekeeping, supply and accounting functions are governed by bureaucracy, but its people-processing (patient care) functions are governed by professional autonomy.

1979–90: the emergence of hierarchy

The Conservative Government elected in 1979 came to power committed to simplifying and decentralising the NHS and cutting bureaucracy. Its consultative document *Patients First* (Department of Health and Social Security and Welsh Office, 1979) proposed the simplification of structures, with health authorities allowed greater discretion to respond to local needs whilst central government withdrew from detailed intervention in local affairs. In the event, a tier of organization was abolished from April 1982. Yet even before this modest reorganisation was complete it was becoming increasingly difficult for ministers to maintain such a hands-off stance. In the context of economic recession, they had come under considerable political pressure to demonstrate that the NHS was using resources efficiently and implementing national policy priorities (Harrison, 1994: 58–68). Rather than leaving local decision makers to their own devices, ministers intervened to compel them to manage resources efficiently. From 1981 onwards the NHS had been required by the government to make efficiency savings, with health authority budgets adjusted to reflect efficiency gains. From 1982, this drive for efficiency gained momentum in the form of initiatives intended to improve accountability, including an annual review process, intended to secure greater adherence to national policies and priorities, and the associated development of performance indicators.

Whilst the 1981–82 NHS reforms were attempts to fine tune the hierarchical relationships between different levels of NHS organisation, the introduction of 'general management' in 1984 represented a significant departure from this approach. These reforms left the statutory structure of the NHS largely unchanged (indeed the Griffiths report which recommended the reforms explicitly rejected another restructuring exercise), but attempted instead to change the nature and status of 'management' in the NHS. Key elements of the reforms, which mark a break with the philosophy of management as diplomacy, included the creation of general manager posts in place of consensus teams at all levels of the NHS and the consequent downgrading of professional influence, signalling a shift from a system

> *based on the mobilisation of consent to one that is based on the management of conflict – from one that has conceded the right of groups to veto change to one that gives the managers the right to override objections. (Day and Klein, 1983: 1813)*

Whereas in 1979 the government had explicitly rejected the notion of general management in the NHS on the grounds that it would not be compatible with professional independence, by 1983 it was enthusiastically implementing general management at all levels of the NHS (Butler, 1994: 14). A manifesto commitment to reduce bureaucracy in the public sector had in the event downgraded 'administration' in favour of 'management' (Learmonth, 2005). The review system mentioned above was extended to lower organisational levels, and efficiency savings were replaced by 'cost-improvement programmes' aimed at reducing costs without impairing services. A further recommendation was for the increased involvement of doctors in local management and the allocation of workload related budgets ('management budgets') to hospital consultants.

These reforms should be seen in the wider context of the 'New Public Management' (NPM), an approach to public administration pursued by governments in various countries attempting to control the growth of public expenditure and gathering momentum during the late 1970s and 1980s. NPM, presented as a shift away from bureaucracy and towards more flexible forms of organisation, was characterised by the importation of business-style managerialism into the public sector and the substitution of market forms of provision in formerly public services (Hood, 1991). (We examine the manner in which these changes became policy in Chapter 6.) However, the introduction of general management and other reforms of this period can also be interpreted as strengthening hierarchical relationships and creating a management culture of command and obedience (Butler, 1994: 14). Nevertheless, their impact on the ground was more nuanced. A review of empirical studies conducted in the period beginning with the implementation of general management (Harrison et al., 1992: 54–92) found that the major influence on managerial agendas was no longer the need to facilitate matters for professionals but rather to respond directly to central government agendas. Moreover, the new general managers were widely regarded (including by doctors) as having a legitimate role, but as yet had made few inroads into clinical autonomy. By the late 1980s, modest changes had occurred in the medical–managerial power balance, but more significant changes had occurred in perceptions of both managerial legitimacy and government–management relationships.

1991–97: constructing markets

Other changes had occurred during the 1980s. 'Compulsory competitive tendering' across the public sector allowed private sector contractors to compete with in-house providers of services; in the NHS, this was applied mainly to such hospital services as catering, cleaning and laundries (Ascher, 1987). Health authorities were also exhorted to develop income generation schemes such as leasing space to shops. These schemes can be seen as symptomatic of a faith in competition and market forms of organisation that resulted in more dramatic subsequent changes described by Klein (2001: 149) as 'the politics of big bang' and Robinson (1999: 2) as 'the greatest change in management and organisation since the NHS was created'. These subsequent changes were the so-called 'internal market' (more technically, quasi-market: see above and Chapter 1) for care introduced in 1991. The proposals for reform were contained in the White Paper *Working for Patients* (Department of Health et al., 1989) and enacted in the subsequent NHS and Community Care Act 1990. Establishment of the quasi-market involved the separation of purchasers and providers of care. Health authorities continued to be centrally funded for the care of the population resident within their boundaries, but no longer had control of their local NHS hospitals and community services, which were transformed over a few years into quasi-independent NHS 'Trusts'. Such Trusts were not guaranteed funding, but would compete with other providers, including non-local Trusts and private hospitals for contracts to treat the purchaser's patients (Harrison, 1991). The system was further complicated by the creation of volunteer GP 'fundholders' who received budgets (based largely on the practice's historic use of services and deducted from health authority allocations) to purchase secondary care for their patients directly from providers (Glennerster et al., 1994). Some GP 'fundholders' held funds to pay only for elective services for their registered patients, while others (variously referred to as 'total fundholders', 'total purchasers' or 'total purchasers in primary care' – hereafter TPPCs) were allocated budgets to pay for all secondary, including acute, care.

The *Working For Patients* reorganisation was based on different organisational assumptions from the earlier general management reforms, summarised by Holliday as follows:

> the shift to general management sought increased efficiency and cost effectiveness in the NHS through the creation of a clear managerial hierarchy [characterised by] a regulatory dynamic. The internal market has an entirely different dynamic … a dynamic of fragmentation and release into a competitive market. It is evident that these two dynamics are distinct … Efficiency … remains a central objective, but it will now be generated, not by an efficient monolith, but by the most efficient units in an internal market. (Holliday, 1992: 59)

As we saw in Chapter 2, both sets of reforms were vehemently, but unsuccessfully resisted by the medical profession. We noted above that the general management reforms did not immediately result in radical changes to the manner in which the NHS operated, and this was also true of the quasi-market. Research evidence suggests that relationships were more usually based on collaboration than competition, with apparent reluctance to engage in competitive behaviour evidenced in the high levels of co-operation between purchasers and providers, with the former generally choosing to place contracts with local hospitals, rather than 'shopping around' for alternatives (Flynn et al., 1996; Flynn and Williams, 1997). GP fundholders, however, were rather more prone to 'shop around' (Mannion, 2005). This lack of competition was also acknowledged by Enthoven, the American economist credited with influencing ministers'

thinking on the design and introduction of the quasi-market (Ham, 1994: 5–6). On a scale of 0 to 10 where 0 represents a centrally planned and managed service and 10 a free market economy, Enthoven rated the NHS market initially between 2 and 3, thereafter falling below this towards more central control (Enthoven, 1999). Perhaps this was not surprising. The prospect of large numbers of patients being transported long distances for treatment was acknowledged by many to be unrealistic, whilst the prospect of money following these patients, with uncompetitive hospitals being forced to close, was politically unacceptable. Thus ministers were reluctant to leave the market to run its course and the fierce commitment to the market which accompanied the launch of the White Paper became progressively diluted (Butler, 1994: 44).

As we noted above, different types of social co-ordination co-exist in the real world, so that markets do not obviate the possibility of hierarchy and bureaucracy within competing organisations. The impact of the quasi-market on medical–managerial relationships has so far been the subject of only a preliminary review (Harrison and Lim, 2003). This suggests that managers were by this time more ready than before to challenge doctors, resulting in decisions where managerial interventions were decisive against medical opposition. Whilst doctors in some locations were drawn into co-operative networks with managers, elsewhere managers were unable to control the acute medical sector or to make other than incremental adjustments to services. Developments in performance indicators begun in the 1980s continued, and centralised management at the Department of Health was enhanced (Klein, 2001: 181–3); despite the rhetoric of markets and competition, central government influence on managerial agendas was further strengthened.

Contemporary NHS organisation

The election to government in 1997 of so-called 'New Labour' brought into government discourses of 'modernisation' and the 'third way' that had originally been developed in its long period of opposition with reference to the party itself (Taylor, 1997: 33). The import of these discourses was partly to distance the party from both its own earlier policies and those of the rival Conservative party, from

> an Old Left preoccupied by state control, high taxation and producer interests; and a New Right treating public investment, and often the very notions of 'society' and collective endeavour, as evils to be undone. (Blair, 1998: 1)

But the discourse also sought 'modernisation' as the means of signalling a perceived need to react pragmatically to contemporary social and global economic changes, rather than trying to resist them (Giddens, 1998: 7). The vagueness of these labels (Powell, 2002) perhaps allowed their application to New Labour's unfolding policies when in government. Despite some vaguely worded publications (Labour Party, 1994, 1995) the party had apparently never considered substantive health policy when in opposition until some six months prior to their election victory; their 1997 manifesto rode largely on rejection of the 'internal market' and a pledge to cut waiting lists. The proposals contained in the White Paper *The New NHS: Modern, Dependable* (Secretary of State for Health, 1997) contained only sketchy details of proposed key institutions and processes such as the new Primary Care Groups (PCGs), NICE (discussed in Chapter 1), the development of local systems of 'clinical governance', arrangements for integrating with the work of local authorities and funding for patients who receive care outside their district of residence. But it did offer an NHS-specific definition of the 'third way':

> neither the old centralised command and control systems of the 1970s [nor] the divisive internal market system of the 1990s [but is] based on partnership and driven by performance. (Secretary of State for Health, 1997: 10)

Thus the third way is contrasted with an implicit 'first way' of hierarchical control and 'second way' of competitive markets. We have seen in the previous section that these are not accurate portrayals; rather they can be seen as myths that serve to obscure the direction of New Labour's own policies (Harrison and Smith, 2003). Ignoring the literal nonsense of the final phrase in the above quotation ('performance' is the *result* of what is being driven), the clear implication is that the third way favours network rather than hierarchy or market, an interpretation subsequently confirmed in a journalist's report of an interview with the NHS's Chief Executive in early 2002:

> ...the [government] aim is to achieve a cultural shift that gives rise to truly patient focused organisations, based on networks rather than hierarchies and driven by locally determined priorities. (Brindle, 2002: 17)

The pragmatic aspect of 'modernisation' was also evident. Shortly after taking office, the government announced that its structure for the NHS would 'go with the grain' of aspects of the Conservatives' arrangements that were perceived to have been of some value, whilst abandoning competition and the market. There were, at least initially, some distinctively Labour policies based on an acceptance that ill-health is causally related to non-individual factors such as social inequalities, material deprivation and the environment that cannot be addressed by the NHS alone. Hence a philosophy of policy integration re-emerged, including 'Health Improvement Programmes', in which health authorities were to work with local government and other NHS bodies to address local health needs through economic, social and environmental policies in addition to healthcare services (Secretary of State, 1997: 26–7). New legislation imposed a duty of co-operation on NHS institutions, both with each other and with local government authorities. Another such initiative, Health Action Zones, allowed NHS institutions to bid for centrally allocated funds to develop multi-agency programmes to improve the health status of their local populations. We shall return to this topic in Chapter 7. At this point we can note that, by 2002, these developments had been overtaken by a renewed emphasis on the provision of services to individual patients.

Reinventing competition

The pragmatic adoption of Conservative organisational forms left NHS Trusts, as before, managerially independent of health authorities, but with the former (ostensibly) competitive annual contracting process replaced with a system of longer term (up to three years) 'service agreements', said to be 'contestable' rather than competitive, that is to be abandoned only in the event of extreme dissatisfaction with providers' services. GP fundholding (GPFH) was formally abolished from 1999, being replaced by PCGs, aggregated groups of GPs which, though legally sub-committees of the health authority, held a cash-limited unified budget for primary, secondary and community care, providing primary and community healthcare and purchasing hospital services. From 2000, some PCGs were translated into Primary Care Trusts (PCTs), with a separate statutory existence, and by 2004 all the new organisations had PCT status. We shall examine this process in more detail in Chapter 6. PCTs are centrally funded according to a formula based largely on the size and demographics of their total practice population with adjustments for factors such as local market forces and 'additional need' for factors not reflected in the age/sex breakdown alone (e.g. estimated unmet need arising from differential uptake of health services by vulnerable groups; Glennerster, 2003: 65–6). These arrangements can be seen as another manifestation of New Labour pragmatism, effectively the re-creation of TPPC on a compulsory basis. Moreover, the government did not repeal enabling legislation (the Primary Care Act, 1997) enacted by the Conservatives immediately before the general election; this has been used to allow changes in traditional GP contractual arrangements, most importantly the treatment of the practice (rather than each individual GP) as the holder of the NHS contract, and employment of some GPs on a salaried, rather than self-employed, basis (Walsh et al., 1999).

We noted above that, on taking office in 1997, the New Labour government purported to have abolished the quasi-market. However, in October 2002 it was announced that the NHS would over the next few years move towards a system in which secondary and tertiary care services would be commissioned by PCTs from a wider range of NHS and private hospitals, including new 'independent sector treatment centres' operated by the private sector and sometimes employing overseas doctors specifically imported for the purpose. In addition to the increasing role envisaged for private sector providers, the creation of Foundation Trusts (FTs), announced in 2002, blurs the public/private boundary in that they are able to undertake joint ventures with the private sector, are subject to a less stringent financial regulatory regime than NHS trusts, are accountable to a new independent regulator ('Monitor') and are not bound by Department of Health directives. Although government intends that all hospitals will achieve FT status, in the short term, only the better performing hospitals have been granted this status, with its greater freedoms and 'lighter touch' monitoring regime.

Although these developing arrangements remain a quasi-market, recent policy emphasis on patient choice suggests that it may move somewhat in the direction of a classical market. The *NHS Improvement Plan* published in 2004 outlined major changes required to move from a centrally directed system to a patient-led system (Department of Health, 2004e), which we shall explore further in Chapter 5. In 2005 proposals to redesign both the way services are delivered (Department of Health, 2005b) and commissioned (Department of Health, 2005a) were published, featuring: pricing of all patient cases at a national standard tariff (purportedly to obviate price competition); the use of casemix measures (Healthcare Resource Groups – HRGs, the UK equivalent of US diagnosis-related groups or DRGs); compulsion on PCTs both to diversify the providers from whom they commission care away from just their local NHS Trust, and to strictly enforce waiting time targets by immediate withdrawal of funds from Trusts that fail to meet them (Department of Health, 2002b); and automatic free choice of any accredited provider for all elective patients at the moment of referral by 2008 (Department of Health, 2005b). These actual and planned developments left the claim to have abolished the Conservatives' 'internal market' somewhat tenuous. These plans also resulted in a halving of the number of PCTs in 2006.

This trend towards re-adopting the policies of the previous government had continued with the invention of 'practice-based commissioning' (Department of Health, 2004f), an apparent return to the principle of GPFH. As we shall see in Chapter 6, participation is voluntary. The organisational forms adopted are varied, often consortia of general practices with budgets for a wide range of secondary services, whilst much early effort in such commissioning seems to be taking the form of defining and contracting for highly bureaucratised 'patient pathways' in an attempt to reduce the proportion of patients requiring hospital care. Other aspects of primary care policy were also moving in directions espoused by the earlier Conservative government, which in 1987 had mooted the desirability of competition in primary care (Secretaries of State, 1987: 12), albeit in vague terms that found no immediate policy manifestation. By 2006, the concept of 'Alternative Provider Medical Services' had appeared, initially as the means of providing primary care services in locations unattractive to traditional GPs but increasingly seen as an opportunity for private corporate healthcare providers to enter the NHS market. The extent to which this will result in such market entries is at present unclear, since entrepreneurial groups of GPs are also active in pursuing such contracts (Walsh et al., 2007: 44).

Regulation and 'clinical governance'

In the discourse of academic political science, the term 'governance' is commonly used to contrast with the term 'government': that is to signify a mode of co-ordination based on networks rather than on hierarchy (see, for instance, Rhodes, 1997 and Chapter 6 below). It is ironic therefore that the term has been officially appropriated to refer to a set of rather hierarchical arrangements. This usage seems first to appear in the White Paper *The New NHS: Modern, Dependable*, but is fleshed out to a considerable degree in the subsequent consultation document *A First Class Service* of June 1998; clinical governance is there 'defined' as

> *a framework through which NHS organisations are accountable for continuously improving the quality of their services and safeguarding high standards of care by creating an environment in which excellence in clinical care will flourish. (NHS Executive, 1998: 33)*

Taken alongside the use of the term 'governance' rather than 'government', this formulation is perhaps calculated to be anodyne; certainly its medical proponents from within the NHS present it mainly in developmental, rather than regulatory or punitive terms (Scally and Donaldson, 1998). Within hospitals, all doctors were required from 2001 to participate in national specialty-based audit programmes as well as in the existing voluntary confidential enquiries into maternal mortality, perioperative mortality, stillbirths and infant mortality, and suicide and homicide by persons with mental illness (NHS Executive, 1998: 35).

However, a key element in the new arrangements was that chief executives (very few of whom were clinically qualified) became responsible for the clinical, as well as the financial, performance of their institutions. New legislation placed upon Trusts a statutory duty for the quality of care, and their accounts were to contain a statement assuring the existence of adequate quality control arrangements (NHS Executive, 1998: 34).

Externally, the hallmark of New Labour's policy was the creation of a new set of well-resourced regulatory bodies, with remits that were both broad in focus and clinically oriented. Despite being presented as independent, these bodies were substantially under government control (Walshe, 2003: 127), providing a form of neo-bureaucracy in which rules were more prominent than hierarchy (Harrison and Smith, 2003). The most prominent of these bodies were NICE (discussed in Chapter 1) and the Commission for Health Improvement (CHI), established in 2000 as a statutory body 'at arm's length from government' (NHS Executive, 1998: 51). CHI was responsible for advising on clinical governance, reviewing the implementation of NSFs (see Chapter 2) and for inspecting NHS provider organisations. Routine 'clinical governance reviews' were conducted of all Trusts every three to four years, and included local compliance with clinical guidelines issued by NICE, and with NSFs. In addition, the Secretary of State or health authorities could initiate inquiries where local problems were suspected. Although CHI had no direct powers of sanction (which were to be applied through the NHS performance management system), it was also responsible for 'independently' publishing performance indicators (including indicators of clinical performance) for the NHS. From 2003, these indicators, along with the results of CHI reviews, contributed to the 'star' system of assessing the overall performance of Trusts, which were classified as having 0, 1, 2 or 3 stars. Organisations with three stars were to be subject to less monitoring (so-called 'earned autonomy') and given the opportunity to take over no-star organisations, which were to receive external advice and support but if necessary be 'subjected to a rising scale of intervention' including mergers with other Trusts (Secretary of State, 2000: 61–5). Within these functions, a tension is clearly discernable. On the one hand, CHI sought wherever possible to be developmental and supportive, a philosophy summed up in the title of its first annual report *Holding up a Mirror to Ourselves* (Commission for Health Improvement, 1999). On the other hand, the government preferred to see CHI more as a 'watchdog'; on the day before it became legally operational, the Secretary of State announced that it would investigate allegations of patient maltreatment in the North Lakeland Trust, referring to CHI's mission to 'root out poor practice'. By 2002, and partly as a result of the Bristol scandal (see Chapter 2), the government had decided in favour of the latter philosophy. From 2004, a new Commission for Healthcare Audit and Inspection (since renamed the Healthcare Commission) took over the role of CHI and the healthcare value-for-money audit responsibilities of the Audit Commission. Unlike its predecessor, it is independent from government to the extent of being responsible to Parliament (Walshe, 2003: 165). From 2005, the 'star' system was replaced by an 'annual health check', employing criteria related to national standards and targets, results of inspections and financial performance and separate publicly available judgements about quality of clinical services and use of NHS resources, with ratings given as 'excellent', 'good' 'fair', and 'weak' (www.healthcarecommission.org.uk/serviceproviderinformation/annualhealthcheck).

In 2001 the government also created a Modernisation Agency (Secretary of State, 2000: 60–1) to build on local experiences of examining and redesigning care from the patient's point of view and to oversee implementation of the *NHS Plan*. The abolition of the Agency in 2005 can be seen as a further manifestation of the downgrading of a developmental philosophy in favour of a more traditional approach to regulation. Other new regulatory agencies created in this period include a National Patient Safety Agency with an accompanying mandatory scheme for reporting adverse clinical events, feeding a single database for analysing incidents and near misses, and a National Clinical Assessment Authority to 'provide a rapid and objective expert assessment of an individual doctor's performance, recommending to the … Trust educational or other approaches' … 'where concern has arisen locally' (2000: 90). The latter organisation was merged into the former in 2005.

In contrast to the piecemeal growth in regulatory bodies under the Conservatives and New Labour's first years in office, greater emphasis is now placed on co-ordination amongst regulators. For example, the Healthcare Commission will now use the findings and evidence of other bodies such as the Audit Commission and 'Monitor', the Independent Regulator of NHS Foundation Trusts, in its regulatory process. The commitment to 'earned autonomy' marks a further change in philosophy under New Labour towards 'enforced self-regulation' (Hood et al., 2000: 292), involving more formal external regulation for poor performers, with good performers rewarded with fewer targets and less regulatory oversight and intervention (Department of Health, 2004d).

Interpreting the 'third way'

We are now in a position to summarise, albeit crudely, the historical pattern of changes to the NHS in terms of the organisational forms outlined in the 'key concepts' section of this chapter. First, the original wartime plans for a health service were essentially for a network of relationships between the then existing public and voluntary hospitals. In contrast, the actual NHS introduced in 1948 had the appearance of a centrally controlled bureaucracy. But as we have seen, such a description was somewhat belied by the strong elements of clan co-ordination exercised through the health professions, especially medicine. Despite its appearance as a kind of nationalised industry, the NHS was not centrally managed. Second, we have seen that bureaucratic styles of co-ordination began to grow from the early 1970s, though the insulation of the medical profession from many of these developments suggests that Mintzberg's (1991) concept of 'professional bureaucracy' provides a better description. Third, although brief attempts were made in the early 1980s to flatten the hierarchical aspects of this professional bureaucracy, the subsequent arrival of 'general management' emphasised this hierarchy, and began to chip away at the mechanisms by which doctors were insulated from it. Fourth, the arrival of the principle (if not always the practice) of competition in the 1990s can be seen as signalling the dominance of two forms of co-ordination, bureaucracy and markets, over the principles of network and clan co-ordination. Since the arrival in office of the Labour government of 1997, this dominance has strengthened, with increasing fragmentation of provider organisations and a proliferation of regulatory institutions, despite the continuation of rhetoric about the promotion of networks based on trust and partnership, and an enabling state (Bevir and Rhodes, 2003: 58). This pattern suggests a general one and a more specific question.

The general question relates to why the NHS is apparently forever being reorganised. The brief history provided in this chapter, along with more detailed treatments elsewhere, (Harrison, 1988; Levitt and Wall, 1984; Webster, 1996) make it clear that the service has been in a perpetual state of reorganisation since the 1970s, a pattern which so far shows little sign of abatement. The NHS is not unique in this respect, for it is a pattern that characterises much of the UK public sector (Hennessy, 1989; Pollitt, 1984). No doubt reorganisation is, in part, an intended instrumental response to problems faced by policy makers. But political considerations are likely to play a part too. First, reorganisation is something that policy makers are generally able to achieve and, moreover, achieve within the constraints of relatively short periods in office. No matter how complex and difficult the problem faced, there is always a plausible-looking organisational solution, whose impact on the problem is unlikely to become evident in the short term. The essentially short-term nature of British politics was famously characterised by Harold Wilson as Prime Minister in the mid-1960s: 'a week is a long time in politics' (Jay, 1996: 390). Second, reorganisations provide endless opportunities for symbolic policy making, to provide public reassurance (Edelman, 1977) that 'something is being done'. The more specific question relates to the specific patterns of reorganisation adopted since 1997. At first sight, this presents a puzzle: why should an ostensibly left-of-centre government pursue policies of which its right-of-centre predecessor would have approved yet felt unable actively to pursue? In this final section, we shall examine three lines of possible explanation, though we shall also see that these are not wholly distinct from each other. The first suggests that New Labour's approach is simply a pragmatic piece of statecraft aimed at presenting a favourable impression of its policies. The second suggests that current policies derive substantially from the spread of contemporary ideas about 'new public management', whilst the third (which in many ways coincides with New Labour's own explanation) attributes the policies as a response to 'globalisation'.

Pragmatic statecraft

The starting point for our first possible explanation is Klein's (1983: 140) famous dictum that governments tend to seek means of centralising the credit for policies that go well whilst diffusing the blame for things that go wrong. We saw in Chapter 1 how highly the NHS ranks in terms of public perceptions of importance, which implies that governments need to regard it as a candidate for acquiring political credit whilst diffusing blame. In this context, the recent growth of NHS funding is hardly surprising. However, we also saw in Chapter 1, neither this nor the ostensibly authoritative decisions of NICE seem to have prevented continuing resource demands. Indeed, as Klein (2005: 53) has noted, opinion poll evidence about public expectations of whether the NHS would improve or deteriorate remains stubbornly unaffected by actual spending decisions. In addition, we saw in Chapter 2 that recent Labour governments have had to address a number of medical 'scandals'. From this explanatory perspective, recent trends in NHS organisation are a political tactic by which responsibility and blame for perceived shortcomings are shifted to independent or quasi-independent healthcare providers and to regulatory bodies that have at least the appearance (Walshe, 2003: 127) of being independent from government. The move to enforced self-regulation might thus be understood in terms of 'the politics of depoliticisation' which allows the centre to retain arms length control, whilst 'placing at one remove the political character of decision making' (Burnham, 2001: 127). At the same time, the maintenance of the concept (and associated logo) of an NHS that is still largely free to patients at the point of delivery, along with rhetoric about the NHS needing to improve performance in return for extra resources, allow political credit to be garnered.

New public management

In general terms, the directions of recent NHS organisational change that we have described are consistent with a bundle of ideas that have been prominent since the 1980s under the label of 'new public management' (NPM) (Hood, 1991). The main ideas that constitute this philosophy can be summarised as the application of private corporate sector principles to public administration. More specifically, NPM seeks efficiency by promoting the break-up of monolithic public sector organisations into autonomous sub-units, whose financial inter-relationships are transparent and ideally constitute a form of trading. This points towards a combination of markets or quasi-markets as the means of governing relationships between organisations (and indeed between sub-units within organisations), and to decentralisation of managerial authority to such units. Such 'entrepreneurial government' also entails a dom-inant position for managers within organisations and clear measures of organisational per-formance. Although there is clearly some affinity between these ideas and the anti-statist preferences of sections of the political right, NPM does not necessarily challenge the need for government intervention in such fields as health and social care. Rather, the guiding idea is that government should 'steer' rather than 'row' (Osborne and Gaebler, 1993), 'outsource' rather than provide public services directly, thereby transforming itself into a 'commissioner', ideally from multiple providers. In stereotypical terms, NPM is presented as being in favour of the taxpayer and consumer, and against bureaucracy (Pollitt, 2003a: 32–3; Power, 1997: 44). Yet, as we have seen, NPM in the NHS has not in practice entailed a turn against bureaucracy, but rather a replacement of hierarchical management by regulation, that is by a different kind of bureaucracy; indeed some commentators have argued that such agen-cies are better considered as engaged in performance management than regulation (Midwinter and McGarvey, 2001). Such regulation, though strictly against the spirit of NPM, can be seen as necessitated by NPM itself (Power, 1997: 44). Government can hardly commission services for people and then profess itself uninterested in their standards, especially where those services have the high political profile of the NHS. Yet the range and technical complexity of public services (and particularly health services) imply that the asymmetry of information between service providers and service users is so great that specialist judgements need to be made by specialist regulatory bodies. NPM has come to provide a philosophical underpinning for governmental reforms in the UK, US and several other countries (Hood, 1991; Pollitt, 2003a), so that its appearance in the NHS can be seen simply as part of this wider project; as conventional wisdom about how to address the contemporary combination of economic constraints and rising public demands.

Globalisation and 'the third way'

Since before coming to power, New Labour has justified third way politics on the grounds that it can deliver the restructuring of the social democratic state required in an era of 'globalisation'. Theories of globalisation point to numerous dimensions of the phenomenon, including unprecedented possibilities of human migration, rapid disease transmission, communication (especially electronically), non-national ('terrorist') aggression and capital flows. The last of these has facilitated the growth of powerful multinational corporations able to threaten host national governments with relocation to lower-wage, lower-tax economies, making it difficult for governments to retain distinct national economies and domestic strategies of economic management (Hirst and Thompson, 1996: 1). A further consequence is that the relative prosperity of different national economies may change, potentially leading to decline in formerly dominant economies (Gilpin, 2001: 146–7). This does not mean that governments are helpless in the face of globalisation, rather that they must respond within constraints, typically seeking to promote open competitive economies with flexible labour markets, high standards of training and lean welfare regimes that both control public expenditure and provide incentives to work (Evans and Cerny, 2003; Jessop, 1999). An additional factor is the increasingly differentiated nature of modern society, characterised by a decline in class politics and the expansion of choice in lifestyle, consumption and sexuality. In a context where old left policies are unsustainable, the 'third way', according to its proponents:

> *implies a thorough-going programme of policy modernisation. It looks to modernise the state and government including the welfare state, plus the economy and other sectors of society … Social democrats … need to overcome some of their worries and fears about markets … it won't do, as writers from the old left suggest, merely to counterpose the state to markets … .The left has to get comfortable with markets, with the role of business in the creation of wealth, and the fact that private capital is essential for social investment … market relations allow free choices to be made by consumers, at least where there is competition between multiple producers … . Markets can also favour attitudes of social responsibility, since participants need to calculate the likely outcomes of what they do, whether they are producers or consumers. This factor helps explain other aspects of the liberating potential of markets, since the decisions the individual makes aren't given by authoritarian command or by bureaucracy. (Giddens, 2000: 32–5)*

As with NPM, there is clearly some affinity between this line of thinking and neo-liberal and anti-statist ideas as promulgated by the New Right, and there are debates about the extent to which the 'third way' is simply a tacit acceptance of the latter (Bevir, 2003; Coates, 2002; Hay, 2002). Nevertheless, as we have seen, this emphasis on markets, choice and individual responsibility is consistent with recent developments in health policy.

Concluding remarks

It is not possible to reach a straightforward conclusion about the explanatory power of the three approaches outlined above. In part, this is because they are not necessarily mutually contradictory and also because they contain some common elements. For instance all imply government aspirations to depoliticise health services, whilst both NPM and globalisation contain assumptions about needs to improve efficiency, and both NPM and the statecraft explanations are concerned with public and consumers. The globalisation explanation does, however, contain a lacuna. It is not clear exactly how opening up the NHS to competition is supposed to improve the UK's economic prospects in a globalised world. Whilst it is possible to argue that changes in other parts of the welfare state, such as education and employment policy, contribute to improving incentives and skills for employment, we saw in Chapter 1 that the 'productionist' justification for state provision has long been superseded by a 'consumerist' justification. Explanations related to pragmatic statecraft and the spread of ideas about NPM therefore seem more plausible. Two final comments can be offered. First, reliance on competing healthcare bureaucracies seems unlikely to be successful in depoliticising the NHS. Public trust in politicians is always much lower than for health professionals (MORI, 2003), so that concerns about 'poor performance' in the NHS tend to be associated in the public's mind with deficiencies in ministerial capabilities. Neo-bureaucracy may be unable to deliver a 'patient led NHS'. Since guidelines downplay differences between individual patients, it is not clear that the end result will be to put patients in control or to deliver services tailored to the circumstances of the individual. Attempts to improve quality by promoting standardisation and limiting the exercise of discretion preclude the application of 'tacit knowledge' (Polanyi, 1967: 34) discussed in Chapter 3. The potential for rules to erode co-operation and trust in clinical settings (McDonald et al., 2005a) and for rule-following to become an end in itself, with potential adverse consequences for patients (McDonald et al., 2005b; Parker and Lawton, 2000), is well documented. Moreover, recent evidence suggests that partnership working has been hampered by the promotion of quasi-markets and regulatory regimes characterised by centrally imposed targets and an intensification of audit and inspection regimes (Glendinning et al., 2005). Second, the creation of a healthcare market may be difficult to reverse, since it creates a range of new provider interests that will resist future policy change. The nationalisation of UK hospitals in 1948 was smoothed by their parlous financial state (Webster, 1988: 3), whilst in the early 1990s the US 'Clinton Plan' for universal health insurance failed in the face of industry opposition (Skocpol, 1996).

Further reading

For a range of approaches to social co-ordination, see Maidment and Thompson (1993). Moran (2004) provides a good book-length introduction to the topic of regulation in the contemporary British state. On quasi-markets in the NHS, see Bartlett et al. (1994). For past and recent regulation in the NHS, see Walshe (2003). On the organisation and management of NHS primary care, see Peckham and Exworthy (2003).

Chapter 5

The Politics of Democracy and Participation

Summary of chapter contents

- Public and user participation: key concepts
- Public and user participation: history and contemporary developments
- Interpreting public and user participation

Public and user 'involvement' refers to participation in some aspect of the governance, design or availability of public services, that is as something more than simply using the service. It relates both to contemporary debates about appropriate governance for specific services such as the NHS and to broader debates about democracy and citizenship in the UK. The latter can perhaps be summarised as manifesting a growing interest in 'participatory' democracy, that is treating public policy as the occasion for public education 'in the widest sense, including both the psychological aspect and gaining of practice in democratic skills and procedures' (Pateman, 1970: 42). One strand of this debate presents participation as the remedy for a so-called 'democratic deficit', as a supplement to the perceived inadequacy of representative democracy, especially in local government: low electoral turnouts, a focus on service provision rather than local voice, poor representation resulting from the 'first past the post' electoral system, and the assumption that the fact of election guarantees representativeness (Stewart, 1997). The view has acquired further credence in a UK context where representative government has been partially replaced over the last 30 years by what has been variously termed the 'new magistracy' (Stewart and Davis, 1994) or the 'appointed state' (Skelcher, 1998), that is the proliferation of public institutions with appointed, rather than elected, governing bodies.

A second strand of current interest in participatory democracy views the process of participation as an end in itself; so-called 'active citizenship' entails 'a concept of both being and of doing' (Prior et al., 1995: 2). It may therefore be valued as an antidote to social fragmentation (Gyford, 1991: 33; see also Pateman, 1970: 22) especially that brought about by the loss of community in areas whose economic existence has depended on now declining industries. A third strand of interest sees participation as part of both neo-liberal critiques of Marshall's (1950) concepts of social rights and social citizenship (and hence of the welfare state) and as a potential response to such critiques (Faulks, 1998; Hayek, 1988; Rees, 1995; Plant, 1992). Increased political participation offers three rather different responses to such critiques. It offers a potential basis for self-help as opposed to passive reliance on state services. In addition, public participation in decisions about the rationing of welfare services would undermine a key neo-liberal argument: that welfare rights cannot be properly or non-arbitrarily enforced because of resource constraints. Finally, participation offers the possibility of political mobilisation in defence of social citizenship; historically, expansions in the definition of citizenship and of the rights consequent upon such definitions have only been obtained through extensive struggle (Giddens, 1982: 171).

There has also been a more specific set of debates about NHS governance, arising especially from the fact of third party payment, discussed in Chapter 1. Since patients are generally in the position of using the services that are provided, rather than choosing from a range in the market, it is logical to argue that patients and public should have some political means of influencing the NHS. One element in these debates focuses upon the way in which, as we shall see below, the (never extensive) formal democratic credentials of NHS governing bodies have been steadily eroded in favour of membership by individuals chosen for their personal abilities rather than their capacity to represent a public perspective (Cooper et al., 1995; Hunter and Harrison, 1997: 124–36; Hutton, 2000: 32–7). Public and user participation has been seen as a necessary counterpoise to managerial influence in the context of a series of critiques and exposés of apparently unregulated managerial behaviour in the mid-1990s, including apparently illicit expenses payments and improper letting of large contracts, as well as critiques of the alleged tendency of government ministers to pack NHS governing bodies with their relatives and political supporters. There is also a long tradition of participation seen as a counterpoise to professional power (Haug, 1973); indeed dealing with expert knowledge can be seen as a core problem of liberal democracy (Turner, 2003).

The first section of this chapter reviews the literature relevant to concepts of involvement. In the second section we outline the history of public and patient involvement in the English NHS. The third section covers the post-1997 official focus upon such involvement in primary healthcare planning and decision making, whilst the final section suggests some theoretical approaches to contemporary developments.

Key concepts in participation

Despite the tendency for public and user participation to be seen as the answer to a wide range of problems, it is not often conceptualised in any very clear way. One reason for this may be that the participation of individuals in the life of a polity (including the consumption of publicly provided services) has been the concern of a number of academic disciplines and has given rise to a number of distinct bodies of literature, though there are some relationships between the concepts that they employ. We begin with brief characterisations of four of these literatures in which we outline some of their main organising concepts. We then suggest some conceptual dimensions by which various NHS participatory arrangements might be classified.

The bodies of literature

The first of our four bodies of this literature concerns democracy and citizenship, the former from political theory and political science, the latter mainly from sociology but with significant contributions from politics. An important cleavage in concepts of democracy is between representative or 'liberal' democracy and direct or participatory 'republican' democracy (so-called because of its derivation from the governance of various European city states especially during the fourteenth and fifteenth centuries: Held, 1996). Some versions of the latter place great stress on political participation as an end in itself and as a means of developing citizens themselves and improving political decisions whilst other versions stress the instrumental value of participation as a means of protecting citizens from others making decisions against their interests. The former provides the model of elective political offices sought by competing elites (Schumpeter, 1943: 1976) that are a familiar element in the British constitution, whilst the latter has been an important foundation for models of worker participation (Pateman, 1970) and community development (Smith and Beazley, 2000; Thomas, 1983).

Citizenship is a notion which historically has carried a complex cluster of meanings; it may imply defined legal or social status, be a means of signifying political identity or a focus of loyalty, carry a requirement to perform duties or the expectation of rights, and serve as a yardstick of good social behaviour (Barbalet, 1988; Faulks, 1998; Heater, 1990: 163; Twine, 1994). Different elements of this cluster have received prominence at particular times. Up to about 1980, *rights* have been predominant, following Marshall's (1950) analysis of the respective development of economic, political and social rights. More recently, however, there has been a burgeoning literature on communitarianism (most notably Etzioni, 1993, 1997) and the emphasis of discussion has changed so as to incorporate a more active perspective in which citizenship entails a moral *duty* to 'take part in constructing and maintaining [the] community' (Meehan, 1993: 177). Although this shift reflects to some extent the impact of the 'new right' and its preference for voluntary effort as a means of relieving the 'burden' on the State, the normative view that citizens should be more active is by no means confined to the political right and indeed underpins a range of policy prescriptions from other points on the spectrum. The work of the left-of-centre Institute of Public Policy Research provides several examples, and the general approach is compatible with the communitarian political philosophy articulated by New Labour both in opposition (*Guardian,* 13 March 1995: 2) and in government (Blunkett, 2002). One strand of the literature on democracy that has recently become prominent relates to 'deliberative democracy', that is to procedures that entail citizens discussing issues rather than forming an opinion in isolation (Fishkin, 1979; Parkinson, 2006; Segall, 2005). We shall see later that these ideas have underpinned various participative processes in the NHS under the label of 'citizens' juries'.

Second, like republican views of citizenship, literatures about pressure groups, networks and 'new social movements' are concerned with proactive social action. Unlike the citizenship literature, however, the focus tends to be both empirical and upon some form of collective action. Self-organised pressure groups are seen as the means by which individuals can represent their interests to government (Baggott, 1995; Grant, 2000), though many analysts see business-based groups as more likely to be effective in capitalist society. 'Policy networks' of institutions and pressure groups, in a particular policy sector, are held together by exchanges of resources but may be dominated by a particular professional or economic interest (Rhodes, 1997; Richardson and Jordan, 1979; Salter and Jones, 2006). As distinct from pressure groups and networks, 'new social movements' are broader and held together by *identity* as much as by interest (Byrne 1997; Dalton and Kuechler, 1990). In the health sector, there are a large number of patient groups, many of which exist to promote services and information in relation to a specific disease or condition (Wood, 2000). Although there are few active links between many such groups, others do form networks (for instance through 'umbrella' organisations such as the British Council of Organisations of Disabled People) whilst some commentators take the view that there is sufficient activism and sense of generalised user identity to speak of a 'user movement' (Barnes, 1999a).

Third, the literature about 'community development' shares the assumptions of active citizenship that 'modern society has seen the destruction of a sense of community … and an over-development of the demand for individual rights at a cost of a sense of responsibility and obligation' (Parsons, 1995: 502). It is argued, sometimes a priori but sometimes on the basis of empirical evidence (see for instance Putnam, 1993; Wann, 1995), that active civic involvement is associated with both economic development and good public services. The term 'community' has been used in numerous ways (Wilmott, 1989: 5) though these may be roughly divided into those which are not necessarily territorially based (such as the 'gay community' or the 'disabled community'), and communities defined spatially as the residents of a neighbourhood. This latter definition implies more than a group of individuals living within a defined space; 'community' makes little sense as a concept unless it assumes or prescribes some notion of affect in the relationships between individuals, perhaps in the form of shared values and identity (Etzioni, 1997: 127). Concepts of community development usually relate to spatial communities, and often stress multifactorial social problems and the need to be involved with a multiplicity of local agencies (Stewart, 1995: 31). Community development was a prominent component of public policy in the 1960s and 1970s in both the US (Marris and Rein, 1974) and the UK (Community Development Programme [CDP], 1977; Loney, 1983; Thomas, 1983), and has also been advocated on behalf of the World Health Organisation (Kahssay and Oakley, 1999). The underlying assumptions of community development programmes vary in terms of their acceptance of the status quo, that is how politically radical they are. The UK Community Development Programme of 1968–78, originally premised on the notion of 'raising [local] people from a fatalistic dependence on [local government] to self-sufficiency and independence' (CDP, 1977: 12), became for some actors a vehicle with which to express class conflict (Loney, 1983: 84ff; Thomas, 1983: 89ff). Thus there is a tension within community development about how far the objective is to help locals to help themselves, and how far there exists the possibility of voicing more radical political demands. The revival in the UK of ideas about community development since the 1990s is built on the less radical strategy of encouraging local groups to compete for nationally allocated development funds (Hoggett, 1997: 10).

Finally, consumerism, classically taken to refer to the exercise of 'effective demand' (that is, desire backed by money) in a market, is necessarily attenuated to matters of information and consumer choice between alternatives in the context of third party payment for health-care. Nevertheless, UK governments have advocated the extension of some of its principles to the NHS (Greener, 2003). Even under third party payment, choice may be exercised through individual rights in relation to market-mimicking mechanisms such as 'vouchers' (OECD, 1993) or through direct payments that enable users to purchase services for themselves (Taylor et al., 1992: 30ff). In this literature, consumption decisions are a matter for individual choice and no social action is implied beyond actually exercising the choice though, as we shall see below, consumers may form pressure groups or even identify themselves as a 'movement'. Since consumer choice implies that providers risk the loss of 'business' if consumers are dissatisfied, there is a natural link to the very large literatures of marketing and market research, quality assessment (which may include data about consumer assessments), quality control and quality assurance. Some advocates of greater user involvement rely very much on the assumption that healthcare providers should be responsive to user demand (Taylor et al., 1992; Williamson, 1992).

Conceptualising participation: the main dimensions

In the context of participation in relation to health services, it is essential to maintain some analytic clarity about the distinction between service *users* (or consumers, or patients) and the more general *public* (or citizens). This distinction differs from that of Beresford and Croft (1990, 1993; O'Keefe and Hogg, 1999), whose concern is to distinguish between a consumerist and a citizenship version of patient/user involvement. Their argument is that claims to services or certain other goods can be based on citizenship claims: the provision of these services will assist the recipient to exercise fuller citizenship than would otherwise be possible. Such claims are held to be distinguishable from claims to services based merely on wants; the latter would be consumerist. We make a different distinction, referring to 'users' rather than 'consumers' because even the citizenship-based claims mentioned above are made by individuals with an immediate use for the service and cannot necessarily be equated with the views of a broader public with no immediate use for the service. To take a crude example, if one suffers from a particular condition, one's interest is in better specific service provision for oneself and, implicitly or explicitly, others in the same situation (Dingwall, 2001). Almost all patient pressure groups focus on a specific interest in the form of a more or less narrow range of medical conditions (Wood, 2000). In contrast, if one's health is generally good, one's interest is in the provision of a broad range of services, balanced against a desire to pay a reasonable level of taxation. (In the context of local government, this divergence of interests has often received historical recognition in legal judgements that recognised a special local 'ratepayer' interest: Gyford, 1991: 9–10.) Whilst it is true that any citizen might become (and probably in the past has been) a patient, it does not follow that the interests of the two can be treated as identical. Indeed if we were to treat them as identical, the same reasoning would apply to NHS staff (who are also likely to be patients at some point in their lives) and the justification for public and user involvement would thereby disappear entirely. The 'public' is a much more diffuse constituency and there exist deep divisions of opinion about just whom it is taken to be. There is surprisingly little explicit debate about this, for these distinctions are usually left implicit in the particular involvement mechanisms that policy makers and analysts advocate. Figure 5.1 suggests some ways of thinking about this. Its horizontal axis distinguishes between whether or not participants have any special knowledge of health or healthcare, whilst its vertical axis distinguishes between whether they simply enter an opinion as an isolated individual or whether they engage in discussion with other participants in order to arrive at an opinion.

	Participants given information	Participants respond on basis of prior knowledge
Participants deliberate collectively	• Citizens' juries etc	• Focus groups
Participants respond as individuals	• Standing panels – questionnaire plus information	• Ad hoc opinion surveys

Figure 5.1   Models of public participation
Source: summarised from Harrison and Mort (1998)

Thus focus groups allow interaction between participants who may or may not have any special knowledge of the topic, whilst the membership of the 'standing panels' operated by several local government authorities in the 1990s (Dowswell et al., 1997) were expected to respond as individuals to questionnaires accompanied by information on the issue under consultation. However, the extreme contrast that illustrates the point we are making here is between the bottom right and top left-hand cells of Figure 5.1. In the former is what might be termed the 'literal' public, members of which respond to participation exercises as individuals without any special knowledge. They may (or may not) be ignorant, prejudiced and unreasoning. The logical mechanism for involving this public is the descriptively representative sample survey. In the latter cell is what might be termed the 'idealised' public. This public is well-informed, probably tolerant, and forms its opinion after due deliberation and reasoning. The logical mechanisms for involving this public are 'citizens' juries' (Barnes, 1999b; Coote and Lenaghan, 1997) and other arrangements in which participants are provided with both expert information and the opportunity to discuss the issues (Bowie et al., 1995; Elster, 1998; Fishkin, 1997; Goodin and Niemeyer, 2003; Parkinson, 2006). Of course (and despite our provocative language) neither approach, nor any other, is self-evidently correct. Rather, we should understand that practitioners of involvement effectively *construct* a 'public' by the participation mechanisms that they adopt (see also Barnes et al., 2003).

A further distinction that we might make is between *active* and *passive* participation. Passive participation occurs where involvement is officially organised, either through agents such as an elected representative or an allocated advocate or through surveys and mechanisms of the kind illustrated in Figure 5.1. In contrast, active participation occurs where users or the public organise themselves proactively, for instance to press for particular developments or services, placing pressure on politicians or managers. Although it can be argued that such active democracy might be irreducibly antithetical to the formal institutions of government and representative democracy (Blaug, 2002), as we noted above it can also be seen as a remedy for a perceived 'democratic deficit'. As we shall see below, proactive patient and carer groups have sometimes had an impact on the NHS. Richardson (1983: 54–67) has argued that discussions of active participation often fail to distinguish between presumed *developmental* and *instrumental* effects. Claimed developmental effects might include enhancement of the dignity and self-respect of participants, the development of their skills and self-confidence for involvement in social and political matters, the opportunity to express their views on larger questions of public policy, and the opportunity to obtain a clearer and more informed view of their own interests. Such effects can be viewed as desirable but, as Richardson also points out, can be viewed more critically as a means for the legitimation of existing arrangements.

Instrumental effects refer to whether participation makes a difference: do official decisions differ from what they would have been in the absence of participation? Relatively little recent research on public participation in the NHS has sought to address this question, concentrating instead on detailed accounts of involvement mechanisms (Harrison et al., 2002b). This serves to remind us of two points. First, we cannot simply predict the effect of participation activity from a knowledge of the processes that it employs. Second, whilst participation may be a valuable experience for individuals in the terms summarised above, it seems likely that its perceived value to them will not be independent of its effectiveness. In other words, willingness to participate is likely to rest on the belief that it might have some effect.

It is possible to build a basic typology of contemporary participation mechanisms by employing the dimensions of consumer/citizen and active/passive. Figure 5.2 provides a sketch of this, together with some examples of how some of the mechanisms that we will discuss later in this chapter might be classified.

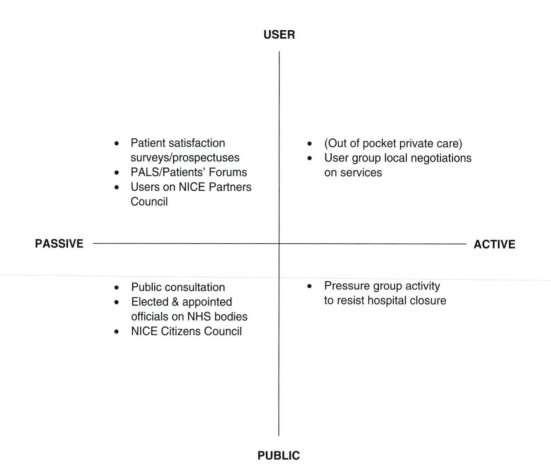

USER

PASSIVE ——————————————————————————— **ACTIVE**

- Patient satisfaction surveys/prospectuses
- PALS/Patients' Forums
- Users on NICE Partners Council

- (Out of pocket private care)
- User group local negotiations on services

- Public consultation
- Elected & appointed officials on NHS bodies
- NICE Citizens Council

- Pressure group activity to resist hospital closure

PUBLIC

Figure 5.2   A typology of participation mechanisms
Source: adapted from Harrison et al. (2002b)

An historical sketch of public and patient participation

Successive governments since 1948 have addressed public and patient participation through a range of structural devices within NHS organisation. In this section we summarise this history through to 1997, considering official mechanisms of public participation separately from the activities of patient pressure groups.

1948–73

Although the wartime coalition government's plans for a post-war health service had involved its governance by joint boards of existing local government authorities (Foot, 1973: 109), and despite the Labour Party's initial preference for direct democracy (Willcocks, 1967: 62) and Morrison's concerns at the potential undermining of elected local government (Webster, 1988: 85), the 1945 Labour government gave only community and ambulance services to the latter. The two remaining elements of the 'tripartite' NHS, the hospitals and family (medical, dental, pharmaceutical and optical) practitioners, were governed by appointed bodies. According to the NHS's official historian:

> *Bevan realised that imperfections in the current system of local government fundamentally under-mined schemes for municipalising health services ... nationalisation [of the hospitals] offered an opportunity to evolve a more rational geographical framework, and a chance to create a system of administration that would be more palatable to the [medical] profession and the voluntary lobby. Bevan held out the attraction of 'worker control' to the profession and to health workers as one of the positive merits of hospital nationalisation and indeed of nationalisation in general.* (Webster, 1988: 83)

Bevan's biographer instead emphasised the legal basis of the new NHS in the minister's duty to provide a comprehensive health service, which implied ministerial power to deliver (Foot, 1973: 192) and, as we saw in Chapter 4, Bevan himself emphasised this. The 1946 National Health Service Act required the new NHS authorities 'to administer the service consistent with the directives of the Minister and relevant regulations' (Webster, 1988: 95) and appointments to the new bodies were heavily influenced by the minister (Webster, 1988: 271–7). The outcome, representing 'the elite of available voluntary effort', was heavy representation of the 'establishment' in the form of businessmen and medical professionals, with only sparse Labour Party or trade union representation (Webster, 1988: 274–81). The new bodies had a strong bias in favour of men and persons over 60 years of age (Webster, 1988: 276). The performance of the various bodies seems to have been undistinguished, with a relatively small core of activists (sometimes having poor relationships with colleagues), poor attendance, and power left to officers and sub-committees (Webster, 1988: 276–7). The arrangements were democratic only in the tenuous sense that many were appointed by a minister who was himself an elected politician. The subsequent Guillebaud Committee rejected the transfer of the NHS to local government (Committee of Enquiry, 1956), and many key issues were until the 1980s dealt with through various joint committees of the medical profession and government; examples of these corporatist arrangements included those for controlling hospital medical posts (Harrison et al., 1990: Ch 4) and the location of general practices (Levitt and Wall, 1984: 176).

1974–90

The NHS reorganisation of 1974 took place in parallel with a reorganisation of local government, and was preceded by discussion of a number of alternative schemes (Levitt and Wall, 1984: 12–17), including two proposals that the NHS should be wholly governed by the new local government authorities (Department of Health and Social Security, 1970; Royal Commission, 1969). In the event, the organisation decided upon took the form of a partial unification of the three parts of the tripartite structure. Community services were transferred from local government to the new health authorities, but the boards holding the contracts of GPs and other family practitioners were merely provided with a statutory link to these authorities, rather than being controlled by them. The (part-time) chairs and members of the new regional authorities were appointed by the Secretary of State (the title used in respect of the most senior ministers after 1968) after consultation with the professions, local authorities, universities, trade unions and voluntary bodies (Levitt and Wall, 1984: 50). The new local health authorities also had part-time chairs appointed by the Secretary of State, alongside nominees (who were not themselves required to be elected councillors) of the relevant local authorities, at least one nominee of the relevant university with a medical school, and the balance (including a hospital consultant, a GP and a nurse) appointed by the regional authority (Levitt, 1979: 57). The period also saw the beginning of the end of Bevan's voluntary principle in that the chairs of the new HAs received an honorarium for their efforts (Levitt, 1979: 57).

The 1974 reorganisation involved another important break with earlier NHS governance arrangements. The old governing bodies had been assumed to be responsible both for managing the service and for representing the user and public interest; indeed, some members had chosen to take, though apparently rather ineffectively, a service user viewpoint (Levitt and Wall, 1984: 254). Under the new arrangements, health authority members were appointed with specific management responsibilities (Levitt and Wall, 1984: 254) in the belief that there would otherwise be a dangerous confusion of roles as had contributed, for instance, to the 1969 scandal over mistreatment of patients at Ely Hospital (Klein and Lewis, 1976: 14–15). The new authorities had fewer members than the old, so that lay participation was much reduced; it became necessary, in an era of political populism, to provide a mechanism for the restoration of local participation (Klein and Lewis, 1976: 13). And so Community Health Councils (CHCs) came to be

> invented almost by accident because, when the plans for a reorganised [NHS] were almost complete, all those involved realised that something was missing: an element which could be … seen as providing a degree of local democracy, consumer participation or public involvement. (Klein and Lewis, 1976: 11)

The CHCs, one for each locality, had the role of representing the views of local users to the relevant health authorities (Levitt and Wall, 1984: 254). Half their membership was nominated by local government authorities, one-third by voluntary organisations, and the remaining one-sixth by regional NHS authorities. CHCs could co-opt additional members (Levitt and Wall, 1984: 254–5) and select their own chairpersons (Hallas, 1976: 13). The early members of CHCs were not sociologically or demographically representative of the population; the middle-aged, the middle class and males were over-represented nationally, though not to the same extent in every region (Klein and Lewis, 1976: 29–36). Although CHCs had some significant powers (most notably to compel proposals to close hospitals to be referred for ministerial determination), and some important successes for individual patients, it has in general been hard to show a significant impact overall (Hallas, 1976: 59; Ham, 1980: 226;

Klein and Lewis, 1976: 135; Lee and Mills, 1982: 142; Lupton et al., 1995; Schulz and Harrison, 1983: 30–3).

Since the detailed plans for the reorganised NHS had been made by a Conservative government but implemented by the Labour government elected in early 1974, modifications were soon made to the original constitution of authorities. The Conservative Secretary of State, Sir Keith Joseph, had wanted their selection to be on grounds of 'management ability' (Klein, 1983: 96), while his Labour successor, Barbara Castle, regarded the arrangements as insufficiently democratic (Castle, 1980: 242). The subsequent consultative document *Democracy in the National Health Service* (Department of Health and Social Security, 1974) proposed that one-third of health authority members should be drawn from local government, that CHCs should provide two members of each, and that two members of NHS non-medical, non-nursing staff, elected by their colleagues, should serve on local health authorities (Levitt, 1979: 57–8). After consultation, it was decided that such changes would be implemented on a progressive basis from 1977, though with only a single CHC representative with only speaking (not voting) rights. In the event the staff nominees were never introduced.

A Royal Commission on the NHS established in 1976 by the Labour government reported in 1979, after the election of the Conservative government in May of that year. It rejected the notion of elected single-purpose health authorities but suggested that the NHS might have a superfluous tier of organisation (Royal Commission, 1979: 324–9). The resulting further reorganisation produced health authorities with membership not dissimilar to that of their predecessors: a part-time salaried chair, a hospital consultant, a GP, a nurse, midwife or health visitor, a trade unionist nominated by the Trades Council (and not an NHS employee), a nominee of the relevant medical school, at least four nominees of the relevant local government authority(ies), and at least seven generalists (Levitt et al., 1995: 67). As before, members were ostensibly representatives of the community at large (Klein, 1983: 96) despite the professional or partisan bases of some of their nominations (Levitt and Wall, 1984: 21).

1991–97

The governance arrangements that accompanied the implementation, from 1991 onwards, of the quasi-market (described in Chapter 4) placed a greater emphasis on authority members' personal contributions. As the White Paper *Working for Patients* put it:

At present [health authorities] … are neither truly representative nor management bodies. Many members, such as those appointed directly by local authorities or on the advice of trade unions and professional bodies, usually regard themselves as representatives. But as a body they are often confronted by the need to take detailed decisions on key management issues. And the actual managers themselves are not members of the authority. The government believes that authorities based on this confusion of roles would not be equipped to handle the complex managerial and contractual issues that the new system of matching resources to performance will demand. The members needed to work in the new system should be appointed on the strength of the skills and experience they can bring to an authority's work. (Department of Health et al., 1989: 64–5)

These words heralded a move, which took effect in April 1991, towards a system of NHS governance based on the commercial model of boards of directors. The new model provided for health authorities and the new NHS Trusts (which were to run hospitals and community services) to have a non-executive chair (appointed by the Secretary of State), and equal numbers of executive and non-executive directors. The former were the full-time salaried chief officers, including the general manager (later re-styled as chief executives) and finance director, whilst the latter received part-time salaries. Not only were these new authorities smaller than their predecessors (by somewhere between one-third and half the size), but much smaller in terms of lay membership; there were no longer local authority appointees or trade union nominees, though trusts were required to have at least two non-executives resident in the local community. Places for health professionals, however, remained through the requirement that trust boards should include nursing and medical directors. In all, there was a clear move away from any principle of representativeness, a move somewhat emphasised by the decision that trusts need only hold a single public meeting each year (Department of Health et al., 1989). Chairs and non-executives of Trusts were somewhat less than typical members of the population; more than half had experience as company directors, three-quarters were male, and 98 percent described themselves as white (Ashburner and Cairncross, 1993).

Further changes followed, including the takeover of NHS regional management by the Department of Health, and acquisition by local health authorities of control over GP and dental contracts, thereby ending a mode of managing the family practitioner services (at arm's length from other services) that had existed long before the inception of the NHS itself (Watkin, 1975: 76). Overall, these changes could be seen as further steps in the transformation of the NHS hierarchy into a more narrowly accountable agent of central government, implicitly dependent for its political legitimacy upon the legitimacy of central government itself. CHCs survived with their role broadened from voicing the views of the community to include closer working with health authorities and GPFHs to identify local needs, monitor and develop services, help to develop and monitor the *Patient's Charter*, help hospitals to obtain patients' views and monitor patterns of complaints. However, they received no extra funds to perform this expanded role (Cooper et al., 1995) and their powers were defined more narrowly than before (Levitt and Wall, 1992: 288).

The NHS quasi-market period of 1991–97, though accompanied by a good deal of rhetoric about choice and closeness to patients, provided few mechanisms to procure this, given that the arrangement was one in which the purchasing was effected by a health authority or GPFH rather than the patient. It was made slightly easier for patients to change GPs and for patients to have information about their GPs' services. It was also assumed that giving purchasing power to GPFHs would empower patients. The quasi-market did, however, spark institutional concern with public involvement in the NHS, mainly as a vehicle for consultation about purchasing (that is, rationing) priorities. There were a number of official appeals to NHS authorities to consult their publics (NHS Management Executive,

1992) and numerous initiatives for so doing, including standing panels of local citizens and public opinion surveys about NHS priorities (Dowswell et al., 1995; Khan and Everitt, 1996; Mort et al., 1999; for a review, see Coote, 1993). Indeed, it has sometimes been argued that a consultation 'industry' has developed (Mort and Harrison, 1999). Perhaps the most widely publicised examples from the period were citizens' juries and similar consultative mechanisms based on notions of deliberative democracy (Bowie et al., 1995; Coote and Lenaghan, 1997; Stewart et al., 1994).

The impact of official involvement mechanisms 1948–97

A number of important points may be drawn from the above account. First, although representative democracy in the local NHS has been considerably attenuated over the years, there is little evidence that the pre-1974 and pre-1991 membership of NHS authorities led to any great degree of responsiveness to patient or public opinion. Second, there was much diversity between CHCs in terms of both specific work and general approach (Cooper et al., 1995; Day and Klein, 1985; Hallas, 1976), but studies suggest that, despite some successes (Levitt, 1980; Webster, 1996: 634), they did not have a significant overall impact (Baggott, 2005; Cooper et al., 1995; Hallas, 1976: 59; Ham, 1980: 226; Klein and Lewis, 1976: 135; Lee and Mills, 1982: 142; Levitt, 1980; Lupton et al., 1995; Pickard, 1997; Schulz and Harrison, 1983: 30–3; Williamson, 1992: 78). They were poorly resourced, sometimes overwhelmed with work, and often unable to strike a balance between seeking to influence NHS plans and responding to patient dissatisfactions. Few felt able to enquire into standards of clinical care and members differed as to how far their role was to represent the community to NHS managers and how far to form a diplomatic bridge between the two. They were often thought unimportant by NHS managers, who felt that they themselves had better information about local healthcare needs and conducted consultation exercises with impossibly short deadlines. CHCs that were deemed to have forfeited NHS management goodwill were subsequently by-passed in consultations, whilst those deemed to have been more co-operative were used by health authorities as part of their own 'legitimation strategy'. Third, experiments with citizens' juries and other deliberative mechanisms helped to raise the political and managerial profile of public involvement, though evaluations have been mixed, with suggestions both that local managers have taken their findings seriously (Barnes, 1999b; Bowie et al., 1995; Elizabeth, et al., 1998; McIver, 1998), and that no real change is contemplated (Newman et al., 2004). Finally, there is little evidence that any of this policy emphasis on consultation changed professionals' relationships with patients. GPFHs did not value responsiveness to patients or public collectively, as opposed to meeting the needs of individuals (Dixon et al., 1998; Kirk et al., 1997; Leonard et al., 1997), whilst in community care, general policy formulations about 'empowering' service users (Taylor et al., 1992) had little impact in practice (Hoyes et al., 1993, though see Crowley et al., 2002 for a counter-example).

Patient pressure groups

In addition to formal top-down mechanisms for involving members of the public and patients in decision making, the period since the creation of the NHS has seen a growth in the number of groups seeking to influence policy from the bottom up. Some health consumer groups in existence today predate the NHS, most notably Macmillan Cancer Relief (formerly the Society for the Prevention and Relief of Cancer), one of the UK's largest charities, which was established in 1911 with the aim of promoting quality cancer care and information for everyone. However, most groups have been created in the last 25 years (Allsop et al., 2004; Wood, 2000). In the NHS context, groups were formed first in the area of maternity and children's services, with activists drawn mainly from the ranks of white middle-class women, many of whom had experienced what they perceived as less than satisfactory NHS care. The National Childbirth Trust (originally the National Childbirth Association) was established in 1956 by an advocate of natural childbirth who had lost her baby due to what she perceived as undue technological intervention. A willingness by women to challenge practices in maternity hospitals is reflected in the establishment of other childbirth organisations such as the Association for Improvements in Maternity Services. Founded in 1960, its focus was on improving access to services and gaining acceptance of fathers' rights to attend births. It has subsequently become more radical, campaigning to increase women's control over childbirth, end routine ultrasound examination and the use of interventions such as induction and electronic foetal monitoring. In 1961 Mother Care for Children in Hospital (subsequently the National Association for the Welfare of Children in Hospital) was formed to campaign for improved parent visiting arrangements for children in hospital. Although the official Platt Report (Central Health Services Council, 1959) had recommended that parents should be allowed to stay with their children in hospital, hospital staff had resisted these proposals. These campaigns for unrestricted contact between parents and children in hospitals, and for fathers to be present at the birth of their children, have resulted in arrangements that are nowadays accepted as normal.

Dissatisfaction with NHS mental healthcare was a catalyst for another wave of pressure groups, many of which were founded by service users or carers as a result of their experiences. Whilst the anti-psychiatry movement of the later 1960s was principally comprised of psychiatrists, the psychiatric survivor or user movement first emerged in Britain with the creation of groups such as the Mental Patients Union in 1973 (Crossley, 1999). At this time the National Association for Mental Health changed its name to MIND and during 1971–72 the organisation's objectives were rewritten to stress its lobbying role. Its Legal and Welfare Rights Service began in 1975 and its proposals for reforming mental health legislation became the basis for the 1983 Mental Health Act Commission Code of Practice (MIND, 2006).

The National Schizophrenia Fellowship (now Rethink) was founded in 1972 by a carer whose experiences appeared in the letters page of *The Times* and resonated with a large number of people with similar stories to tell. SANE (Schizophrenia: a National Emergency) was founded in 1986 by a campaigning journalist whose newspaper articles about the care of people with schizophrenia helped raise the public profile of the condition. SANE has subsequently been successful in keeping these issues on the policy agenda (Rogers and Pilgrim, 2001).

The 1980s and 1990s saw the formation of several groups campaigning for improvements in the cancer care provided by the NHS. Marie Curie Cancer Care was founded in 1952 as the Marie Curie Memorial Foundation and pioneered work providing specialist homes for the care of cancer patients and providing nursing for patients at home, both of which were revolutionary at the time. However, both Marie Curie and Macmillan have focused much of their more recent effort on filling gaps in NHS provision by, for example, specialist nurses or hospice care. Subsequent groups in this field were established by people with direct experience of cancer treatment within the NHS as patients or carers. Cancer BACUP was founded in 1984 by a young doctor with advanced cancer and whose own experience was that patients were in desperate need of good quality information, practical advice and emotional support, which too often were unavailable. These experiences were published in the *British Medical Journal*, thereby attracting the attention of medical professionals and the media. Today Cancer BACUP provides cancer patients and their families with up-to-date information, practical advice and support in an attempt to reduce the fear and uncertainty of cancer. The 1990s also saw a flurry of activity in relation to breast cancer care with the creation of the Breast Cancer Coalition founded in 1995 by women with personal experience of the disease, bringing together individual, regional groups and national organisations to campaign for improvements in access to breast cancer services and to support and train members to become patient advocates. Breast Cancer Care (originally the Mastectomy Association, founded by a patient and run from her home on a voluntary basis between 1973 and 1981) gained momentum during this period. Their Pink Ribbon Appeal was launched in 1995, with celebrity patrons and financial self-sufficiency achieved during the late 1990s.

In recent years there has been an increasing trend towards the formation of formal alliances between patient groups, offering benefits such as the ability to pool resources, learn from other alliance members, provide a mutually supportive environment and to provide greater understanding of and access to policy networks. The Long-Term Medical Conditions Alliance (LMCA) founded in 1989 is apparently 'enormously well regarded in the Department of Health as one of the most effective lobbying voices and one of the most effective organisations in relationships with ministers' (LMCA, 2003). Whilst many mental health groups have engaged in at times acrimonious struggles with the medical profession, opposition to government proposals to reform mental health legislation have served to unite service users, carers, voluntary sector organisations, NHS managers, and professionals with common concerns about the proposals. The Mental Health Alliance is a coalition of over 60 organisations involved in lobbying politicians and challenging the coverage of mental health legislation in the media. The involvement of groups raises questions about the risk of their or their representatives' co-optation by government (Baggott et al., 2005: 294–5); it is also possible that groups that become service providers in contract to governmental bodies lose some of their ability to develop radical ideas (Barnes et al., 1999). Finally, some commentators have identified the risk that patient groups that have adopted an 'empowered consumer' approach risk co-optation into government agendas for the creation of active and engaged citizens; consumerist ideas and rhetoric 'have frequently been adopted uncritically as symbols of a new determination to speak and act for themselves by individuals and groups who are not necessarily familiar with their ideological associations' (Beresford and Wallcraft, 1997: 90).

Contemporary developments in participation

The New Labour governments of 1997 and 2001 espoused an unprecedented degree of policy concern with patient and public participation, often expressed in a rhetoric of active citizenship and community responsibility (Blears, 2003; Chandler, 2001). This broadly communitarian view sees the rights associated with citizenship (such as healthcare free at the point of delivery) as implying a moral duty to participate in the construction and maintenance of the community (Milewa, 2004). Critical commentators have interpreted this as an attempt to shift what have traditionally been seen as responsibilities of the state onto other agencies and onto citizens themselves through partnerships, community 'empowerment' initiatives and increasingly onto 'responsible' individual citizens (Newman et al., 2004; Rose, 1996). In keeping with this approach, the Expert Patient Programme (EPP) aims to give patients more control over their care though 'a self-management course giving people the confidence, skills and knowledge to manage their condition better and be more in control of their lives' and is also aimed at patients with chronic disease (Department of Health, 2001b). Take-up for the EPP has been slower than envisaged (Kennedy et al., 2004). In general, however, the concrete manifestations of participation policy have followed the pattern described in Chapter 5: a range of new (sometimes short-lived) institutions, coupled with a drive towards a healthcare market. In this section, we examine each of these facets of policy.

Institutional developments

CHCs were never popular with governments and had narrowly escaped abolition in 1982 (Webster, 1998: 143). English CHCs (though not their Welsh equivalents) were finally abolished in 2003 (Department of Health, 2003a), by which time a number of other bodies intended to involve local people in health services decision making and hold NHS policy makers to account had begun to be established. These included an Independent Complaints Advocacy Service (ICAS) to provide advice and support to people who wish to complain independently about the NHS, a Patient Advocacy (subsequently 'Advice') and Liaison Service (PALS) to address patient concerns, provide on the spot help and information about health services and tell people about the complaints procedure, and a Patient and Public Involvement Forum (PPIF) in every NHS trust and primary care trust to 'provide direct input into how local NHS services are run' (Secretary of State for Health, 2000: 94). In 2003 the Commission for Patient and Public Involvement in Health (CPPIH) was established as a non-departmental public body to oversee these new arrangements, reporting to the government, and liaising with regulatory bodies such as the Healthcare Commission (see Chapter 4) to ensure that information and opinion from PPIFs are acted upon. However, PPIFs soon

experienced difficulties. Eleven percent of members (who, unlike non-executive directors of NHS organisations, received no remuneration) resigned their positions after six months, citing amongst their reasons lack of time and inadequate support (Gaze, 2004). This may have been seen as a sign of CPPIH failure and soon afterwards the government announced that, as a result of a review of such bodies, CPPIH would be abolished and its functions transferred to other departments (Department of Health, 2004h). This was followed in 2006 by plans to replace PPIFs with Local Involvement Networks (LINks), funded through local authorities for every social service local authority area (Department of Health, 2006).

A further development, local authority health scrutiny, came about as a result of the replacement in most local government authorities of the traditional system in which much decision making took place in functional executive committees in which all elected council-lors participated (Stoker et al., 2003). The new system, introduced by the Local Government Act of 2000, provided for decision making by a smaller group of 'executive' councillors, leav-ing the need to define a role for 'non-executive' councillors. The notion of 'overview and scrutiny committees' (OSCs) consequently emerged; non-executive councillors were to act effectively as 'backbenchers' scrutinising decisions and council services and holding the Executive to account. OSCs are also able to scrutinise the work of external service providers that might impact on the well-being of the local population so that many OSCs have the power to scrutinise the NHS (Coleman, 2003). NHS organisations have a statutory duty to consult OSCs on any proposal that is a 'substantial' development or variation in services. Evidence to date suggests that, whilst OSCs have provided a forum for improved network-ing between NHS and local government agencies, they have not succeeded in engaging the public to any significant extent (Coleman, 2006).

To these new institutions have been added changes to existing institutions. From its begin-nings NICE (see Chapter 1) has had a Partners' Council with members drawn from patient and carer organisations, health professions, NHS management, quality organisations, indus-try and trade unions to provide advice and opinion in its technology assessment process (NICE, 1999). However, discontent by patient group representatives at the priority given to scientific versus other forms of evidence (such as patient views) led to the formation of Patient Involvement in NICE (PIN) as an intended counterweight (Quennell, 2003). More recently, the creation of a NICE Citizens' Council is a logical response to the potential diver-gence of public and patient interests outlined above. This a group of 30 people chosen from around 4,400 individuals who responded to invitations to people not normally involved in the NHS to 'help NICE find out what members of the public think about key issues'. The impact on NICE appraisals remains unclear (Davies et al., 2005), though one analyst has stressed the novelty of NICE as a new form of 'dialogic' organisation (Davies, 2007). Another change to existing institutions is the opportunity for NHS Trusts to become FTs (see Chapter 4), ostensibly a 'new form of social ownership where health services are owned by and accountable to local people' (Department of Health, 2002a). Local citizens are invited to become members of the trusts, with representation on the board. However, the turnout in the first round of elections to the board has been extremely low (Klein, 2004).

Policy related to participation shows no sign of stabilising. Recent White Papers have proposed a duty on commissioners and providers 'systematically and rigorously' to discover what people want, especially difficult to reach groups, a role for elected local councilors as advocates for their communities, 'local triggers' that will require Primary Care Trusts to take action where public satisfaction or service quality fall below an acceptable level (Secretary of State for Health, 2006) and measures to strengthen OSCs (Secretary of State for Communities and Local Government, 2006).

Patient Choice

Following a 2001 Labour manifesto commitment to give patients more choice, a national consultation was launched in September 2003 asking people to identify the types of choice they wanted in healthcare and the changes needed to support them, whilst ensuring that the expansion of patient choice could be made 'fair for all' (Department of Health, 2003b: 5). Although the government estimated that over 110,000 people were 'reached' by the consultation, only 773 (including 314 NHS bodies) written responses were received, with a further 2,500 patients and staff responses to a survey conducted by MORI. A recurring theme amongst the responses was the need to ensure that 'all of us – not just some among the affluent middle classes … share in decisions about our health' (Department of Health, 2003b: 7). Policies of expanding choice for NHS patients are, however, also seen as the means of tailoring services to individual requirements, putting an end to the 'one size fits all' mentality seen as characterising service delivery in the past. However, the notion of tailor-made care sits uneasily with its conceptualisation as a commodity to be traded in the market (see Chapter 4) and consisting of a series of standard patient pathways with remuneration to providers in the form of national standard tariffs. Such standardisation (which also underpins the national guidelines produced under the auspices of NICE) downplays differences between individual patients and it is not clear therefore how it can put patients in control or give them a greater voice. It also remains to be seen whether a policy of greater choice can reduce the potential inequalities which critics of the policy fear (Appleby et al., 2003; see also Propper et al., 2006).

As we saw in Chapter 4, the government has placed great emphasis on expanding the choice of providers for elective inpatient care. PCTs were required to ensure that patients referred for elective hospital care were offered a choice of four or five providers at the point of referral by the end of 2005, with this choice being extended by 2008 to the right to choose any healthcare provider that meets the Healthcare Commission's standards and whose charges do not exceed the national tariff. Initial results from pilot studies suggest that many patients who had waited for treatment were keen to exercise choice of an alternative provider, though it is not known whether patients will still choose to travel further for speedier treatment after 2008, once the maximum waiting times for inpatient treatment have been reduced to 18 weeks from referral, compared with many months for those exercising choice in the pilot studies. The initial pilots included advisers to provide patients with support and information to exercise choice, which may go some way towards addressing concerns that the policy will favour the middle classes, who are better equipped to take advantage of choices offered. However, the full implementation of choice at the point of referral will not include patient advisers except 'where PCTs identify particular challenges in securing choice for all parts of their community' (Department of Health, 2004a: 10).

Interpreting participation as policy

Identifying the precise contribution of the various campaigning, awareness raising and participation processes in which health consumer groups are engaged to specific policy outcomes is not easy. The Mental Health Alliance was successful in getting the government to withdraw the Mental Health Bill from its legislative timetable for 2003, whilst the LMCA is consulted on all major policy developments relevant to people with long-term conditions and the alliance claims that it has 'succeeded in exerting a noticeable influence on the development of new policy on choice and on the NSF' (LMCA, 2003: 4). A recent national study concluded that cancer and mental health groups were influential in shaping policy, though without approaching the level of influence of health professional institutions (Baggott et al., 2005: 294–6). Yet studies at a local level suggest a patchy impact of group activity, with a tendency for officials to respond selectively to user views that coincide with professional or managerial thinking (Barnes and Wistow, 1994; Barnes et al., 1999; Harrison et al., 1997; Milewa et al., 1999; Stalker, 1997). However, local pressure group campaigns occasionally highlight 'scandals' that lead to national action. For instance, it was parents of babies who had died after heart surgery at Bristol Royal Infirmary (see Chapter 2) that triggered investigations by the General Medical Council and subsequent disciplinary action against the doctors involved.

Despite the plethora of initiatives to increase patients' and public participation in the NHS, it is difficult to discern evidence of their impact on decisions. In 2004, CHI produced a report summarising its conclusions on participation from over 300 inspections of NHS organizations. It concluded that participation 'is not yet having a major impact on policy and practice … despite a plethora of … initiatives. It is almost as if there is a brick wall between the activities going on and any changes on the ground that happen as a result' (CHI, 2004: 2). The Department of Health subsequently published examples of participation's impact on such matters as the choice of colour schemes for hospital wards, the provision of new services (including bone scanning, water births and multiple sclerosis clinics) and the development of quality standards. However, the report also drew attention to CHI's findings and exhorted NHS organisations to shift the focus of their work from involvement processes to outputs and outcomes:

> It is this type of behaviour that has led to the building of the brick wall. Whilst the NHS is stuck behind it, it is not fulfilling its duty under section 11 of the Health and Social Care Act 2001. What it is doing is merely ticking the box. (Department of Health, 2004c: 9)

How might we interpret this picture of proliferating and rapidly changing, but largely ineffectual, official participation initiatives? This section briefly considers four overlapping theoretical approaches.

Symbolic politics

The first theoretical approach that might help us to understand the politics of participation in the NHS is what has been termed 'symbolic politics' (Edelman, 1971, 1977; see also Elder and Cobb, 1983). By definition, a symbol stands for something other than itself. The analysis here hinges on distinguishing between 'referential symbols', that is shorthand ways of referring to objective phenomena, and 'condensation symbols', that is symbols that also evoke emotions connected to the phenomena (Edelman, 1971: 6). It is easy to see how many of the terms connected with the subject-matter of this chapter can be seen as falling into the latter category. 'Democracy', 'choice' and 'partnership', for instance, are powerful condensation symbols that carry positive connotations. This is not just a question of political language, though that is important in communicating symbols, but of political acts more generally, which themselves work as a form of communication that serves to reassure and to encourage political quiescence. As Edelman puts it:

> *Political forms ... come to symbolise what large masses of men [sic] need to believe about the state to reassure themselves ... Political acts, speeches and gestures involve mass audiences emotionally in politics while rendering them acquiescent to policy shifts through that very involvement. (Edelman, 1971: 2, 15)*

In our specific context of participation in the NHS, Fairclough has argued that

> *Blair has referred to ... 'experiments in democracy' ... , for instance focus groups and citizens' juries, which allow the government to develop its policy in a way that incorporates public opinion from the start ... . This includes a certain dispersal of government, which is indicated by the concept of 'participation' ... . Many groups and people who have hitherto not been involved in government are being drawn in [but] ... it entails a new form of control that ... shap[es] the culture, discourse and language of the dispersed agents of government ... (Fairclough, 2000: 5)*

The replacement of CHCs (which were sometimes troublesome to NHS managers) with a range of institutions (such as PALS, PPIFs, ICAS and LINks) can be seen as redirecting discontent with NHS services to the micro level, thereby channelling it in directions that do not challenge overall policy. One interpretation that might be drawn from all this is that policy makers are simply cynical; their aim is to ensure that policy is *seen* to be addressing some problem, rather than to make some change in the circumstances thought to be problematic. Arnstein's well-known (1969) description of many participation processes as 'therapy' is perhaps an example of such a view, albeit not expressed in terms of symbolic politics. On this interpretation, the theory of symbolic politics would find it difficult to explain New Labour's rapid and consistent reorganisation of the institutions of public and patient participation that we have described. Edelman's own interpretation goes beyond such simple cynicism, however; he argues that much of politics is in fact symbolic:

> *There is no implication here that elites consciously mould political myths and symbols to serve their ends ... What we are talking about is social role taking, not deception. (Edelman, 1971: 20)*

In other words, the symbols are as meaningful for politicians as for everyone else.

Post-democracy

The notion of 'post-democracy' derives from the work of Crouch (2000), though it also draws on ideas about globalisation discussed in Chapter 4. Briefly, the argument runs as follows. Global financial deregulation and the growth of powerful multinational corporations have reduced the policy options of national governments to those that are favourable to business elites. Yet governments must still seek re-election from a fragmented, self-interested electorate who may not share the concerns of business. Consequently, politicians must devote considerable effort to discovering these concerns and addressing them. As Crouch scathingly notes, this constitutes

> *the reduction of politicians to something more resembling shopkeepers than rulers, anxiously seeking to discover what their 'customers' want in order to stay in business. (Crouch, 2000: 13)*

Governments are thus torn between needing in some way to prevent voters from feeling excluded, whilst at the same time avoiding unmanageable conflict or the derailment of business-friendly strategies. The effect is the same as in the 'symbolic politics' explanation summarised above, though for a different reason. Participation mechanisms must both collect public (including patient) opinion, but simultaneously channel it in directions that do not threaten core policies. Thus consumerist institutions such as PALS, PPIFs, ICAS and LINks depoliticise discontent with NHS services by redirecting it to the micro level, rather like complaining to the shopkeeper. Similarly, scrutiny of the NHS by OSCs can be seen as the means of tying-up local politicians in the formidable technical detail of health issues. This kind of analysis also links easily to theories of co-optation:

> *Policy making elites may choose to co-opt ... interest groups into compliance with government policies ... by creating sham 'corporatist' institutions and ideologies. (Dunleavy and O'Leary, 1987: 163–4)*

Moreover, the use of voluntary organisations as subcontracted providers of NHS services potentially blunts their opportunity for political campaigning (Barnes et al., 1999). The totality of this line of explanation fits well with New Labour's explicit concerns to respond to globalisation (see Chapter 4) and its overall strategy of occupying the political centre ground. But like the cynical version of symbolic politics, it has difficulty in explaining the persistent enthusiasm of New Labour for remaking the institutions of participation.

Responding to individualism

The theory of 'post-democracy', described above, provides one possible link between globalisation, New Labour's 'third way' politics and the institutions for participation in the NHS that we have described. An alternative means of making such a link can be derived from the arguments of 'third way' proponents about individualism. Amongst several dilemmas that third way politics is said to address, Giddens identifies individualism: 'all western countries … have become culturally more pluralistic, with a proliferation of lifestyles' (1998: 34). Whilst some government rhetoric has represented this as leading directly to a need for greater consumer choice of public services (Newman and Vidler, 2006: 195ff), Giddens's view is that this new individualism is not mere selfishness, but rather is associated with a decline in the importance of custom and tradition as sources of authority on how people should live. This effectively means, as another sociologist puts it, that people need 'to constitute themselves as individuals: to plan, understand, design themselves as individuals' (Beck, cited in Giddens, 1998: 36). This means that individuals can no longer take for granted how they should live, but rather must make active decisions about it: in Giddens's words, 'All of us have to live in a more open and reflective manner than previous generations' (1998: 37; for a fuller account, see Giddens, 1991: 74ff).

A stronger statement of this new individualism is that consumption has displaced working as 'the cognitive and moral focus of life, the integrative bond of society and the focus of systemic management … the hub around which the life-world rotates' (Bauman, 1992: 49). This consumerism 'knows no boundaries. It neither respects domains once immune from its effects, nor supports existing markers of cultural territory' (Lyon, 1999: 76). In addition to such matters as religion (Lyon, 1999: 77), such radically extended consumerism encompasses human bodies and individuals' identities, which are closely interrelated. Thus contemporary sociologists have noted the recent growth in 'what might be termed body "projects", including … body-piercing, tattooing, exercise, cosmetic surgery, diet, and the use of make-up, all of which are designed to improve, beautify or remodel the flesh' (Ashe et al., 1999: 125; Giddens, 1991: 177). As we saw in Chapter 1, this form of analysis can extend to healthcare; 'consumerist medicine' has become the rule, driven by post-1960 emphases on choice in lifestyle, the expectation of good health and good medical services and, by the 1970s, a cult of fitness and a notion of the body as a sexual commodity for individual investment (Pickstone, 2000: 12–16). This consumerism exacerbates the inherent demand/supply mismatch which results from consumer 'moral hazard' and the increasingly widespread availability of health and treatment information from sources such as the Internet which are not mediated by the physician actually treating the patient. It thus increases the level of demand encountered by such systems and tends to delegitimise their attempts to ration care.

A consequence of these new individualisms and their rejection of tradition is that political legitimacy is no longer provided by habitual or historical ways of reaching authoritative decisions; instead, legitimacy must derive from citizens exercising their preferences through

democratic means (Giddens, 1998: 66, 74). But, as we noted earlier in this chapter, the traditional British constitutional domination of Parliament by governments creates a 'democratic deficit'. The logic of this line of analysis is that traditional liberal UK democracy needs to be supplemented both by greater service user choice and by other mechanisms of public and service user participation, such as citizens' juries, focus groups and other institutions developed in the NHS since 1997. It is, however, less able to provide a convincing explanation for the development of OSCs, whose role is not to focus on individuals' experiences.

Responsibilisation

A fourth interpretation of the public and patient participation arrangements described above is as manifestations of what Foucault (1991) terms 'governmentality'. In the modern state, government can be seen as taking place at a distance from formal centres of power (Larner and Walters, 2000), 'responsibilising' individuals by transferring what have traditionally been seen as the responsibilities of the state onto individual citizens (Newman et al., 2004). Such arrangements seek to regulate 'the conduct of conduct' by encouraging individuals to adopt cultures, values and attitudes that lead to the government of the self through self-discipline, self-motivation and self-regulation that accord with governmentally desired norms, shaping the conduct of individuals in a direction that does not challenge the state (Hindess, 2001: 44). In general terms, a great deal of the rhetoric of government and other proponents of the 'third way' stresses the importance of citizens being seen as having duties alongside the rights conferred by the welfare state (Freeden, 1999). In the specific health policy sector, as we noted in Chapter 1, obvious manifestations of such governmental aspirations are the recommendations of the Wanless Report (Wanless, 2002) and subsequent consultation documents that individuals should become 'fully-engaged' in protecting and promoting their own health. But similar aspirations for citizens to become more actively engaged both in choices about their own healthcare and in decisions about the shape of NHS services can also be attributed to governmentality. Thus patient choice of service provider clearly makes the patient partially responsible for the outcome. The provision of information to members of citizens' juries and OSCs potentially co-opts them into the views of the experts who provide the information, whilst the various institutions for supporting individual patients (such as PALS) can be seen as means of reinforcing consumerism.

Concluding remarks

As noted above, these four theorisations of contemporary policy for public and patient participation in the NHS have much in common and little that is contradictory. Thus it is not easy to distinguish definitively between their respective explanatory power, though it is worth noting that the latter two approaches presuppose some expectations by policy makers of substantive impact, whilst the others base their explanations on the fact of having the policy in existence. But all can be linked in some way to the multifaceted phenomenon of 'third way' politics and it is perhaps best therefore to regard them simply as strands within broader New

Labour ideology, rather than as competitive explanations. Of course the fact that the 'third way' provides a plausible explanation for participation policies does not provide evidence for the validity of the assumptions, most importantly about globalisation and the new individualism, that underpin it. Rather, it might be argued, treatment of these supposed facts as problems that must be addressed is in effect self-fulfilling (Newman and Vidler, 2006).

Further reading

For an overview of the concepts of democracy, see Held (1996). On public and patient involvement see Wood (2000), which examines the politics of Patients' Associations in Britain and America. For NHS public and/or patient involvement the following are recommended: Baggott et al. (2005) (patient pressure groups), Barnes (1999b) (citizens' juries), Barnes et al. (1999) (user involvement).

Chapter 6

The Politics of Healthcare Policy Making

Summary of chapter contents

- The policy process: key concepts
- NHS policy making: history and contemporary developments
- Interpreting the contemporary policy process

The notion of 'policy' is both contested in the academic literature (for a review, see Colebatch, 1998) and may be used differently by politicians, civil servants, managers and professionals. At its most general, 'policy' may be understood as the means by which politics is connected to government activity in the real world; the Secretary of State for Health does not treat patients, nor does the Home Secretary chase burglars. Some widely (though not universally) agreed characteristics of policy are as follows. First, 'policy' usually denotes not just a single decision but rather a stance towards some topic or type of case. Thus it may refer to a cluster of related decisions or actions, or to a collection of cases to be dealt with in a consistent fashion. The latter further implies coherent organisational arrangements for ensuring consistency. Second, 'policy' usually implies a claim to be backed by some kind of authority. It therefore implies some normative force, for instance specifying what *ought* to happen or how organisational members ought to act in given circumstances. It may therefore be distinguished from the 'practice' that actually occurs in the relevant circumstances. Policy and its implementation may or may not coincide. Third, 'policy' implies a claim to both instrumentality and expertise; it is assumed both that policy reflects intentions (Levin, 1997: 19–27) and that policy makers and implementers possess the necessary knowledge to calculate 'what works'. Statements of policy may be expressed in terms of ends (objectives), such as 'reduce inflation' and/or means, such as 'control the money supply more tightly'. We might distinguish between *enacted policy*, that is what governments do in terms of legislation, regulation, expenditure, executive action and so on, and *espoused policy*, that is what governments say in speeches and documents that they are doing or intend to do. Espoused and enacted policy may or may not coincide. For instance, ministers may lie or indulge in after-the-event rationalisation, or may (as we discussed in Chapter 5) have 'symbolic policies' merely designed to reassure the public that 'something is being done' about some perceived problem. Finally, 'policy' is not uniquely associated with any particular level of organisation. National governments, local government authorities, NHS institutions, and even departments within organisations may all have 'policies'. Much public policy is intended to regulate the activity of private organisations or individuals, and may consist of no more than a law that specifies what must be done (Colebatch, 1998: 32). As we have glimpsed in Chapter 4, the last 20 years has seen an increasing trend for public policy to be implemented via private organisations, including the purchase of NHS medical treatment from private hospitals.

The first main section of this chapter outlines some of the most important concepts and theories related to public policy. The second and third explore policy making processes in relation to the organisation of the NHS up to 1997 and then more recently in order to assess how the process has changed over the last 20 years. Finally, we review a range of potential theoretical interpretations of this change.

Key concepts in the policy process

There are numerous theoretically oriented accounts of policy making (for a review, see Sabatier, 1999). In this section we present a summary version of a model usually known as the 'policy process' or 'stages' model, derived originally from the work of Lasswell in the 1950s. Our version has just three stages, but versions in the specialist policy analysis literature tend to have more; for instance, Lasswell (1956) and Jenkins (1978) both have seven, Hogwood and Gunn (1984) have nine, and Rose (1973) has 12. Our three stages are as follows. First, the public *policy agenda*: we need to consider how and why issues come to the attention of government, and how they are defined or 'framed'. Second, the consideration of *alternatives and choices*: we need to consider how 'rational' are policy choices, and what analyses support the evaluation of these choices. Third, *implementation*: we need to consider whether and how choices are put into action.

Shaping the public policy agenda

As we have glimpsed in earlier chapters, a range of groups from outside the formal institutions of government may seek to influence the policy agenda. Such groups may include campaigning 'cause groups', seeking to promote their specific values through and within policy, as well as 'interest groups' with more material interests in influencing policy, for instance patient pressure groups (Wood, 2000), trades unions and as noted in Chapter 1, private financial institutions seeking to provide capital for schemes such as the Private Finance Initiative. (For a general discussion of pressure groups, see Baggott, 1995.) Although we normally think of groups seeking to place issues on policy agendas, it is important to remember that they may wish to do precisely the opposite and to prevent issues from reaching the agenda, so-called 'nondecision-making' or 'unpolitics' (Bachrach and Baratz, 1962; Crenson, 1971). Groups do not necessarily seek to influence government directly, but may also seek to influence other policy process actors such as Parliament and its committees, the public, political parties and the news media. There are also numerous 'think-tanks', usually associated with a particular section of the political spectrum; important contemporary examples are the Institute for Public Policy Research and Demos (both left of centre), and the Adam Smith Institute, the Institute for Economic Affairs and Civitas (all right of centre). Finally, various international agencies, such as the World Bank and World Health Organisation, along with the institutions of the European Union, are engaged in influencing UK national policy but are also targets for UK policy to influence. (For a detailed introduction to some of the actors in UK public policy, see James, 1997.)

Hogwood and Gunn (1984: 108) use the term 'issue' to encompass perceived problems, opportunities and uncertain trends. Given a multiplicity of actors, it is perhaps unsurprising that issues may be perceived as potentially requiring government action, without any consensus or clarity about their definition. Problems do not simply exist, but are rather subjectively perceived and socially constructed. The concept of 'framing' is sometimes employed as a narrower term within the general notion of issue definition to signify that different actors (individuals or agencies) in the policy process may have particular ways of seeing issues, including 'cognitive maps' or 'conceptual lenses' of how problems arise and what might be appropriate solutions (Allison, 1971). Frames may also be a product of actors' own educational or occupational backgrounds; lawyers may tend to see problems as amenable to legal solutions, and we introduced the concept of the 'medicalisation' of problems in Chapter 1. The manner in which issues are framed and defined is important for two reasons. First, as we shall see below, it affects the likelihood that the issue will reach the political 'agenda'. The time and capacity of agencies to deal with issues are finite, whilst the issues that might be addressed are potentially infinite, so that a selection process must occur. There is not one single policy agenda; Cobb and Elder (1972) distinguish between the 'systemic agenda' of government in general and the narrower 'institutional agendas' of particular agencies. We should also note that there is no definitive policy agenda, though political party manifestos, the Queen's speech and news media reports offer important clues. Second, the manner in which a problem or issue is framed and defined is likely to go some way towards determining the kinds of policy that would logically address it.

Early studies of policy agendas sought to identify the features that made it more likely that issues would receive government attention. The work of Hall et al. (1975: 475ff) in the field of social policy suggested that, in addition to particular factors in particular cases, three factors generally help to bring an issue to the policy agenda. First, it is important that government believes that the issue in question is one which is legitimately within the scope of governments in general, as well as one where party ideology allows involvement. Second, government needs to believe that possible policies are technically and financially feasible. Third, government assesses the identity of probable winners and losers from possible policy on the issue, and its effect on support for the government. In addition, Hall et al. noted that a perceived present or future crisis enhanced the probability of an issue attaining agenda status. Similar conclusions were reached by Solesbury (1976) in the field of environmental policy; the importance of the issue's legitimacy in current political terms, the role of perceived crises, and linkages with other issues are examples (1976: 384–95). However, Solesbury goes further, noting that

> *There may be nothing distinct or sequential about the search for attention, legitimacy and action. They may equally well proceed together or in parallel. Rather, they should be regarded as three tests which the nascent issue must pass in order to remain on the agenda for debate and decision. Only a failure to pass all three tests would remove the issue from the agenda completely. (1976: 395)*

As we saw in Chapter 3, this rejection of the need for policy making to take place in a sequential fashion was extended to full theoretical status in the context of US government by Kingdon (1984), who specifically addresses the question of why policy ideas often exist for many years before being applied to a specific problem and becoming 'an idea whose time has come'. Kingdon's work is an example of the application of 'evolutionary' theories to the policy process (Baumgartner and Jones, 1993; John, 1998: Ch 8).

Alternatives and choices

The notion of 'rationality' is central to studies of decision making; its central feature is the choice between alternative possible means for reaching desired objectives ('ends'), taking into account the relative costs and the relative efficacy of each alternative (for reviews, see Carley, 1980; McDonald, 2002: Ch 2). Its underlying assumptions may be summarised as follows. First, actors have a clearly defined 'utility function', a clearly ranked set of objectives at which their actions are directed. Second, actors are aware of all alternative strategies for achieving their objectives. Third actors are aware of all the costs and (intended and unintended) consequences associated with each alternative strategy. Finally, actors evaluate and choose from these alternative strategies so as to maximise the expected utility in terms of the original objectives. Simple 'ex-post' or retrospective evaluation focuses on evaluating the success of a chosen policy after it has been implemented (and allowed to run for an appropriate length of time) using data (perhaps including costs and outcomes) collected during that period. However, 'ex-ante' or prospective evaluation seems to have become increasingly utilised over the last 30 years. Typically, it aims to *forecast* the likely success of alternative policies or programmes by utilising the findings of earlier empirical research, perhaps based on modelling of probable costs and microeconomic analysis of cost-effectiveness, cost-utility or cost-benefits. (For an account of these techniques in a health context, see Drummond et al., 2005.) As we saw in Chapters 1 and 3, this interest has led to the creation of public institutions, such as NICE, focused on 'getting evidence into professional practice'. This perspective on rationality is a technical definition that we shall employ throughout this chapter, different from everyday usage. Even for its proponents, it is an unattainable ideal, but serves as a guide for policy and decision making and provides a logical underpinning for techniques such as operations research and statistical 'management science'.

Table 6.1 Lindblom's models of decision making

Rational-comprehensive (root)	Successive limited comparisons (branch)
Clarification of values or objectives distinct from and usually prerequisite to empirical analysis of alternative policies.	Selection of value goals and empirical analysis of the needed action are not distinct from one another but are closely intertwined.
Policy formulation is therefore approached through means-ends analysis. First the ends are isolated, then the means to achieve them are sought.	Since means and ends are not distinct, means-end analysis is often inappropriate or limited.
The test of a 'good' policy is that it can be shown to be the most appropriate means to desired ends.	The test of a 'good' policy is typically that various analysts find themselves agreeing on a policy (without their agreeing that it is the most appropriate means to an agreed objective).
Analysis is comprehensive; every important relevant factor is taken into account.	Analysis is drastically limited: • important possible outcomes are neglected. • important alternative potential policies are neglected. • important affected values are neglected.
Theory is often heavily relied upon.	A succession of limited comparisons greatly reduces or eliminates reliance on theory.

Source: adapted from Lindblom (1959: 81)

This approach has been criticised on the grounds that actors do not in fact behave in accordance with such assumptions, and moreover that unavoidable limitations in information availability and human ability to process information necessarily preclude such behaviour. In their place, Simon coined the notion of 'bounded rationality' to signify that decision making is intendedly rational within the above constraints. He observed that decision makers are often faced with multiple, competing goals, implying that they deal with objectives serially (one at a time) since they are incapable of paying attention to everything at once, and necessitating trade-offs between objectives (Simon, 1957: Ch 5). Moreover, decision makers are limited in their cognitive capacities (memory, information processing, calculation, attention span), so that they are prone to use 'rules of thumb' based on habits, existing routines and standard procedures of the organisations in which they work. As a consequence, decision makers seek to 'satisfice' (another term that Simon seems to have coined), rather than to maximise, that is to produce an outcome that was 'good enough' rather than the 'best'.

Simon's retreat from assumptions of rationality has been continued by other theorists. Lindblom (1959: 81) compares what he terms the 'rational-comprehensive' model of policy making with the 'successive limited comparisons' model. He argued that the former ('root') model, was the one advocated in textbooks and other literature aimed at influencing how policy makers *should* behave (1959: 79). In contrast, however, the second ('branch') model was the one actually practised by policy makers. Lindblom's comparison is summarised in Table 6.1. Lindblom stresses that the 'branch' method is methodical, rather than just the absence of method, implying that it was for him both a description of how policy decisions are made and a prescription for how they ought to be made (1959: 85).

Lindblom's paper and his subsequent writings (Braybrooke and Lindblom, 1963; Lindblom, 1965, 1977) provoked a good deal of academic interest and the term 'incrementalism' became associated with what he had earlier described as the 'branch' model.

Lindblom (1979) later conceded that the original had not made sufficiently clear distinctions between *incremental analysis* (that is the 'branch' method), *incremental change* (policy change occurring gradually, in small steps) and *'partisan mutual adjustment'* , a system of politics in which actors adjust their actions to take account of the anticipated actions of others, thus producing outcomes 'better described as happening rather than decided upon' (1979: 522). Indeed, as Harrison et al. (1990: 8–13) have noted, there is no *necessary* causal link between these three phenomena. (For a general review of Lindblom's work, see Gregory, 1989.) Some responses to the work of Simon and Lindblom saw incrementalism and bounded rationality as defeatist and sought a middle way between rationalism and incrementalism (Dror, 1964; Etzioni, 1967). However, the progression away from rationality was continued in other theories, notably the 'garbage can theory' of Cohen et al. (1972), which argues that the decision outputs of organisations verge on the random. Although this is an extreme view, it was subsequently an important influence on the work of Kingdon (1984), outlined above.

Implementing policy

There are four main ways in which governments can act on the real world, often in combination. First, *legislation* may be enacted in the form of Acts of Parliament or statutory regulations. (For a brief account of the UK legislative process, see Jones et al., 2001: 354–7, 386–7.) Although until perhaps 20 years ago, a large proportion of regulation within the British state was *self-regulation*, with bodies allowed to govern their 'own' sector of the economy, there has more recently been a marked trend for such self-regulation to be replaced by statutory regulation, as we saw in Chapter 4 (Moran, 2003). Second, *public expenditure* entails the allocation of financial resources to government departments, government agencies, local government authorities and programmes. The last category may entail substantial allocation of resources to the private and voluntary sectors; private and voluntary sector organisations (such as private nursing homes and charities providing drugs services) are often publicly funded to deliver services on behalf of the government. Third, *controlling the 'machinery of government'* entails creating, organising, reorganising and abolishing public sector organisations. Many areas of the public sector are now run by 'executive agencies', often 'hived off' from existing government departments, with the avowed aim of allowing them to operate 'at arm's length' from the government in accordance with a 'performance agreement' (Common, 1995; Efficiency Unit, 1988; Gains, 2004). In the health sector, such agencies include the Medicines and Healthcare Products Regulatory Agency. (For a general overview of the period 1960 to 1983, see Pollitt, 1984; for a history of the Department of Health, see Butcher, 2002: Ch 2; Day and Klein, 1997; Rayner, 1994; Wilding, 1967.) Finally, *management* involves appointing and dismissing individuals, specifying rules and procedures, establishing performance standards and targets, and providing rewards and sanctions.

None of these 'levers' add up to policy that is 'self-implementing', a problem that has been recognised in the literature since the appearance in 1973 of the first edition of Pressman and Wildavsky's (1979) empirical study of the failure of the federally funded Oakland Project to provide economic regeneration in an area of the US's west coast. The overall message of the

Table 6.2   Gunn's conditions for 'perfect implementation'

1   'Circumstances external to the implementing agency do not impose crippling constraints'. These might include natural factors, such as droughts or epidemics.

2   'Adequate time and sufficient resources are made available to the programme'. Time is not trivial, since most agencies have existing tasks to handle, so that new programmes are essentially competing for organisational attention.

3   'The required combination of resources is actually available at the appropriate time'. Resources are not just money; even plentiful funds may not be able to overcome (eg) skills or vaccine shortages, at least in the short term.

4   'The policy to be implemented is based upon a valid theory of cause and effect'.

5   'That the relationship between cause and effect is direct and that there are few, if any intervening links'. In essence, this is the point raised by Pressman and Wildavsky. To make the same point mathematically, the total probability of a set of independent links all 'working' is the probability to the power of the number of links; thus 10 links with a 95 percent probability of each working gives 0.95 to the power 10, equal to about 0.57, or only 57 percent probability of the whole thing working!

6   'That dependency relations are minimal', that is that multiple organisations will co-operate with each other as required to implement the policy. Presumably the same mathematics applies as in 5 above.

7   'That there is understanding of, and agreement on, objectives' of the policy throughout the implementation process.

8   'The tasks are fully specified in correct sequence', implying that the policies are capable of being reduced to a set of detailed instructions to relevant actors.

9   There is 'perfect communication and co-ordination' with no conflicts within the implementing organisation and everyone understanding what is required of them.

10   'Those in authority can demand and obtain perfect compliance'; that is, everyone will do as they are told.

Source: adapted from Gunn, 1978

study is neatly summed up by the 'Heath-Robinson' style cover illustration and full title of the book:

> *Implementation: How Great Expectations in Washington are Dashed in Oakland; Or, Why it's Amazing that Federal Programs Work at All, This being a Saga of the Economic Development Administration as Told by Two Sympathetic Observers Who Seek to Build Morals on a Foundation of Ruined Hopes*

In short, their overall conclusion was that policies dependent on numerous links in a causal chain, including a multiplicity of agencies, were very difficult to implement successfully. This recognition that implementation is difficult, or indeed impossible in any precise sense, is manifest in a range of classic studies produced in the 1970s and 1980s. Gunn's (1978; Hogwood and Gunn, 1984) analysis continued the 'top-down' approach to implementation begun in the Oakland study. He argued that for 'perfect implementation' to occur, ten conditions would have to be met, as shown in Table 6.2. It should be noted that Gunn is not suggesting that such perfection is actually achievable; rather he is using the idea as a means of understanding why implementation is so difficult, and perhaps how it might be improved. (Logically minded readers might note that Gunn's formulation seems to contain some redundancies; for instance perfect implementation might not require both 9 and 10 or both 7 and 8.)

Other theorists, notably Dunsire and Lipsky, have argued on various grounds that 'top-down' implementation is simply not possible. Dunsire (1978) offers an analysis which, although apparently rather abstract, is carefully illustrated with an example of his local railway station being closed down! First, he notes, organisations are not as it were standing around waiting for something to implement: any new policy has to be fitted into the train of existing activities, probably using some of their components. Second, organisational hier-archies are characterised by (ascending) generality of perspective and consequent lack of detailed knowledge. Each tier will have its own concepts, style of operation and language; such different 'languages' are compounded by in-jokes, and stereotypes of other parts of organisation. As a result, in communications terms an organisation is a 'Tower of Babel'. (For an application of this metaphor to the NHS, see Klein, 1984.) Implementation necessarily involves a communication problem and an interpretation problem: messages for superiors must be summarised to a higher level of generality, whilst messages for subordinates must be made more specific, often differently for different subordinates. Third, managers cannot therefore specify precisely what subordinates should do (even if they have been promoted from the bottom, they will not have performed every job there). As a result, it is an officer's job to specify for him/herself what an order from above means, and what is to be passed on downwards, and in practice a superior will often check with a subordinate that a proposed instruction is the right one to give.

Lipsky's (1980) approach to implementation is very much geared to the situation of public service professionals (including police, probation officers, teachers and doctors), whom he labels, perhaps confusingly, 'street-level bureaucrats'. He begins by noting how in 'schools, police and welfare departments ... and other agencies ... workers interact with and have wide discretion over the dispensation of benefits or the allocation of public sanctions' (1980: xi). Consequently:

> *the decisions of street-level bureaucrats, the routines they establish, and the devices they invent to cope with uncertainties and work pressures, effectively become the public policies they carry out (Lipsky, 1980: xii) ... The processing of people into clients, assigning them to categories for treatment by bureaucrats, and treating them in terms of those categories, is a social process. Client characteristics do not exist outside of the process that gives rise to them. (1980: 59)*

Moreover, as we saw from the example of doctors in Chapter 1, street-level bureaucrats ration access to service; this is achieved, at best, by 'benign modes of mass-processing that... permit them to deal with the public fairly, appropriately and successfully. At worst, they give in to favouritism, stereotyping and routinising' (Lipsky, 1980: xii). Lipsky's conclusion is that it is infeasible to establish hierarchical control of such services and that 'it is dys-functional to most street-level bureaucracies to become more responsive' to clients (1980: 101). Finally, it has been argued that policy and implementation are not clearly conceptu-ally distinguishable. Barrett and Fudge (1982) draw from a series of case studies the con-cept of the 'policy-action continuum' consisting of ongoing explicit and implicit negotiation 'between those seeking to put policy into effect and those upon whom action depends' (1982: 25). In this view, there is nothing special about 'policy'; rather it is a mat-ter of sets of actors interacting in various ways, drawing upon their respective resources and power relationships (1982: 29).

An historical sketch of NHS policy making

'Policy process' models of the kind rather brutally summarised above contain a number of stages which can be represented as more or less logical, but in respect of which no claims to sequential occurrence or overall rationality are made; the possibility of errors, iterations and implementation failures is fully recognised. For our purposes, it is merely a device by which to introduce some theories about particular aspects of the process; the model has been subjected to a wide range of criticisms (for summaries, see John, 1998: 22–37; Parsons, 1995: 79–80; Sabatier, 1999: 6–7) and few authors would claim that the model accurately represents or explains real-world policy processes. But policy practitioners themselves often maintain distinctions between the stages (Stewart, 1996), perhaps partly because many of their job roles are defined by them, for example in terms of 'policy making' and management, or 'politics' and 'administration'. Moreover, as we saw in Chapter 3, many aspects of the 'evidence-based medicine' phenomenon imply a similar kind of distinction between those who decide what is to be done and those who put it into practice.

The ability to make some kind of clear distinction between stages of the policy process is crucial to rationality in the technical sense given above. Without the ability to decide what is desired, consider effective means of achieving it, and put those means into practice, claims to rationality will be difficult to sustain. In this and the following main section, we examine the policy processes employed in connection with various reorganisations of the English NHS in order to see how clearly different stages can be identified, and how these processes have changed over the last 30 years. Our focus here is therefore rather different from Chapter 4, on processes of designing and implementing organisational changes rather than on the substance of the changes. The policy process in this area is of special interest because formal organization is a matter which naturally lends itself to top-down treatment precisely because it is formal; we expect a formal organisation to be consciously designed. Moreover, the NHS is formally a highly centralised organization: directly funded and politically 'hands-on', as a result of the Secretary of State's legal duty and powers. In this section, we discuss three specific moments of NHS reorganisation which manifest a progressive dissolution of identifiable stages in the policy process.

The blueprint: the 1974 reorganisation

The antecedents of the 1974 reorganisation of the NHS are to some extent traceable back to the service's earliest years. The Conservative governments of 1951 to 1964 were responsible for both the development of the *Hospital Plan* (Ministry of Health, 1962) and several reports on the administrative structure of professions and institutions (for a summary, see Harrison, 1988: 12–14). The Labour governments of 1964 to 1970 exhibited a more sustained and integrated emphasis on questions of management and organisation. First, they instituted, and accepted the recommendations of a number of further reports on such topics. The Salmon committee, established in 1963 by the Conservatives, recommended a comprehensive, hierarchical management structure for hospital nursing (Ministry of Health, 1966), and similar principles were extended to community nursing by the subsequent Mayston report

(Watkin, 1978: 113). A series of joint reports of the (then) Ministry of Health and the medical profession (usually termed the 'Cogwheel' reports after the logo on their cover) urged physicians to recognise their interdependence with each other and with the organisation, and proposed a series of committees within hospitals as the means of integrating specialties and relating them to the local administration (Ministry of Health, 1967). The subsequent Zuckerman and Noel Hall reports of 1968 and 1970 respectively recommended career structures for NHS scientists and technicians, and pharmacists, respectively (Watkin, 1975: 341–9).

The second manifestation of the Labour governments' interest in management and organisation was their concern with the macro-level organisation of the NHS. Consideration of possible reorganisation of local government had begun in the mid-1960s (Wood, 1976) and extensive efforts were made to ensure that the design of a reorganised NHS was both consistent and integrated with parallel changes then being planned. This design was carefully developed over a period of several years and included extensive consultation via two Green Papers (DHSS, 1970; Ministry of Health, 1968), both of which discussed organisational design and the functions of each tier in detail, and an equally detailed White Paper (DHSS, 1972a). The reorganisation was preceded by several years of extensive conceptual work by the management consultants Messrs McKinsey and the Health Services Organisation Research Unit at Brunel University. The plans survived changes of government from Labour to Conservative in 1970, and back in January 1974, with only minor changes such as the Conservatives' even more explicit emphasis on management (Klein, 1983: 91).

The new form of organisation adopted health districts as the operational level of the new service, which was to run hospitals, clinics and community services; they were largely designed around the (nominally 250,000) 'catchment' populations of existing district general hospitals. Such hospitals, designed and located in accordance with the Conservatives' earlier *Hospital Plan,* normally contained an accident and emergency department, all the main medical specialties (with at least two consultants in each) and often a maternity unit. Above this were two higher levels of organisation. The intermediate level had a mainly planning function, its boundaries being coterminous with local government, which continued to be responsible for environmental health and personal social services. (In some cases, these two levels were conflated.) Above this were regions, retained at the insistence of the 1970–74 Conservative government.

These and further details of the new organisation were conveyed to the NHS in a document which became known as the 'Grey Book' (DHSS, 1972b), a detailed and densely packed 174 page organisational prescription of structures, and institutional, managerial and professional roles and relationships, including elaborate consultative mechanisms and formal powers of veto. It is difficult to convey the character of this volume in a few sentences, but to describe it as a 'blueprint' is not an exaggeration. Successive chapters discuss organisation in general and of particular skill groups, and management and planning processes. The document contains 16 detailed diagrams of different segments of government and NHS organisation, specifying functions and relationships between statutory bodies, and managerial and professional relationships within and between them, including the system of 'consensus decision making' outlined in Chapter 4. An appendix contains 27 detailed role specifications, together with definitions of key terms such as 'manager', 'accountable', 'monitor' and 'co-ordinate'. The blueprint was uniformly implemented throughout the service in April 1974, at the same time as corresponding changes to the structure of local government. The character of the Grey Book reflected the specific approach to organisation developed in the Health Services Organization Research Unit at Brunel University (Jaques, 1978; Rowbottom et al., 1973), apparently built on the assumption that most organisational problems were rooted in misunderstandings of role. But its approach was also consonant with contemporary received wisdom which stressed planning, integration of social policy and the various health and social services (Glennerster, 1981), professional specialisation, and large-scale institutional operation (Committee on the Functions of the District General Hospital, 1969), eschewing any need for the kinds of pilot studies then taking place in other policy sectors (Burch and Wood, 1983: 200–3). In summary, the history and outcome of the 1974 reorganisation of the NHS manifest a clear distinction between stages of the policy process; there was a long period of careful planning and design of the new policy, which transcended changes of government and was then adopted almost in its entirety by the government of the day, and implemented nationally and uniformly.

1974 to 1989: blueprints abandoned

The style of policy making did not immediately change with the new Conservative government of 1979. Indeed, until 1982 matters were much as before. The Royal Commission on the NHS, established in 1976, had proceeded very much along the conventional lines, investigating problems, reviewing alternatives and recommending change. Following its report (Royal Commission, 1979), a consultation document was issued (DHSS and Welsh Office, 1979) which contained a commitment to abolish a tier of NHS organisation with effect from 1982: another blueprint, albeit a minor one. The policies for NHS reorganisation which followed were, however, 'made' in a different way, taking the form of a series of 'policy accidents' as a result of which new policies emerged in a somewhat unplanned fashion. The content of these new policies also differed from 1974 in that they did not take the form of blueprints; rather, each consisted of a central 'bright idea', expressed in somewhat general terms and without much institutional detail. Such policies were necessarily defined by implementation at least as much as by their original content and they therefore represent a weakening of distinctions between stages of the policy process. We illustrate this by means of two important NHS organisational reforms of the 1980s, the introduction of 'general management' and of community care, both associated with the late Sir Roy Griffiths, and both taking forms not intended by those who commissioned them.

In the case of general management, Harrison (1994) has shown the series of accidents that occurred. The government attempted in 1982 to commission an inquiry into NHS 'manpower'. The person offered its chair declined the offer. Ministers and officials did not have an immediate substitute in mind and sought advice from a number of industrial confidants; Griffiths, then Managing Director of the Sainsbury supermarket chain, who had no previous contact with government, was proposed and was subsequently offered the role. He declined on the ground that if there were problems with the size of the workforce, that was only a symptom of a deeper problem, one of management; he would accept the chair only if the terms of reference were changed to focus upon NHS management. The government conceded this. The eventual policy recommendations were radical and included the abolition of the system of consensus team decision making and its replacement with individual general managers (later, chief executives). But the recommendations were also vague; the report (NHS Management Inquiry, 1983) took the form of a 24 page, double-spaced, typescript letter from Griffiths to the Secretary of State, containing only the sketchiest account of the functions of the new arrangements proposed, and indeed no concrete recommendations whatsoever on a number of matters (such as responsiveness to service users) which were held to be key topics for reform. Despite a good deal of resistance from the NHS over a prolonged period, and the diffidence of the Secretary of State, the new arrangements, which had been neither planned nor anticipated, were accepted by the government when it became clear that they had the Prime Minister's support. Thus the roles of the new general managers and the shape of local organisational structures were left to emerge.

In the subsequent case of community care, Wistow and Harrison (1998) have shown how Griffiths, now with some NHS experience and known to policy makers, was asked in 1986 to examine what was recognised to be an intractable problem of community care. A central government which had clearly demonstrated hostility to local government and its powers and had already moved to abolish the many local authorities (Stoker, 1988) could hardly be expected to anticipate that Griffiths would recommend the allocation of the lead role in community care to local authorities, and that the financial resources to support this should be transferred from the central Social Security budget to local authority coffers (Griffiths, 1988). Yet that is what happened. Despite various attempts to sabotage the recommendation, including the official publication of the report on the eve of a statutory holiday, while Griffiths himself was recovering from surgery, some 15 months later the Prime Minister was eventually convinced that there was no logical alternative. Nevertheless, there was a further two years before implementation in 1993 during which time other important details of Griffiths's recommendations, such as the role of 'care managers', were left to emerge.

The quasi-market emerges

Even before the end of the Griffiths community care story, a further policy accident had begun to occur: the Prime Minister's decision, made in haste in reaction to media reports of paediatric cardiac surgery cancelled as a result of NHS funding shortages, to establish a 'prime ministerial review' of the NHS. Her decision, announced in January 1988 on the *Panorama* television programme, came as a surprise to ministers (Klein, 2001: 149). The eventual outcome was the White Paper *Working for Patients* (Secretaries of State for Health, 1989), which proposed the NHS quasi-market described in Chapter 4. The policy process was very different from that of the 1974 reorganisation in four respects. One difference was a characteristic shared by the policy accidents described above; the process of initial design of the reforms was shorter and more closed. The review of the NHS was conducted informally, largely in secret and uninformed by expert opinion from the field (Lee-Potter, 1997), by a team consisting almost entirely of ministers. The remaining three differences, however, seem to have signalled a move towards a new style of policy making: a deliberate eschewing of blueprints in favour of the promulgation, in vague terms, of a core set of ideas combined with an invitation to relevant actors (which they could not easily refuse) to constitute the formal institutions which would embody these ideas. The specific differences were as follows. First, the White Paper, though some 102 pages long, devoted substantial space to Scotland, Wales and Northern Ireland and had a generously spaced and repetitive text containing only the barest account of the purchaser/provider split, the role of health authority purchasers, NHS trusts (providers) and GPFHs. It promised further details in a forthcoming series of working papers. Eleven eventually appeared, some with as few as 12 generously spaced pages, and many (see, for instance Secretaries of State for Health, 1989) also largely innocent of substantive content. As Klein has summarised it 'the White Paper's proposals were little more than outline sketches, even when supplemented by a series of working papers' (1995: 198). Second, and presumably as a result, even by the formal implementation date of April 1991 fundamental matters such as the contracting process had not been thought through, in some cases with disastrous results for individual institutions (Harrison et al., 1994). Relationships between institutions were adapted as perceived to be necessary. Some of these amounted to far more than minor adjustments; for instance the relative emphasis given to competition and co-operation, the relative importance of the logically inconsistent models of GPFH and health authority purchasing (Harrison, 1991), and whether acute and non-acute services should be combined in one Trust all varied substantially between 1991 and 1996. Third, the implementation arrangements were not uniform, but centred upon a process of annual waves of volunteers for trust or fundholding status. The criteria for admission of volunteers to the new status were developed 'on the hoof' in parallel with the application process. This allowed ongoing adjustments; thus initial criteria for acceptance of volunteers were relaxed over time to ensure the apparent success in implementation terms of the approach.

The Review had no formal terms of reference, but both the context in which it was announced and most of its deliberations indicated that it was considering alternative ways of funding the NHS (Butler, 1992: 5–8). The resulting White Paper was both brief and vague, the very antithesis of a blueprint, and reached conclusions that had little to do with the problems that precipitated the Review. An incomplete new model of NHS organisation emerged and developed to address the resulting uncertainties.

Contemporary healthcare policy making

The changed policy process for NHS reorganisation described in the preceding section can be seen as having two elements. First, there has been a shift away from the presentation of a 'blueprint' as the intended endpoint of reorganisation, and its replacement by what might be termed the 'bright idea', a rather unspecific vision of how to proceed. Second, the process changed from one where expert advice significantly shaped the content of the blueprint to one involving the translation by incentivised local actors of the bright idea into specific organisational arrangements which accord with the (often vague) philosophy behind that idea. We might term this 'manipulated emergence' (Harrison and Wood, 1999). The Conservative government continued to operate in this manner almost to the moment of losing office at the 1997 general election. It enacted legislation (the NHS Primary Care Act 1997) which made provision for volunteers to make proposals for breaking down the existing rigid division between primary and secondary care, including the strict financial regime of separate budget heads which underpinned it. Unspecified new organisational forms could be proposed, and initial approval by the Secretary of State on a case-by-case basis could later be replaced by blanket approval to generic new developments.

Re-creating primary care organisation: 1997–2006

Early in its office the new Labour government made limited use of the 1997 Act by approving minor schemes (such as for salaried GPs) in some localities, but greater government attention was given to a further NHS reorganisation to replace the 'internal market' system which had been bitterly criticised by the party while in opposition. The initial proposals appeared in a White Paper *The New NHS: Modern, Dependable* (Secretary of State for Health, 1997) which, despite 86 pages and several diagrams, is quite insubstantial. Considerable repetition of central ideas is accompanied by only the sketchiest details of key institutions and processes such as the management of the proposed new PCGs (see Chapter 4), NICE, local systems of 'clinical governance', arrangements for integrating with the work of local authorities, and funding for patients who receive care outside their home district. Though the 1997 White Paper was far from a blueprint of the 1974 variety, a consultation document (Secretary of State for Health, 1998) was issued some seven months later containing reasonably detailed accounts of the constitutions and functions of the two new regulatory institutions CHI and NICE, though (as we saw in Chapter 1) the functions of the latter seem to have been subsequently reinvented. However, the 'bright idea' approach practised by the Conservative administration remained discernible in Labour policy. The White Paper gave only bare details of policy content (though certain of these were fleshed out in the later document) thus providing for policy to emerge from implementation.

As we saw in Chapter 4, elements of compulsion were present in that fundholding was to be abolished and membership of geographically defined PCGs was to be compulsory for GPs from 1999. However, a choice of entry levels to PCG status was offered, apparently providing the opportunity for GPs collectively to decide how far to engage in a wider role than that of the traditional practitioner. Level 1 PCGs would merely advise on the health authority's commissioning of services; level 2 PCGs would have devolved responsibility for commissioning but remain part of the health authority; the highest level of PCG status was the PCT, independent of the health authority but accountable to it for commissioning care and in some cases providing community services. PCGs were relatively popular with GPs, since their management arrangements gave substantial control to an executive committee on which GPs were in a majority. Initial take-up of PCT status in 2000 was therefore slow, but accelerated rapidly, with over one-third of the new organisations in this category by 2001 (Peckham and Exworthy, 2003: 153) perhaps fuelled by the desire of some GPs to maximise their independence from the health authority, even at the price of sacrificing their built-in governing majority for management arrangements modelled on those of hospital trusts (see Chapter 4). But these choices were already redundant; in 2001 the government announced that all PCGs would become PCTs by 2004 (Department of Health, 2001a).

As we saw in Chapter 4, a new contract was agreed for GPs in 2004, a key element of which was the 'Quality and Outcomes Framework' (QOF) which specified 146 evidence-based indicators of quality and paid practices for meeting 'points' targets derived from these indicators (Roland, 2004). Although the principle of paying GPs for achieving quantifiable targets was not new, QOF went well beyond previous contracts in terms of both the number of targets and the proportion of income (some 20 percent on average) dependent on their achievement. The clinical elements of the 2004 QOF related to ten diseases, often based on existing clinical guidelines and NSFs. Examples of QOF targets are the percentage of patients with heart disease treated with aspirin, and the proportion of patients with blood pressure in excess of 150/90 whose level is subsequently reduced below that figure. QOF is designed to be regularly reviewed, and changes made in 2006 included the addition of seven new disease areas. It is important to note that official statements surrounding the introduction of QOF presented it as an enabling device within which GPs could prioritise the targets most relevant to their own practice (NHS Confederation/British Medical Association, 2003: 20). Some of the new targets (such as for 'chronic kidney disease') proved professionally controversial, but there is little evidence that practices have used their ostensible freedom to refrain from pursuing these, or indeed any of the targets. Practices were predicted to achieve 700–750 (from a maximum of 1050) points in total, but mean achievement for 2004–05 was approximately 950 (Cole, 2005: 457). Moreover, evidence is emerging that pursuit of QOF points has led practices to reorganise themselves for this purpose, with highly bureaucratised procedures and new forms of internal hierarchy, even amongst the GP partners themselves (McDonald et al., forthcoming).

A final contemporary development in primary care policy is the appearance in 2005 of 'practice-based commissioning' (PBC) which, as we saw in Chapter 4, allows general practices to choose to hold budgets to commission secondary care services (Department of Health, 2004g), an apparent return to something like GPFH, often through consortia of practices, though sometimes singly. Participation in PBC is voluntary so far as individual practices are concerned, though there are various incentive payments and the ability to retain savings from new commissioning patterns. PBC has been officially presented very much as the means by which GPs might, amongst other things, secure 'a greater variety of services' for patients (Department of Health, 2004g: 4), and early anecdotal evidence suggests that tightly controlled 'patient pathways' are seen as one means of making savings. Although participation in PBC is not required of GPs, PCTs have been placed under some government pressure to ensure that general practices do opt in, with the result that by 2006 some 96 percent of practices had done so (www.dh.gov.uk/en/policyandguidance/organisationpolicy/

commissioning/practice-basedcommissioning/DH_4131190, accessed 30 March 2007), though it is not yet clear how far these choices will genuinely translate into new commissioning patterns.

Creating Foundation Trusts

In early 2002, the government announced the establishment of Foundation Trusts (FTs), a new status initially only available on application by existing hospital trusts with '3-star' performance ratings (see Chapter 4). FTs were politically controversial (for a summary, see Baggott, 2004: 183–5). They were to be freed from the direct control of the Secretary of State, regulated by a new regulator ('Monitor') responsible to Parliament rather than government and, as we saw in Chapter 5, have boards that included governors elected by a self-selected group of local people. FTs have a range of freedoms not possessed by other Trusts, most importantly the ability to set their own conditions of employment and to enter into joint ventures with private sector organisations (Pollock et al., 2004: 72). Twenty FTs came into existence in 2004, apparently the product of a lobby group of Trust managers, though the government has stated that all NHS organisations will eventually be eligible (Klein, 2006: 228). The total stood at 59 by early 2007, with a further 27 applications under consideration (http://monitor-nhsft.gov.uk/register.php, accessed 23 March 2007).

Interpreting the contemporary policy process

We can begin by noting that the policy-making processes that we have described in this chapter are very particular examples, related to the restructuring of the mainstream NHS institutions responsible for commissioning and delivering health services. They are important for that reason, but they do not constitute the whole of policy. In other matters, the contemporary health policy process has been different. For instance, we saw in Chapter 2 that New Labour has implemented evidence-based medicine energetically, bureaucratising the policy of scientific medicine developed by their Conservative predecessors, producing 'scientific–bureaucratic medicine'. This preference for bureaucratic, rule-driven solutions to policy problems is pervasive in New Labour's approach, leading to the many new regulatory institutions described in Chapters 2, 3 and 4. But as we have seen in this chapter the approach to designing and redesigning the core institutions of the NHS has been different. We might summarise as follows. First, the approach to seeing organisational redesign in terms of a 'blueprint' had gradually been abandoned before New Labour came to office. Although it is doubtful if this was initially a conscious strategy by the Conservatives, experience with the largely accidental circumstances surrounding the two Griffiths reports seems to have allowed the conscious adoption of policy based on 'bright ideas' to be fleshed out in the implementation process, when it came to allowing the arrangements for the post-1991 quasi-market to emerge. Thus any clear distinction between 'making' and 'implementing' policy becomes difficult to sustain. Second, the Conservative government had also invented 'manipulated emergence', that is the creation of a new organisational status for which existing organisations could be persuaded to volunteer. This creation of a 'bandwagon' of early adopters upon which others would wish to climb was, as we saw in Chapter 4, highly successful in the production of NHS Trust hospitals and GP fundholders. Third, New Labour adopted elements of these approaches after 1997 in order to bring PCT and FT status, and PBC, into existence. In this section we consider four possible interpretations of all this. It is important to note that, unlike in earlier chapters, our interpretations relate to a trajectory of policy that predates the election of the New Labour government in 1997.

Governance

We briefly noted in Chapter 4 that contemporary academic concepts of 'governance' are not synonymous with 'government' or with hierarchical or bureaucratic control (as implied in 'clinical governance'). In analyses of UK politics, the term is often used as a contrast to the so-called 'Westminster model' of government, which

> *focuses on: parliamentary sovereignty; strong cabinet government; accountability through elections; majority party control of the executive (that is, Prime Minister, cabinet and the civil service); elaborate conventions for the conduct of parliamentary business; institutionalised opposition; and the rules of debate. (Rhodes, 1997: 5)*

As Rhodes further observes, studies of politics that adopt this perspective tend to focus very much on the formal institutions, powers and procedures of government (1997: 6). Over the last 15 years, however, some scholars have ceased to regard this as helpful, in part from a recognition that it might overstate the powers of executive government and in part because contemporary governments might be less able to operate in the 'top-down' manner assumed by the Westminster model. On the latter point, some analysts point specifically to the role in public policy of numerous levels of governmental institutions and of self-organising networks of organisations (Rhodes, 1997: 7–16). Others adopt what is perhaps a broader concept of governance to signify that contemporary governments are less able simply to control society as markets become more aggressive, citizens more demanding and organisations of all kinds more proactive in forming networks and alliances. Hence 'the actual role that the state plays in governance is often the outcome of the tug-of-war between the role the state wants to play and the role which the external environment allows it to play' (Pierre and Peters, 2000: 26). As a consequence, rather than simply governing 'top-down', governments engage in 'governance by transaction … [that is] the creation of frameworks in which other actors can perform' (Hill and Hupe, 2002: 181). The creation of organisations and incentive systems is an obvious example of such frameworks.

Government policies for the reorganisation of the NHS since about 1990 can in some respects be seen as specific manifestations of governance. This is perhaps clearest in the case of the creation of GPFH where, given the ownership status and considerable variation in size and administrative resources of general practices, it might well have been politically difficult simply to decree that GPs should hold budgets for secondary care. Similar reasoning might well apply to our other primary care examples of PCT creation, QOF and PBC, but is less obviously applicable to the creation of Trust and FT hospitals where, as we have seen, governments have in the past simply reorganised by decree. Moreover, its focus on the lack of power of governments simply to impose policy suggests that governance offers a better explanation of 'manipulated emergence' than of policy as 'bright idea', which suggests an element of uncertainty on the part of policy makers as to exactly what was to be implemented.

Prevailing assumptions about policy and management

A broader approach to understanding the appearance of 'manipulated emergence' and policies as 'bright ideas' is through the changing context of prevailing assumptions, independent of party politics, about government, policy and organisation in the UK. For the 1960s and early 1970s, these overlapping assumptions might be briefly characterised as follows. First, there was a strong belief in the role of science and technology, not just literally (as in the 1964–70 Labour government's policies for computing, space exploration and the Concorde aeroplane) but also in respect of *social* technologies. These included the application to the public sector of corporate planning techniques, programme planning budgeting systems, management by objectives, work study and operational research (Friend and Jessop, 1969; Spiers, 1975). Policy-related research was also valued; it underpinned the 1974 NHS reorganisation (as we saw above) but also the earlier Royal Commission on Local Government of 1966–69, which was the first such enquiry to have a research staff and budget. Second, expertise was valued, supporting a belief that policy and administration could and should be separated (Self, 1972), with elected politicians determining clear policy directions and implementation being left to officials. Our description of the 1974 NHS reorganisation has provided one example of this; local government examples include the Maud report (Committee on the Management of Local Government, 1967) and the Bains report (Department of the Environment, 1972). Third, there was a set of related assumptions about the value and feasibility of planning at all levels as a means of determining the future; this was the period of economic planning, the National Plan and Regional Economic Planning Councils, but also of the *Hospital Plan* (see above) and of comprehensive planning systems in health and in social welfare. Finally, there was an acceptance of much of the 'Fordist' notion that there is a single 'best way' of production: mass production by a large integrated organisation (Hoggett, 1990). We have already noted the development of the NHS district general hospital and increasing specialisation within medicine as examples, though (as we saw in Chapter 2) this reasoning was not fully applied in organisations such as hospitals, where professional autonomy was important in designing human services for individual clients.

These assumptions had greatly changed by the 1980s. First, faith in technocratic solutions to social problems had been somewhat overtaken by the recognition that fast-moving events can render carefully thought-out policies obsolete; something of a preference for 'gut feeling' developed in its place. Second, a suspicion of experts had developed and there was something of a resurgence of politics, especially when informed by strong ideological conviction. As a consequence, professionals were no longer immune from scrutiny and public sector managers were expected to work under tighter political control. Third, faith in planning and bureaucracy as the means of social co-ordination was increasingly replaced by a preference for interactive, especially market, approaches. No doubt this was partly ideological, stemming from Conservative beliefs about the virtues of markets and the perceptions of professions as cartels, but it was also a result of manifest planning 'disasters' (Hall, 1980; see also Hood, 1976). Fourth, there had occurred outside the arena of public policy a shift to so-called post-Fordist approaches to industrial production, entailing replacement of the Fordist assumption of one best way of operation by 'the progressive decentralisation of production under conditions of rising flexibility and centralised strategic control' (Hoggett, 1990: 5). Finally, beneath all these was anti-statism, a complex of assumptions about why the state cannot solve social and economic problems, theorised by authors such as Bacon and Eltis (1976) and Niskanen (1971).

These post-1980 assumptions can clearly be discerned in policy for reorganising the NHS since the early 1990s. The replacement of blueprint by 'bright idea' exemplifies in general terms gut feeling and suspicion of experts and professionals, whilst the specific 'bright ideas' that have been implemented reflect a preference for interactive methods of social co-ordination such as markets and perhaps also a degree of anti-statism. It is perhaps not far-fetched to apply the idea of post-Fordism to the 'production' of policy: progressively decentralised under conditions of increasing flexibility (that is, emergent) and increasingly centralised strategic control (that is, incentivised). However, it is more difficult to see 'manipulated emergence' as connected to these revised assumptions about government.

Backward mapping

We noted in the first section of this chapter that theorists of policy implementation varied in their view of how far to conceptualise the process as 'top-down' or 'bottom-up'. One writer in the latter category is Elmore (1979) whose concept of 'backward mapping' aimed to provide an approach to policy implementation research that avoids the unrealistic assumptions implicit in top-down models. (As we saw, Gunn's model of 'perfect implementation' shows the number and implausibility of such assumptions.) Elmore's solution was to

> begin ... not with a statement of intent, but with a statement of the specific behaviour at the lowest level of the implementation process that generates the need for a policy. Only after that behaviour is described does the analysis presume to state an objective ... Having established a relatively precise target at the lowest level of the system, the analysis backs up through the structure of the implementing agencies ... In the final stage of analysis, the analyst or policymaker describes a policy that directs resources at the organisational unit likely to have the greatest effect. (Elmore, 1979: 604)

Note from the final sentence that this approach can be applied both by analysts seeking to understand the results of an implementation exercise and (though Elmore focuses mainly on analysis) as a strategy by which policy makers can secure more effective implementation. Whilst we cannot say whether policy makers were knowingly pursuing Elmore's approach, 'backward mapping' does have a great deal in common with 'manipulated emergence' in that both start with asking, in effect, 'what do we want these people (in this case NHS managers and physicians) to do?' If it is desired to engage them in adopting some new organisational form (Trusts, GPFH, PCT, FT, PBC) then it may be effective to incentivise these actors to choose the new status, with the expectation that the volunteers will be those most able and willing to adopt it successfully, serving also as a message to others that the future lies in this particular direction. Elmore also sees organisations and the expertise within them as 'instruments to be capitalised upon and modified in pursuit of policy objectives ... Organisations can be remarkably effective devices for working out difficult policy problems' (1979: 607). Elmore's model therefore incorporates some of the elements of policy as 'bright idea' rather than blueprint. We should note that, as an approach to explaining New Labour policy, backward mapping implies some sort of 'lesson-drawing' (Rose, 1993) from the experience of their predecessors in a context where, as we have seen in Chapter 4, there have been other important continuities in NHS policies. A final point is that backward mapping can be seen as a form of rationality, albeit somewhat different from the form described above, in the sense that it is a calculated strategy for implementing and learning from a partly developed and possibly contentious policy.

Contingent policy styles

As we noted at the beginning of this section, the policy processes that we have examined in this chapter are very particular; they relate to the restructuring of the mainstream NHS institutions responsible for commissioning and delivering services. In other areas of health policy, both Labour and Conservative governments since the mid-1980s have been quite prepared to be directive in the implementation of clearly specified plans, so that the 'bright idea' and 'manipulated emergence' approaches are not pervasive across policy topics; governments seem to employ a mix of approaches (Richards and Smith, 2002: 238). This raises the question of whether different policy styles are systematically employed in different circumstances. A number of analysts have examined this possibility in relation to international differences (Lijphart, 1999; Richardson, 1982), rather than in relation to different types of policy. In their examination of UK policies for families, long-term care, pensions and the labour market, Larsen et al. (2006) have shown that top-down approaches occur where a policy involves large expenditure increases, affects relatively weak groups and/or is politically or ideologically driven. Conversely, a more negotiable approach is adopted when dealing with strong external organisations, where reforms are service-oriented, where policy involves changes in current administrative arrangements and/or represents a new policy direction. Again, these observations do not seem to help us to analyse our observations about NHS policy making. For instance, many of the organisational innovations that we have described are both ideologically driven and represent a new approach to administrative arrangements.

A number of other analysts have proposed policy typologies based on types of issue such as principle, cost and benefit distribution, and type of regulation (Hogwood, 1987; Lowi, 1972). The framework of issue types proposed by Thompson and Tuden (1956) is constructed around whether or not participants share objectives, and whether or not participants share beliefs about how particular objectives are likely to be achieved. For each of the four decision types resulting from these situations, Thompson and Tuden propose an ideal-typical decision strategy. First, where participants agree about both objectives and how to achieve them, 'computation', that is working out a technical solution, is appropriate. Second, where there is agreement about objectives, but disagreement about how to achieve them, 'judgement' by experts is appropriate. Third, where participants disagree about objectives but agree about the causation of the various possibilities, negotiated 'compromise' is the appropriate decision strategy. Finally, where participants agree about neither objectives nor how various possibilities might be achieved, 'inspiration' is the appropriate strategy. Such inspiration might emanate from a charismatic leader, but might also emerge from the interaction within a diverse group of decision makers. Although Thompson and Tuden are careful to stress that such clear-cut decision types are unlikely to occur in the real world, and we might also think that their distinction between objectives and means of achieving them is difficult to apply to real situations, we can nevertheless see that their framework does offer some points of contact with our account of policy making. Thus we might argue that the situations in which governments came to introduce the organisational innovations that we have described were characterised by uncertainty about exactly how to proceed and knowledge that there would be opposition in any case. Hence we can perhaps characterise the combination of the 'bright idea' and 'manipulated emergence' as an example of 'inspiration' as posited by Thompson and Tuden.

Concluding remarks

Our four approaches to interpreting policy making fall into two groups. Both the 'governance' and 'prevailing assumption' approaches offer broad explanations of changes in the way governments seek to get things done. These approaches are both broadly consistent with the facts of these changes, and can perhaps be seen as setting the context within which the policies that we have described were developed. However, neither provides us with a specific explanation; the first is better in respect of manipulated emergence than 'bright idea', whilst the second is exactly the opposite. The remaining two approaches are more specific and provide a description that is consistent with what policy makers seem to have done. Both imply that 'bright idea' and manipulated emergence are strategies consciously chosen to deal with uncertainty about how to design new arrangements and to overcome potential opposition. These are plausible assumptions, though we should note that they have not yet been investigated in detailed research.

Further reading

The encyclopaedic volume by Parsons (1995) is a vital resource for students of public policy theory, though not a linear read. John's (1998) book assesses a range of theoretical approaches. For empirical studies of policy making in the NHS see Marinetto (1999). Kingdon's (1984) book-length treatment of agenda setting provides empirical case study material to examine policy processes in a US context. For evaluation of policy processes Pawson and Tilley (1997) is recommended.

Chapter 7

The Politics of Contradiction:
Three Case Studies

Summary of chapter contents

- Policy tensions: consumerism and evidence-based medicine, devolution and uniformity, choice and health inequalities
- NHS policymaking: history and contemporary developments
- Interpreting the contemporary policy process

In this final chapter, we depart from the formula employed in earlier chapters in order to present three case studies that illustrate significant contradictions in the contemporary politics of healthcare. The first case examines the tensions created by simultaneously applying separate and contradictory policies, namely the prioritisation of both lay (consumerist) and expert ('evidence-based') opinions. The stories of the drug beta interferon and the measles-mumps-rubella 'triple vaccine' are told in some detail in order to illustrate the twists and turns of real politics. The second case examines the devolution of control of the NHS in Scotland and Wales to new executive bodies, consequent upon the creation of elected assemblies as part of wider political devolution in the UK. We examine the consequences for both NHS organisation and for the pursuit of uniformity of healthcare provision and access. The third case goes beyond geographical variations in access to treatment to examine the wider issue of health inequalities and the way in which policies for addressing them seem to be constrained by New Labour's political and ideological commitment to the 'third way'. Our final section briefly reflects on the politics of contradiction.

Consumerism and evidence-based medicine

The potential tension between policies that stress consumerism and patient participation on the one hand, and evidence-based medicine on the other hand is clear. Crudely, the first suggests that people should have the services that they desire, whilst the second suggests that they should receive the services that (according to the evidence) are good for them. In principle, the contradiction can be overcome if people come to appreciate and value the evidence, thereby bringing demands into line with it. In this section, we present two recent cases that illustrate that it is by no means guaranteed that healthcare consumers will demand what the evidence suggests would be good for them. The cases concern, respectively, the drug beta interferon employed in the treatment of multiple sclerosis (MS) and the measles-mumps-rubella (MMR) triple vaccine for children. In the former case, many patients wished to consume despite the 'scientific' evidence of poor cost effectiveness; in the latter case, many parents wished to avoid the vaccine for their children despite lack of any 'scientific' evidence that the vaccine can trigger autism.

Beta interferon and relapsing-remitting multiple sclerosis

Clinical trials have shown that beta interferon reduces the frequency of relapse in relapsing-remitting MS patients and may influence the duration of relapse (NICE, 2002: 4), but economic evaluations of the drug suggest rather low levels of cost effectiveness (Forbes et al., 1999; Nicholson and Milne, 1999; Parkin et al., 1998). Even before it was licensed for use in the UK, the high unit cost of the drug and estimates that it would consume 10 per cent of the national drug budget (New, 1996) had begun to fuel concern at the Department of Health. Following the launch of the drug in 1996, a number of health authorities took decisions not to fund treatment, but in 1997, two months after Labour's election victory, the High Court ruled against North Derbyshire Health Authority's decision to deny drug treatment to MS patients (Dyer, 1997). When the initial work programme for NICE was produced in 1999, beta interferon was listed as one of the first technologies to be appraised. As NICE subsequently acknowledged, the process was much more protracted than initially envisaged (NICE, 2002).

The process began with the request from the Department of Health and the National Assembly for Wales to appraise the drug in August 1999. NICE wrote to interested parties (manufacturers, national patient/carer groups and professional bodies) on the same day asking that any submissions to NICE regarding the drug should be made by November 1999, although this deadline was subsequently extended to February 2000 following discussions between the manufacturers and the two government departments (NICE, 2001). NICE also commissioned a review of the published evidence of clinical and cost effectiveness from the Northern and Yorkshire Drug and Therapeutic Centre. All of this information was considered at the first meeting of the Appraisal Committee held in May 2000. Following this, the Committee prepared its Provisional Appraisal Determination (PAD) which it circulated to consultees as strictly confidential material. However, the findings along with those for Glatiramer acetate, another drug for the treatment of MS, were leaked to BBC News in June

2000. Their discussion in a BBC news item prompted NICE to issue a press release the following day confirming 'that other than for those patients who are already receiving these medicines, they should not be made available in the NHS at the present time. This is because, on the basis of a very careful consideration of the evidence, their modest clinical benefit appears to be outweighed by their very high cost.' Meanwhile BBC News reported the comments of Peter Cardy, the Chief Executive of the MS Society: 'I can only say that there are going to be tens of thousands of people waking up this morning with the icy fingers of dread closing round their hearts. [NICE]… has taken away from them the only hope they have ever had of relief from this disease' (BBC, 2000). The Conservative health spokesman accused the government of distorting the workings of NICE by 'slipping in affordability' as one of the criteria it considered and turning NICE into an 'arms-length rationing mechanism for ministers.' In the context of emotive media images and criticism from political opponents, the Prime Minister responded in the House of Commons by defending the need to consider affordability as a general principle, and pointing to the large increase in NHS resources since Labour's election victory.

In July the Appraisal Committee met to consider its provisional determination in the light of feedback from consultees and agreed a Final Appraisal Determination (FAD) which was submitted to NICE and circulated to consultees. In addition to MS patient groups, the Royal College of Nursing, the Association of British Neurologists and various pharmaceutical companies all submitted appeals against the FAD. The NICE Appeal Panel decision published in November 2000 upheld appeals on a number of grounds, including failure by the Appraisal Committee to explain the basis of its conclusion that beta interferon was 'not cost effective, when compared with alternative uses of current resources', and acceptance that the long-term benefits of treatment with beta interferon may not have received full consideration. The Appraisal Committee had expressed serious reservations about the economic models submitted, but maintained that, 'on the basis of current evidence, neither beta interferon nor glatiramer is cost-effective for the NHS'. In addition, new evidence was also presented for consideration by the manufacturers of the drug. All of this resulted in a decision by NICE in December 2000 to commission further economic modelling and to extend the evaluation process. In January 2001 NICE wrote to consultees requesting their views on its proposals to commission the development of a new economic model and identifying where stakeholders could become involved. Manufacturers were invited to make available further data that they might have, including patient-specific data from clinical trials.

The Appraisal Committee met in July 2001 to consider the results of the new economic modelling exercise and subsequently produced a PAD which was sent to the consultees (including patient/carer organisations, professional bodies and manufacturers) in August 2001. Because of media speculation surrounding its content, NICE's Chairman, on the recommendation of two of the Institute's Executive Directors, took the decision, in line with NICE policy, to publish the PAD on its website. Further modelling took place in response to comments from consultees and the Appraisal Committee met to agree the FAD in October 2001, sending it to consultees and publishing it on the NICE website a few days later. However, the Department of Health had already announced that it had entered into a 'risk-sharing scheme' with the pharmaceutical companies concerned under which it would fund beta interferon prescribing. Under this agreement the Department of Health would fund the drug for an agreed period during which time an assessment would be made to establish its cost-effectiveness. (NICE, 2001)

As is usual with NICE appraisals, cost effectiveness would be assessed in terms of cost per quality-adjusted life year (QALY). Although NICE has never publicly adopted a standard threshold of cost effectiveness at which it would recommend NHS adoption of a technology, a retrospective analysis of appraisal determinations in its first year suggested that positive recommendations were generally associated with a cost per QALY of £30,000 or less (Raftery, 2001). However, in view of the 'special factors' which were not quantified in reaching the FAD (such as the impact of treatment on the severity, as opposed to the frequency, of relapses and possible cost offsets against personal social services expenditure), the threshold was set at £36,000. If actual benefit is equal to or greater than this, the Department of Health will continue to purchase the drug at the price agreed at the outset of the scheme. If, however, actual benefit is less, the price to the manufacturers will be reduced to a level that restores the cost per QALY to £36,000. NICE's response was to issue a press release immediately saying that it had had no involvement in these discussions, had no knowledge of the details and was continuing with the appraisal process. The final guidance was published in February 2002 recommending on grounds of cost effectiveness that beta interferon should not be funded.

Comments by a Liberal Democrat MP in January 2002 suggesting that 'the fact the Department of Health is rushing out an announcement on its plans for "risk sharing" is a vote of no confidence in NICE' received a swift denial and by February 2002 NICE was insisting that the government had not 'over-ridden the NICE decision' since 'the [risk-sharing] scheme would not exist had not NICE undertaken its appraisal and reached the conclusion that as things stand, the drugs are not cost-effective.' Whilst government has portrayed the risk-sharing scheme as evidence-based medicine in action, critics suggest that the scheme is 'scientifically unsound' (Mayor, 2001; Sudlow and Counsell, 2003: 388). The beta interferon guidance was originally due for review in November 2004 but data are not now expected until 2007; in any case it seems unlikely that manufacturers will be required to reimburse the government if the drug proves to be ineffective, since new drugs are likely to supersede beta interferon within a few years (Sudlow and Counsell, 2003). A subsequent report from NICE cited evidence that four of its guidelines, including the use of beta interferon for MS, had been 'over-implemented' (White, 2004).

We saw in Chapter 1 that NICE seems to have been established on pragmatic grounds, largely to deal with the issue of demand for new drugs. But other pragmatic considerations have surfaced. In the case of beta interferon, the government appears to have backtracked on its commitment to evidence-based medicine when faced with the prospect of antagonising both an important patient group and the pharmaceutical industry. It was not the first time that NICE had antagonised the latter. When NICE recommended in October 1999 that the NHS should not fund the influenza drug zamanivir (Relenza) due to the inadequacy of the evidence submitted by the manufacturer, the industry's reaction was one of outrage (McDonald, 2000). A leak of NICE's decision was followed by a drop in the price of the manufacturer's shares. The company's immediate response was to announce job losses in the UK, to warn government that the policy could result in further large-scale disinvestment in its UK base, and to threaten legal action. Other drug companies joined in the protests against NICE's decision. NICE subsequently approved Relenza for use in 'at-risk adults' after a further evaluation using additional data from the manufacturer. In the case of Relenza, it seems likely that had the government not intervened, then the pharmaceutical companies who manufacture the drug would have sought a judicial review and it is possible that the manufacturers of beta interferon would have taken legal action (Crinson, 2004). A further example of government preparedness to sidestep NICE came only days after the beta inter-feron announcement. The Department of Health pre-empted any ruling by NICE on the drug imatinib mesylate (Glivec) for chronic myeloid leukaemia, writing to regional health directors saying that they should make funds available for Glivec despite the fact that NICE's appraisal was not expected for some months (Barbour, 2001).

The politics of seeming to deny the chance of benefit to patients with dread diseases such as MS or cancers are clearly seen as risky by policy makers. Highly publicised variations in access to the drug Herceptin for a specific type of breast cancer have prompted the Secretary of State for Health to intervene, first by asking NICE to fast-track its assessment of the drug in July 2005 and then in the following November, questioning a ruling by a Primary Care Trust not to fund the drug. The PCT subsequently reversed its decision. The Court of Appeal later ruled against a PCT decision to deny the drug to a patient with early-stage breast cancer, despite the PCT's argument that the drug was licensed only for the treatment of later-stage disease.

The MMR triple vaccine

Although government appears to have bowed to pressure in the case of beta interferon, con-sumerist medicine has prompted a rather different response in relation to the MMR triple vaccine. The combined MMR vaccine was introduced into the UK childhood immunisation schedule in 1988 (Badenoch, 1988). In February 1998, a group of clinical researchers pub-lished a paper in *The Lancet* reporting an association between autism and intestinal abnor-malities in 12 children and raising the possibility of a link with MMR vaccination. The authors acknowledged that the study did not prove an association between the MMR vaccine and autism, but suggested that further investigations were needed to examine the 'possible relation to this vaccine' (Wakefield et al., 1998: 641). At a press conference publi-cising the research, the lead researcher argued that it would be safer to give children the measles, mumps and rubella vaccines in three separate doses. Responding to the media cov-erage shortly after publication of the paper, the Department of Health Chief Medical Officer (CMO) sought to dispel concerns about a link between the vaccine and autism, emphasis-ing that 'immunisation policy is built on scientific evidence of benefit and risk' and strongly recommending that parents continue having their children vaccinated with the triple vaccine. He also drew attention to what he saw as the 'inevitable increased risk' of separate vaccines which would result in children being exposed to serious infections for far longer than neces-sary, due to the necessity of spacing them out (Calman, 1998). This statement was faxed to all GPs, doctors, nurses, health visitors and pharmacists involved in the immunisation programme and to all health authorities and NHS Trusts. It contained a joint statement from the BMA and several medical royal colleges and nursing organisations fully supporting the Chief Medical Officer's advice and strongly advising all parents to continue with the present MMR vaccination programme.

The following month, a group of around 30 experts in virology, gastroenterology, psychiatry and epidemiology met at the request of the CMO. It concluded that there was no evidence of a link between the triple vaccine and autism or bowel disease, and that there was no reason to amend the current MMR vaccination policy. In June 1999 a large study, involving nearly 500 children and conducted by researchers from the same hospital as the original study, found no evidence of a causal association between MMR vaccine and autism (Taylor et al., 1999). In July 2000 the All-Party Parliamentary Group on Primary Care and Public Health concluded that the MMR vaccine was safe and expressed concerns about the fall in uptake that had resulted from the fears about the triple vaccine.

Despite the mounting scientific consensus against a link and some scientific flaws in the original study, media coverage tended merely to indicate that there were two competing bodies of evidence rather than offering an evaluation of the case for and against (Hargreaves et al., 2003). Indeed, some commentators felt that the media had adopted an uncritical approach to the original study, portraying the lead researcher 'as a David ranged against the Goliath of the medical establishment, who has suffered personal and professional persecution as a result' (Fitzpatrick, 2002). In December 2000, the same researcher published a further paper documenting 170 cases of children who developed autism shortly after receiving the triple vaccine, concluding that 'for MMR, autism and inflammatory bowel disease, a significant index of suspicion exists without adequate evidence of safety' (Wakefield and Montgomery, 2000). At a press conference a month later the CMO dismissed these findings as highly selective by excluding studies that did not support the author's views (Unnamed, 2001). At the same time, a £3 million publicity campaign to provide information to parents and health professionals was announced.

Nevertheless, many parents continued to defer or refuse MMR vaccination for their children; the rate for England fell from over 90 percent in 1997 to 82 percent by 2002/03 (National Statistics, 2004). The media also encouraged the campaign for single vaccines, which were presented as an issue of choice and rights and were taken up in these terms by opposition politicians. Newspapers reported that some GPs, faced with financial incentives to reach target vaccination levels, were threatening to strike children off their registers if their parents failed to consent to the MMR vaccine (BBC, 2002), though the Department of Health drew attention to the right of parents to choose. However, a court case suggested that when two parents cannot agree, 'evidence-based medicine' trumps individual choice. Upholding a decision that children should receive the MMR as requested by their fathers, but despite their mothers' opposition, the judge dismissed the evidence against the vaccine as 'junk science':

> While you can never prove a negative, there was strong scientific evidence that the risks of not immunising children were real and in many instances serious – tetanus, meningitis C, mumps, measles and rubella presenting what was characterised as a plausible risk of severe illness and death. (England and Wales Court of Appeal (Civil Division) Decisions, 2003)

The refusal of the Prime Minister to declare whether or not his baby son had received the vaccine also received widespread newspaper coverage, with politicians and journalists alike calling upon him to state his position. In April 2002, a few months after this refusal to comment, demand for imports of single vaccine alternatives to the triple vaccine had increased by up to 60 times the figure for 2000 (Meikle, 2002). The (Labour) Chair of the House of Commons Science and Technology Select Committee was subsequently reported as saying that the Prime Minister 'certainly could have helped check the fall-off in vaccination levels by standing up and declaring that his son had been given it. He should have demonstrated that what was good enough for the rest of the population was good enough for his family' (Rogers and O'Reilly, 2004).

The tension between government's commitment to both consumer sovereignty and 'evidence-based medicine' is reflected in its advice to parents:

> *The NHS in the 21st century recognises patients' right to choose ... Choice is a key part of NHS practice, but the Government's advisers and the Department of Health can't recommend anything that is likely to increase the risks of catching and spreading measles, mumps or rubella ... It would be wrong for the NHS to give parents options that health experts around the world advise are less safe for children. The best evidence is that MMR is the safest way to protect children against measles, mumps and rubella. (NHS Immunisation Information website www.mmrthefacts.nhs.uk/library/experts.php)*

Recent evidence suggests that fears over the vaccine are reducing, with MMR vaccination uptake rates increasing (Wilkinson, 2007).

How are we to interpret this case of tension between consumerism and evidence-based medicine? The reasons for resistance to the triple vaccine are rather different from those underlying the beta interferon case. First, mass childhood immunisation programmes with their assumptions of blind compliance sit uneasily with the discourse of patient and citizen empowerment and increased self-reliance and are easily attacked in anti-statist language. Second, it is important to note that there is a history of anti-vaccine sentiment and anti-vaccine pressure groups that goes back into the nineteenth century (Wolfe and Sharp, 2002) in part based on objections to compulsory treatment of people, especially children, who are not presently ill. The scare resulting from the publication of the 1998 *Lancet* paper can be seen as drawing on this history. Third, although parents who refuse the vaccine are depicted as acting in an irrational or unscientific manner through adopting mistaken lay perceptions of risk, they can be seen as making 'rational' calculations of risk and benefit to their children. As levels of immunisation amongst the population increase, the decision to forego vaccination may become more attractive, since whilst the unknown risk of vaccine damage remains constant, the risk of unvaccinated children becoming infected falls. Hence, if parents are not persuaded by arguments that specific risks to their offspring will be greater if they forego vaccination, they are unlikely to be swayed by arguments not to opt out of mass immunisation programmes to protect the greater good. Such arguments trade on the values of social solidarity upon which the NHS was founded, but which are somewhat at odds with the consumerist health policies promoted under New Labour. People who display little consumerist orientation with regard to other aspects of healthcare may choose to focus on risks and benefits to their own children.

Diversity and devolution

Since the 1970s, Scotland and Wales have had both separate funding arrangements and some differences in formal organisation from England (for an early comparison, see Williamson and Room, 1983). As a result, they have historically received higher levels of NHS funding per capita than England (Glennerster, 2003: 192; Greer, 2004: 28), a situation effectively institutionalised by the so-called 'Barnett formula' developed in the late 1970s. This calcu-lated a baseline allocation of funding to Scotland and Wales which is still used as the basis of increments. Thus whatever allocations are agreed between the UK Treasury and the Department of Health are applied pro rata to the population of the other countries (Stewart, 2004: 102; for a general discussion, see Glennerster, 2003; McLean and McMillan, 2003). This means that Scottish and Welsh allocations are not needs-based in the same sense as the English capitation formula discussed in Chapter 1. Moreover, Wales and (especially) Scotland have political cultures that, albeit for different reasons, were often less than enthu-siastic in implementing reorganisations originating in the English NHS, especially those associated with the Conservative governments of the 1980s and early 1990s (Greer, 2004: 67–9, 129–34; Stewart, 2004: 103–4). The election in 1997 of a New Labour government committed to political devolution for Scotland and Wales opened up the possibility of greater intra-Britain differences, which are the subject of this section. Devolution took different forms in the two countries.

Shortly after New Labour's election victory, a referendum was held in Scotland, asking whether there should be a Scottish parliament and, if so, whether it should have powers of taxation. Assent was given to both questions by substantial majorities (Jones et al., 2001: 272) and legislation in 1998 created the new parliament, to which the first elections were held in 1999 based, unlike Westminster elections, on proportional representation. As a con-sequence, both the initial and subsequent (2003) elections produced a Scottish Labour government that relied for a majority on support from the Liberal Democrats. Although the UK (Westminster) Parliament has overriding sovereignty and reserves to itself powers over policy areas such as defence, macroeconomic policy and social security, some policy areas, including health, are delegated to the Scottish Parliament (Stewart, 2004: 101–2), which may enact primary legislation. Indeed, health and community care is the largest single ele-ment in the Scottish Executive's budget (Marnoch, 2003: 255). The Executive has power to reallocate within its total budget and may marginally increase income tax rates, though it has not done so to date (Stewart, 2004: 103). The referendum result in Wales was only margin-ally in favour of devolution. The outcome was the creation of a National Assembly for Wales without powers of taxation, and able to enact only secondary legislation (Chaney and Drakeford, 2004: 122), though this may change in future. The Welsh Assembly Government, which is responsible for providing the NHS in Wales (Greer, 2004: 133), has a budget the bulk of which relates to health and other areas of social policy (Chaney and Drakeford, 2004: 122–4). The first term of the Assembly produced a Labour/Liberal Democrat coalition Executive, whilst the subsequent (2003) election produced a narrow Labour majority. It is important to note that both Scotland and Wales have nationalist parties (the Scottish National Party: SNP, and Plaid Cymru) that form the second-largest party in the Parliament and Assembly respectively (Jones et al., 2001: 272, 277), though the SNP gained seats whilst Plaid Cymru lost seats in the 2003 elections.

Substantive diversity

We can briefly summarise the diversity that has so far resulted from political devolution in Britain as taking two substantive forms; service entitlement and organisational arrangements. Both Wales and Scotland have adopted high-profile divergences from England in terms of patient entitlement. The divergence in Wales is stark and easily stated; prescription charges were initially frozen at their 2001 rate, halved in 2006 and, in accordance with Labour's manifesto for the 2003 Assembly elections, completely abolished in 2007 (Chaney and Drakeford, 2004: 126). A parallel move in Scotland was the abolition of charges for eye tests in 2006.

However, there has been further service divergence in Scotland that requires more explanation. First, there is some evidence that Scottish patients receive earlier access to some new treatments than do their counterparts in England and Wales, and may occasionally have access to drugs not available elsewhere in the UK. This occurs because the remit of NICE, described in Chapter 1, covers only England and Wales, though the Scottish NHS may adopt NICE guidance in respect of non-drug interventions. In place of NICE's function in relation to drugs, Scotland has the Scottish Medicines Consortium (SMC), established in 2001, which operates on a somewhat different basis from NICE. In particular, the SMC has a much shorter appraisals process, which does not involve expert witnesses at meetings, and which does not consult on draft guidance (Cairns, 2006: 136). These arrangements make it possible for the SMC to aim to produce recommendations within three months of the appearance of new drugs, whereas NICE appraisals have taken much longer. However, NICE has recently shortened its appraisal process for certain types of drug. It is also possible that the Scottish NHS may make different decisions from the English NHS in relation to drug availability. Studies that have compared the work of NICE and the SMC (Cairns, 2006; Watts, 2006) have observed that most drugs that have been considered by both bodies have received essentially similar recommendations. Nevertheless, there is no automatic reason why this should be so and where occasional differences do occur, the adverse publicity can be considerable. During 2006, the SMC made a decision to recommend the drug bortezomib as a treatment of last resort for patients with progressive multiple myeloma who had not responded to other treatments. In contrast NICE did not recommend the drug. The SMC decision was to recommend the drug for only a very narrow group of myeloma patients but one tabloid newspaper headline represented this as 'Medical apartheid: Another life-extending drug joins list of medicines given to Scots but denied the English' (Watts, 2006: 875).

Second, Scottish residents have since 2002 been universally entitled to free long-term 'personal care', that is assistance with an individual's daily personal tasks that do not require a health professional (Greer, 2004: 87). Elsewhere in Britain, such care (as opposed to healthcare, requiring professional input) is means-tested. Marnoch (2003) has documented the story of this high-profile political development, which provided the first major instance of conflict between Westminster and the Scottish Executive. Events began with the publication of the report of the Royal Commission on Long-Term Care of the Elderly (1998), which recommended that personal care should be provided from general taxation, irrespective of the recipient's means or the setting in which the care was delivered. After some delay, the recommendation was rejected by the UK government on the grounds that it would benefit those who were able to provide for themselves, rather than the poorest people (Stewart, 2004: 112). The Labour-led Scottish Executive had also planned to reject it, but found itself faced with an alliance of other parties, including the SNP and its own Liberal Democrat coalition partner, that supported the recommendation (Marnoch, 2003: 259). In mid-2001, the Executive committed itself to free care, provoking financial retaliation from an angry UK government, which refused to return to Scotland consequent savings made in the Whitehall budget (Greer, 2004: 89). The Executive's decision has been interpreted as demonstrating the necessity of the Labour Party in Scotland to accede to nationalist sentiment (and the SNP opposition's advocacy of free care) by not seeming to be controlled from Whitehall (Greer, 2004: 89; Marnoch, 2003: 258).

Organisational arrangements for the NHS can be seen both in instrumental terms, as a mechanism for delivering health services, and in expressive terms, that is as a means of expressing a wider philosophy. Thus, for instance, a preference for social co-ordination through markets (see Chapter 4) can be seen as expressing a set of both normative beliefs about the value of competition and assumptions that much of healthcare can be reduced to a set of clearly definable procedures. Decisions about how to organise the NHS in Scotland and Wales are therefore more than just technical decisions but express political values too. As noted above, organisational differences between England and Scotland (less so in the case of Wales) predate political devolution. Whilst there was little formal flexibility in policies set in Westminster, the dependence on local collaborators at the implementation stage created opportunities for dilution or divergence in the execution of policy. For example, the creation of the quasi-market met with much resistance from the medical profession in Scotland (Forbes, 1999). Although NHS Trusts were created in spite of this opposition, GPFH required the active support of the doctors concerned and thus made little progress (Greer, 2004: 79). Resistance to market reforms can be understood as a response by Scottish medical elites to threats to their power base, but resistance was not confined to the medical profession. Managers were reluctant to promote competition, preferring instead to pursue collaboration and stability. The quasi-market reforms can be seen as diametrically opposed to the values of collective responsibility and benevolent authoritarianism which underpin Scottish social welfare institutions and are reflected in the actions of elites involved in these institutions (Greer, 2004). The idea of the health 'consumer' at the heart of market reforms sits uneasily in a system which has traditionally been characterised by a willingness to take responsibility for its population and to decide what is in their best interests. It is understandable, therefore, that following devolution, Scotland's health system has begun to diverge significantly from the increasingly market-based model in existence in England. Moreover, the Scottish Executive inherited a structure that was already beginning to diverge from England in the sense of being more hierarchical and less market-oriented, as local policy makers prepared for devolution. After devolution, Trusts and the purchaser/provider split itself were abolished and replaced by integrated geographically organised bodies with an emphasis on engaging clinicians through 'managed clinical networks' (Greer, 2004: 79–82) defined as

> linked groups of health professionals and organisations from primary, secondary and tertiary care, working in a co-ordinated manner, unconstrained by existing professional and [organisational] boundaries, to ensure equitable provision of high quality clinically effective services throughout Scotland. (Scottish Executive, 1999)

Such networks have been created to redesign health services, each network focusing on a specific condition (such as stroke or diabetes) or treatment for a condition (for example, intravenous nutrition). There are no FTs in Scotland. In summary, the new Scottish arrangements can therefore be seen as emphasising professionalism rather than management or competition (Greer, 2004: 63ff) and as resisting the English NHS's involvement with the private sector, though without rejecting PFI schemes. In 2005 the Scottish Executive (2005b) launched *Delivering for Health*, a response to *Building a Health Service Fit for the Future: a National Framework for Service Change in the NHS in Scotland,* (Scottish Executive, 2005a), a report prepared by the National Framework Advisory Group under the chairmanship of Professor David Kerr. Both the 'Kerr Report' and the Scottish Executive's response recommended changes to the design and delivery of healthcare to address challenges such as an aging population and inequalities in access to care and health outcomes. The themes of partnership working and the shifting of some services closer to patients, into communities and away from hospitals, echo similar trends in English health policy. However, unlike in England these changes have not been accompanied by major reorganisations or market style reforms, although 'tariffs' are to be used as the means of benchmarking costs and reimbursing cross-boundary flows.

In early 2007, with the next Scottish Parliamentary election in prospect, the Scottish Executive decided to pay in full the staff pay award which was to be paid only in stages in England (*BMA News*, 24 March 2007: 4). Scotland's implementation of a ban on smoking in enclosed public places in 2006 also preceded similar bans in Wales (April 2007) and England (July 2007). Due to the system of proportional representation in the Scottish parliament, Scottish Socialists and Greens have a significant presence, which helps shape some of the debates and may explain why a greater emphasis appears to have been placed on issues such as health inequalities and the role of poverty in Scottish health policy.

Compared with Scotland and England, medical elites have played a much smaller role in influencing Welsh health policy. The Welsh Assembly government inherited a pre-devolution history of attempts to integrate health and other relevant services locally, and to address the wider determinants of health outcomes, though this approach had suffered setbacks under the Conservative government of the mid-1990s (Greer, 2004: 135–7). Although the quasi-market was introduced in Wales, GPFH was relatively poorly supported (Greer, 2004:

134). The Assembly's approach since devolution has been to reject strong performance management and foundation hospitals and avoid private sector involvement in provision of services. PFI schemes were not pursued as vigorously as in other parts of the UK (Greer, 2004: 154) and may not be employed in future (Chaney and Drakeford, 2004: 134–5). In contrast to the centralised, top down processes in England, Welsh health policy emphasises localism and trust in public service employees, joint working with local government and collaboration with health service providers. Although (unlike in Scotland) health boards will continue to act as commissioners of care, maintaining an arms length relationship with NHS trusts, there are no FTs (Chaney and Drakeford, 2004: 134–5), and so far no payment-by-results and no practice-based commissioning. Health boards have boundaries coterminous with those of local authorities, and there are requirements for these bodies to jointly formulate and implement a 'Health, Social Care and Well Being Strategy' for their area. The Welsh approach to integration therefore differs from the Scottish approach, concentrating instead on the local community integration (Greer, 2004: 128ff) rather than professional integration. As we noted in Chapter 5, CHCs have been retained in Wales, and indeed strengthened (2004: 127).

The logic of political devolution is that the polities to which power is devolved will decide to proceed in different ways. This has proved to be the case with both the organisation of the NHS and with a small number of potentially high-profile aspects of patient entitlement. We can explore the significance of this divergence from three perspectives. First, and most obvious, there is a tension between the UK government's strongly espoused aspiration to end 'postcode rationing' and its pursuit of political devolution, a pursuit that could hardly fail to result precisely in intra-UK postcode rationing. Indeed, it is perhaps surprising that the divergence has not been greater. Second, we can examine the organisational divergence in instrumental terms, asking about its impact on patients and the public. This is not an easy question to answer, both because of the difficulty in procuring comparable data across the UK (Alvarez-Rosete et al., 2005) and because it is not clear what outcomes we should look for, or over what period. One preliminary attempt to make such comparisons has concluded that the single striking difference is the relative success of the English NHS in reducing waiting times compared with Wales, where such times had increased between 1996–7 and 2002–3 (no comparable Scottish data were available) (Alvarez-Rosete et al., 2005: 949). Given the heavy emphasis in the English NHS on waiting times as a key performance measure, this outcome is perhaps to be expected. Otherwise, the study found no changes in health indicators that might be attributable to devolution, though the pattern of changes in public satisfaction with various aspects of the NHS over the same period seems to favour England (2005: 949). Perhaps ironically, the Welsh approach of focusing on local planning, the wider determinants of health and social care rather than the target-driven regime operated in England, has been singled out by the Welsh auditor general as a factor contributing to widening inequalities in access to care between Wales and the rest of Britain (National Audit Office Wales, 2005). This seems to have led to the replacement of the Welsh Health Minister by a physician committed to greater emphasis on central planning and performance management, including waiting times, and perhaps an example of re-convergence within the UK. Finally, we can regard the divergence of Scotland and Wales from England in expressive terms, that is as a manifestation of underlying political cleavage. The implication is that the ideology of the 'third way' has less purchase in Scotland and Wales than in England, despite the fact that the largest parties in the Scottish parliament and the Welsh Assembly were until the May 2007 elections nominally the same as in the UK government. Following these elections the Scottish Nationalists became the largest party (with 47 seats, compared with 46 seats for the Labour Party), with Alex Salmond, the SNP leader, becoming first minister. In Wales, the Assembly election also resulted in a significant shift in the distribution of seats between parties. Labour remains the largest party and formed a government despite losing its overall majority due to the failure of opposition parties to agree a coalition deal. At the time of writing, it is too early to draw conclusions on the likely impact of these changes on health policy.

Choice, responsibilisation and health inequalities

Health inequalities are not a new phenomenon; evidence of an inverse relationship between socioeconomic status and health dates back to ancient times (Whitehead, 1997). Despite steady overall improvements in life expectancy over the last century, and the formal claims of the NHS to provide universal access to comprehensive healthcare, 'the distribution of ill-health continues to follow the contours of disadvantage' (Graham, 2000: 6). Strictly speaking 'health inequalities' denote an empirical state of affairs, without any attached value judgement; for instance, it is just a matter of fact that life expectancy at birth is higher than life expectancy at 60 years of age. In contrast, the phrase 'health inequity' denotes 'differences in health which … are considered unfair and unjust' (Whitehead, 1990: 5; see Harrison and Hunter, 1994: 54–61 for a discussion of more precise operationalisations of the term). However, the health policy discourse usually employs the term 'health inequalities', so we have retained this usage in what follows.

The recent history of UK health policy concern with health inequalities can perhaps be seen as dating from the Working Group on Inequalities in Health, established in 1977 under the chairmanship of Sir Douglas Black, formerly Chief Scientist at the Department of Health and at the time President of the Royal College of Physicians. The resulting Black Report (Black et al., 1980) highlighted marked differences in mortality rates between occupational classes, for both sexes and at all ages, including perinatal and infant mortality. The Report's comparison of mortality rates between 1951 and 1971 showed a steady improvement in social classes I and II (respectively, professional and intermediate professional/management), whereas in classes IV and V (respectively, semi-skilled and unskilled workers) they had either changed very little or had deteriorated. It also noted a class gradient for most specific causes of death and for self-reported rates of longstanding illness. The report also found inequalities in the use of services, with 'severe under-utilisation by the working classes', especially in relation to preventive services, and the receipt of less good primary care (1980: 198). The report also stressed the importance of 'specific features of the socio-economic environment … such as work accidents, overcrowding [and] … smoking which are strongly class-related … and also have clear causal significance' (1980: 199). However, it went on to conclude that *there is undoubtedly much which cannot be understood in terms of the impact of so specific factors, but only in terms of the more diffuse consequences of the class structure: poverty, working conditions, and deprivation in its various forms. (Black et al., 1980: 199)*

In addition to a radical overhaul of health services to achieve a better match between utilisation and need, the report also called for a wide range of measures to be taken outside the NHS to improve the material conditions of poorer groups in society. The report had been commissioned by a Labour government, but was submitted to the relatively new Conservative administration in 1980. It was not welcomed. Notoriously, it was published in a limited quantity in typescript form, without widespread press notification or distribution to the NHS, on the day before a public holiday (Townsend and Davidson, 1982: 4). In its Foreword, the Secretary of State effectively rejected the report:

It will be seen that the Group has reached the view that the causes of health inequalities are so deep-rooted that only a major and wide-ranging programme of public expenditure is capable of altering this pattern ... I cannot ... endorse the Group's recommendations. I am making the report available for discussion, but without any commitment by the government to its proposals. (Jenkin, 1980)

Throughout the 1980s the Conservative government rejected the idea that health inequality was related to material conditions, citing factors such as individual behaviour and statistical artefact as alternative explanations (Baggott, 2000). Much of the data used to inform the Black report dated from the early 1970s but *The Health Divide*, an update of the evidence published in 1987, found that the situation had:

grown worse rather than better over the last decade. There is evidence that the number of children living in poverty has increased ... that welfare benefit policy has failed to improve the living standards of poorer people to any appreciable extent and that poorer nutrition, housing and working conditions abound. (Whitehead, 1992: 393)

This report also received a cold governmental reception (Townsend et al., 1988: 7–10), though it may well have helped to stimulate research interest into what were diplomatically termed 'health variations' (Graham, 2000) and to generate new interests in ill-health as related to people's 'lifecourse' rather than static social class attributions. By the early 1990s, the government had begun to take an interest in the overall health of the nation, publishing a consultative paper of that name (Secretary of State for Health, 1992) which set out a series of targets for health improvement in such areas as coronary heart disease, stroke, cancer, mental health, sexual health and accidents, and commended collaboration between the NHS and other public agencies (for a fuller summary, see Baggott, 2000: 62–4). However, the targets were not explicitly aimed at inequalities, and it seems likely that the desired inter-agency working would have been inhibited by the co-existence of the NHS quasi-market described in Chapter 4.

New Labour and health inequalities

After its election victory in 1997, health inequalities were central in New Labour's early policy discourse; as the incoming Secretary of State for Health put it in an official press release:

Inequality in health is the worst inequality of all. There is no more serious inequality than knowing you'll die sooner because you're badly off. (Department of Health, 1997)

Whilst in opposition, the Party had continued to make political capital from Conservative inactivity in relation to health inequalities and committed itself, if elected, to commission an independent inquiry into the topic (Shaw et al., 1999: 2). The inquiry was duly commissioned in 1997, to be chaired by Sir Donald Acheson, a former Department of Health CMO. Several other relevant policy developments occurred in this immediate post-election period, including the creation of a new ministerial post for public health and of 'Health Action Zones' (HAZs) in localities of poor health, and a Green Paper (consultative document) entitled *Our Healthier Nation*, which sought to 'reject the old arguments of the past' and recognised the importance of 'social, economic and environmental factors tending towards poor health' (Department of Health, 1998: 3), aiming 'to improve the health of the worst off in particular' (1998: 2). However, it also highlighted the role of lifestyle factors, asserting that 'People can improve their own health, through physical activity, better diet and quitting smoking. Individuals and their families need to be properly informed about risk to make decisions' (1998: 3).

HAZs were established in response to competitive bids in 26 localities in 1998–9. They were intended to identify and address local health needs, develop services that were more responsive to needs, and develop inter-agency partnerships across NHS, local authority and voluntary sector boundaries. The focus varied, including clinical, behavioural and broader environmental issues, and HAZs were modestly supported by central funds for some three years, though they had originally been mooted as having up to seven years of operation (Bauld and Judge, 2002: 1–6). The principle of area-based schemes such as HAZs has been criticised by analysts on the twin grounds that earlier similar interventions have not been effective, and that even deprived areas will usually contain a majority of non-deprived individuals, so that schemes are not appropriately targeted (Shaw et al., 1999: 175–7). The official evaluation of HAZs reports mainly in terms of claims by project managers, which are themselves primarily made in terms of processes and structures rather than claims about reductions in inequality (Bauld and Judge, 2002: 287–8), though it is arguable that three years is too short a period to detect any changes. In any event, the HAZ programme has not been renewed. The Acheson report was published in 1998. Constrained by terms of reference that required it to work within the government's then rather tight financial strategy, it set out a summary of the current evidence on the extent of, and trends in, health inequalities that was generally welcomed by analysts, but produced recommendations that were unprioritised, uncosted and sometimes vague (Shaw et al., 1999: 180–1). The government response took the form of an 'action report' detailing current efforts to address specific potential causes of inequalities, such as encouraging breast feeding, healthy eating, and salt reduction, and the provision of nicotine replacement therapy, and a White Paper *Saving Lives* (Secretary of State for Health, 1999). The latter contained clear targets for improving overall population health, but not for reducing health inequalities; the latter were left to health authorities to establish locally.

However, the later *NHS Plan* announced the intention to set national inequality targets (Secretary of State for Health, 2000), which were published in 2001. The government subsequently completed a 'cross-cutting review' of health inequalities which assessed the progress that had been made and identified priorities for future action. This highlighted the link between deprivation and poor health and presented evidence that 'those in greatest need of public services often have the lowest levels of use and the poorest access' (Department of Health/HM Treasury, 2002: 6). It also identified, as had Acheson, that in order to tackle the underlying determinants of inequalities, action would be required across government. *Tackling Health Inequalities: A Programme for Action* (Department of Health, 2003c) was launched in 2003, backed by 12 government departments and intended to lay the foundation for meeting targets to reduce inequalities in infant mortality and life expectancy by 2010. However, a status report published in 2005 showed continuing widening of inequalities as measured by infant mortality and life expectancy at birth (Department of Health, 2005c). The subsequent White Paper *Our Health, Our Care, Our Say* (Secretary of State for Health, 2006) announced plans to tackle inequalities and improve access to community facilities by, for example, increasing the quality and quantity of primary care services in 'under-doctored' areas and ensuring joint working between local health and social care commissioners to understand and address local inequalities. In keeping with the rights and responsibilisation themes of previous policy documents (see Chapter 5) the White Paper promises to give people 'more choice and a louder voice' whilst at the same time encouraging them to do more to 'assess their lifestyle risks and to take the right steps to make healthier choices' (2006: 7).

In addition to all this, the New Labour government has adopted policies beyond the NHS which might be seen as addressing wider determinants of health, such as poverty and substandard housing, through such means as a national minimum wage and centrally funded renovation of local authority housing. However, critics have suggested that the minimum wage was set too low, the allocation for housing renovation inadequate, and welfare reform policies (such as 'New Deals' for groups such as the unemployed and the disabled and attempts to reduce the numbers claiming invalidity benefit) seek to curb welfare spending, rather than improving the lot of marginalised groups. The number of children living in poverty has reduced since 1998, though still falls far short of the aspiration to halve child poverty levels by 2010–11. Income inequality initially rose after 1997, before falling in 2004–05 to a similar level to 1996–97. A recent report from the Institute for Fiscal Studies observes 'the net effect of eight years of Labour government has been to leave inequality effectively unchanged' (Brewer et al., 2006: 1). New Labour also established a Social Exclusion Unit (some of whose projects were health related) though income inequalities were not within its remit (Shaw et al., 1999: 184).

There are two broad, and perhaps complementary, explanations for the evident gap between government aspirations to reduce health inequality and its relative lack of success.

First, there is a puzzlement factor; in comparison to other NHS targets (such as reducing waiting lists for inpatient care) an understanding of the relationship between policy and outcomes is more uncertain, especially since many of the factors contributing to health inequalities lie outside the remit of the NHS. Thus available explanations of health inequalities include; lifestyle and environment differences between social classes, health as a determinant of class (sick people are forced into lower-class occupations and *vice versa*), unemployment, housing quality, cultural and/or genetic differences between ethnic groups, income inequality, changing gender roles, and geographical differences in deprivation (for summaries, see Baggott, 2000: 226–35). The policy implications of these various explanations differ considerably, ranging across the use of taxation to compress income differentials, disincentivising unhealthy behaviour, improving welfare benefits, and investing in public housing. Second, many such measures are, as Shaw et al. (1999: 183) put it, not seen as 'practical politics'. Increased taxation of higher incomes would risk alienating 'middle England', whilst others (such as tobacco or alcohol control, or new food standards) would threaten capitalist enterprises and thus economic growth.

These difficulties mean that despite measures such as those described above, a good deal of the policy burden of health inequalities has been deflected onto the NHS, where it has three manifestations, all of which are consonant with 'third way' assumptions. First, the opening-up of markets to private healthcare providers has been seen as a means of improving access to care, both in general and specifically in 'under-doctored' areas, respectively through creation of the 'independent sector treatment centres' and 'alternative provider medical services' (described in Chapter 4). Second, there has been a continuing discourse about individuals' responsibility for their own health. As we saw in Chapter 1, the 'fully engaged scenario' outlined in the Wanless reports involves individuals taking much greater responsibility for their own health, resulting in a reduced requirement for health services and better health for all, with life expectancy increasing and expenditure requirements estimated at under half of current NHS expenditure. However, the differential distribution of wealth and income in society means that for many individuals the ability to exercise healthy choices is severely constrained. Furthermore, it is not clear that such approaches will result in the reduced demand for care intended. Estimates suggest that about 25 percent of the health of a developed population is attributable to the healthcare system, with the remainder determined by the social and economic environment, the physical environment and human biology and genetic endowment (Canadian Institute for Advanced Research, 1997). Third, equality has effectively become reconceptualised as the equal right of patient choice, for instance through the right to choose a health service provider described in Chapter 5. However, there is a good deal of evidence to suggest that the expansion of patient choice will have an adverse effect on equality (Fotaki et al., 2005), mainly because wealthy and articulate populations are better able to take advantage of choice (Mukamel et al., 2004). Publishing performance data in order to allow healthcare consumers to make informed choices has been shown to benefit more affluent patients who are more likely to act on this information (for a review of this literature see Fotaki et al., 2005).

In summary, New Labour's ideological attachment to the 'third way' and its underlying assumptions can be seen as having constrained its attempts to address health inequalities, by directing them largely away from income redistribution and measures perceived as damaging to industry, and into NHS policy. Whilst some elements of the latter, such as ensuring more equal provision of primary care services, are clearly capable of genuinely addressing some aspects of inequalities in access to services, other elements seem simply to repeat the preference of previous governments for treating inequalities as remediable at the level of the behaviours of individuals.

Concluding remarks

Our cases of the politics of contradiction illustrate a truism of policy and politics; action taken on one agenda often has consequences for other agendas. Second, our cases show how highly political healthcare has become. It is notable that our cases are all in some sense about 'fairness', perhaps the most contested of normative political concepts. Is it more important that people should have the services that they want or that some overarching rationality should be applied? How important is it for citizens of the UK to be treated alike? If it is important, then how meaningful are ideas about devolution, or indeed administrative decentralisation more generally? And how much social and economic 'engineering' can the state realistically attempt in order to protect its least powerful subjects? Finally, contradictions may be resolved in various ways, or indeed may simply persist. The beta interferon and health inequalities contradictions have been dealt with, respectively by an ad hoc policy modification and by wholesale redefinition of the problem as something that can be addressed by existing policy approaches. The MMR vaccine problem has died down, partly over the course of time and partly as a result of firm resistance by the government, though history suggests that controversy will recur with future vaccines. The UK government has not concerned itself with differences in organisational philosophy, and there is perhaps a suggestion that Welsh policy is moving marginally towards that of England. Intra-UK variations in service entitlement have so far caused only brief media controversies, but the logic of devolution is that they will further widen over time, thereby providing a potent source of future political controversy.

Further reading

The edited volume by Graham (2000) provides various chapters examining health inequalities in the context of policy development and policy impact. For devolution and health policy, Greer (2004) provides a comparison of health policy in the territories of the UK and charts its divergence since devolution. More details on NICE appraisal processes and the clash between consumers and NICE can be found in the various documents which outline appraisals, evidence and debate on the NICE website at www.nice.org.uk/

Glossary of abbreviations

AHCPR – Agency for Health Care Policy and Research (USA)
BMA – British Medical Association
BRMA – Board of Registration of Medical Auxiliaries
CHC – Community Health Council
CMB – Central Midwives' Board
CMO – Chief Medical Officer (of Department of Health)
CPPIH – Commission for Patient and Public Involvement in Health
CPSM – Council for Professions Supplementary to Medicine
DHSS – Department of Health and Social Security (Department of Health after 1988)
DRG – Diagnosis-related group (casemix measure)
EBM – Evidence-based medicine
EBP – Evidence-based practice
EPP – Expert Patient Programme
FAD – Final Appraisal Determination (by NICE)
FT – Foundation Trust
GDP – Gross domestic product
GMC – General Medical Council
GNC – General Nursing Council
GP – General (Medical) Practitioner
GPFH – General Practice Fundholder/Fundholding
HAZ – Health Action Zone
HRG – Healthcare resource group (casemix measure)
ICAS – Independent Complaints Advocacy Service
LINk – Local involvement network
MMR – measles, mumps, rubella ('triple' vaccine)
MS – multiple sclerosis
NHS – National Health Service
NICE – National Institute for Clinical Excellence, renamed National Institute for Health and Clinical Excellence in April 2005
NPM – New public management
NSF – National Service Framework
OSC – Overview and Scrutiny Committee
PAD – Provisional Appraisal Determination (by NICE)
PALS – Patient Advice and Liaison Service
PBC – Practice-based Commissioning
PCG – Primary Care Group

PCT – Primary Care Trust
PFI – Private finance initiative
PPIF – Patient and Public Involvement Forum
QALY – Quality-adjusted Life Year
QOF – Quality and Outcomes Framework
R and D – Research and development
RCT – Randomised controlled trial
SMC – Scottish Medicines Consortium
TPPC – Total Purchasing in Primary Care
UK – United Kingdom (England, Scotland, Wales, Northern Ireland)
UKCC – UK Central Council for Nursing, Midwifery and Health Visiting
US – United States (of America)

References

Aaron, H.J. and Schwartz, W.B. (1984) *The Painful Prescription: Rationing Hospital Care*. Washington, DC: Brookings Institution.

Abbott, A.D. (1988) *The System of Professions: An Essay on the Division of Expert Labour*. Chicago, IL: University of Chicago Press.

Abel-Smith, B. (1960) *A History of the Nursing Profession*. London: Heinemann.

Abraham, J. (1997) 'The science and politics of medicines regulation' in M.A. Elston (ed.), *The Sociology of Medical Science and Technology*. Oxford: Blackwell.

Abraham, J. and Lewis, G. (2001) *Regulating Medicines in Europe: Competition, Expertise and Public Health*. London: Routledge.

Addicott, R., McGivern, G., and Ferlie, E. (2006) '"Joined-up" knowledge management through managed clinical networks', *Public Money and Management*, 26(2): 87–94.

Agency for Health Care Policy and Research (AHCPR) (1993) *Acute Pain Management: Operative or Medical Procedures and Trauma*. Publication 92-0023. Rockville, MD: United States Department of Health and Human Services.

Albrecht, G., Fitzpatrick, R. and Scrimshaw, S. (eds) (2000) *The Handbook of Social Studies in Health and Medicine*. New York: Sage.

Alford, R.R. (1975) *Health Care Politics*. Chicago, IL: University of Chicago Press.

Alford, R.R. and Friedland, R. (1985) *Powers of Theory: Capitalism, the State and Democracy*. Cambridge: Cambridge University Press.

Allen, D.E. (1979) *Hospital Planning: the Development of the 1962 Hospital Plan*. Tunbridge Wells: Pitman Medical.

Allison, G.T. (1971) *Essence of Decision: Explaining the Cuban Missile Crisis*. Boston, MA: Little, Brown.

Allsop, J. (2002) 'Regulation and the medical profession', in J. Allsop and M. Saks (eds), *Regulating the Health Professions*, 79–93. London: Sage.

Allsop, J. and Mulcahy, L. (1996) *Regulating Medical Work: Formal and Informal Controls*. Buckingham: Open University Press.

Allsop, J. and Saks, M. (eds) (2002) *Regulating the Health Professions*, 79–93. London: Sage.

Allsop, J., Jones, K. and Baggott, R. (2004) 'Health consumer groups in the UK: A new social movement?', *Sociology of Health & Illness*, 26(6): 737–56.

Alvarez-Rosete, A., Bevan, G., Mays, N. and Dixon, J. (2005) 'Effect of diverging policy across the NHS', *British Medical Journal*, 331: 946–50.

Alvesson, M. and Lindkvist, L. (1993) 'Transaction costs, clans and corporate culture', *Journal of Management Studies*, 30(3): 427–52.

Andersen, T.F. and Mooney, G.H. (eds) (1990) *The Challenge of Medical Practice Variations*. Basingstoke: Macmillan.

Annandale, E. (1989) 'Proletarianisation or restratification of the medical profession? The case of obstetrics', *International Journal of Health Services*, 19(4): 611–34.

Appleby, J. (1992) *Financing Health Care in the 1990s*. Buckingham: Open University Press.

Appleby, J. and Boyle, S. (2001) 'Extra time', *Health Service Journal*, 1(Nov.): 22–5.

Appleby, J., Harrison, A. and Dewar, S. (2003) 'Patients choosing their hospital may not be fair and equitable', *British Medical Journal*, 326: 406–7.

Argyris, C. and Schon, D.A. (1977) *Theory in Practice: Increasing Professional Effectiveness*. San Francisco, CA: Jossey-Bass.

Armstrong, D. (1976) 'Decline of the medical hegemony: a review of government reports during the NHS', *Social Science and Medicine*, 10: 157–63.

Armstrong, D. (1983) *The Political Anatomy of the Body*. Cambridge: Cambridge University Press.

Arnstein, S. (1969) 'A ladder of citizen participation', *Journal of the American Institute of Planners*, 35(4): 216–24.

Ascher, K. (1987) *The Politics of Privatisation: Contracting Out Public Services*. London: Macmillan.

Ashburner, L. and Cairncross, L. (1993) 'Membership of the "new style" health authorities: continuity of change?', *Public Administration*, 71(3): 357–75.

Ashe, F., Finlayson, A., Lloyd, M., Mackenzie, I., Martin, J. and O'Neill, S. (1999) *Contemporary Social and Political Theory: An Introduction*. Buckingham: Open University Press.

Bachrach, P. and Baratz, M.S. (1962) 'The two faces of power', *American Political Science Review*, 56: 947–52.

Bacon, R.W. and Eltis, W.A. (1976) *Britain's Economic Problem: Too Few Producers*. London: Macmillan.

Badenoch, J. (1988) 'Big bang for vaccination', *British Medical Journal*, 297: 750–1.

Baggott, R. (1995) *Pressure Groups Today*. Manchester: Manchester University Press.

Baggott, R. (2000) *Public Health: Policy and Politics*. London: Macmillan.

Baggott, R. (2004) *Health and Health Care in Britain, third edition*. London: Palgrave Macmillan.

Baggott, R. (2005) 'A funny thing happened on the way to the forum? Reforming patient and public involvement in the NHS in England', *Public Administration*, 83(3): 533–51.

Baggott, R. Allsop, J. and Jones, K. (2005) *Speaking for Patients and Carers: Health Consumer Groups and the Policy Process*. Basingstoke: Palgrave Macmillan.

Baker, M.R. and Kirk, S. (eds) (1996) *Research and Development for the NHS: Evidence, Evaluation and Effectiveness*. Oxford: Radcliffe Medical Press.

Barbalet, J.M. (1988) *Citizenship*. Milton Keynes: Open University Press.

Barbour, V. (2001) 'Imatinib for chronic myeloid leukaemia: a NICE mess', *Lancet*, 358: 1478.

Bardsley, M., Coles, J. and Jenkins, L. (1987) *DRGs and Health Care: the Management of Case Mix*. London: King's Fund.

Barnes, B., Bloor, D. and Henry, J. (1996) *Scientific Knowledge: a Sociological Analysis*. London: Athlone Press.

Barnes, M. (1999a) 'Users as citizens: collective action and the local governance of welfare', *Social Policy and Administration*, 33(1): 73–90.

Barnes, M. (1999b) *Building a Deliberative Democracy: an Evaluation of Two Citizens' Juries*. London: Institute for Public Policy Research.

Barnes, M. and Wistow, G. (1994) 'Achieving a strategy for user involvement in community care', *Health and Social Care in the Community*, 2(6): 347–56.

Barnes, M., Harrison, S., Mort, M. and Shardlow, P. (1999) *Unequal Parties: User Groups and Community Care*. Bristol: Policy Press.

Barnes, M., Newman, J., Knops, A. and Sullivan, H. (2003) 'Constituting "the public" in public participation', *Public Administration*, 81(2): 379–99.

Barr, N. (2001) *The Welfare State as Piggy Bank: Information, Risk, Uncertainty and the Role of the State*. Oxford: Oxford University Press.

Barrett, S. and Fudge, C. (eds) (1982) *Policy and Action*. London: Methuen.

Bartlett, W., Propper, C., Wilson, D. and Le Grand, J. (eds) (1994) *Quasi-markets in the Welfare State*. Bristol: University of Bristol School for Advanced Urban Studies.

Bauld, L. and Judge, K. (2002) *Learning from Health Action Zones*. Chichester: Aeneas Press.

Bauman, Z. (1992) *Intimations of Postmodernity*. London: Routledge.

Baumgartner, F. and Jones, B. (1993) *Agendas and Instability in American Politics*. Chicago: University of Chicago Press.

BBC (2000) *MS patients 'denied drug'*, 21 June, http://news.bbc.co.uk/1/hi/health/799403.stm

BBC (2002) 'Scrap GP vaccine payments', 26 February, http://news.bbc.co.uk/1/hi/health/1842236.stm

Beck, U. (1992) *The Risk Society: Towards a New Modernity*. London: Sage.

Becker, H.S., Geer, B., Hughes, E.C. and Strauss, A.L. (1960) *Boys in White: Student Culture in Medical School*. Chicago: University of Chicago Press.

Benton, P.L., Evans. H., Light, S.M., Mountney, L.M., Sanderson, H.F. and Anthony, P. (1998) 'The development of Healthcare Resource Groups - version 3', *Journal of Public Health Medicine*, 20(3): 351–8.

Beresford, P. and Croft, S. (1990) *From Paternalism to Participation: involving people in social services*. London: Open Services Project and Joseph Rowntree Foundation.

Beresford, P. and Croft, S. (1993) *Citizen Involvement: a Practical Guide for Change*. London: Macmillan.

Beresford, P. and Wallcraft, J. (1997) 'Psychiatric system survivors and emancipatory research: issues, overlaps and differences', in C. Barnes and G. Mercer (eds) *Doing Disability Research*. Leeds: The Disability Press.

Berg, M. (1997a) 'Problems and promises of the protocol', *Social Science and Medicine*, 44(8): 1081–8.

Berg, M. (1997b) *Rationalising Medical Work: Decision Support Techniques and Medical Practices*. Cambridge, MA: MIT Press.

Beveridge, W. (1942) *Social Insurance and Allied Services: Report*. Cmnd 6404. London: HMSO.

Bevir, M. (2003) 'Narrating the British state: an interpretive critique of New Labour's institutionalism', *Review of International Political Economy*, 10(3): 455–80.

Bevir, M. and Rhodes, R.A.W. (2003) 'Searching for civil society: changing patterns of governance in Britain', *Public Administration*, 81(1): 41–62.

Black, D., Morris, J., Smith, C. and Townsend, P. (1980) *Inequalities in Health: Report of a Research Working Group*. London: Department of Health and Social Security.

Blair, T. (1998) *The Third Way: New Politics for the New Century*. London: Fabian Society.

Blau, P.M. (1955) *The Dynamics of Bureaucracy*. Chicago, IL: University of Chicago Press.

Blaug, R. (2002) 'Engineering democracy', *Political Studies*, 50(1): 102–16.

Blears, H. (2003) *Communities in Control: Public Services and Local Socialism*. London: Fabian Society.

Blunkett, D. (2002) 'How Government can help build social capital'. Speech to the Performance and Innovation Unit Seminar on Social Capital, 28 March, http://www.homeoffice.gov.uk/civil_renewal/piuspeech.htm

BMA (1989) *Special Report of the Council of the British Medical Association on the Government's White Paper 'Working for Patients'*. London: BMA.

BMA (2004) *The BMA's Handbook of Ethics and Law*. London: BMA.

Bourdieu, P. (1986) 'The forms of capital', in J. E. Richardson (ed.), *Handbook of Theory and Research for the Sociology of Education*, pp. 241–58. New York: Greenwood Press.

Bourn, M. and Ezzamel, M. (1986) 'Organisational culture in hospitals in the National Health Service', *Financial Accountability and Management* 2(3): 203–25.

Bovens, M., Peters, B.G. and t'Hart, P. (eds) (2001) *Success and Failure in Public Governance*. Aldershot: Edward Elgar.

Bowie, C., Richardson, A. and Sykes, W. (1995) 'Consulting the public about health service priorities', *British Medical Journal*, 311: 1155–8.

Boyd, K.M. (ed.) (1979) *The Ethics of Resource Allocation in Health Care*. Edinburgh: University of Edinburgh Press.

Braverman, H. (1974) *Labor and Monopoly Capital: the Degradation of Work in the Twentieth Century*. New York: Monthly Review Press.

Braybrooke, D. and Lindblom, C.E. (1963) *A Strategy of Decision: Policy Evaluation as a Social Process*. New York: Free Press.

Brewer, M., Goodman, A., Shaw, J. and Sibieta, L. (2006) *Poverty and Inequality in Britain: 2006*. London: Institute for Fiscal Studies.

Brindle, D. (2002) 'The big picture', *NHS Primary Care Magazine*, February: 16–17.

Brittan, S. (1975) 'The economic contradictions of democracy', *British Journal of Political Science*, 5(1): 129–58.

Brook, R.H. (1991) *Health Services Research: Is It Good for You and Me?* Santa Monica, CA: RAND Corporation.

Brown, B., Crawford, P. and Hicks, C. (2003) *Evidence-Based Research: Dilemmas and Debates in Health Care*. Maidenhead: Open University Press.

Browning, G. (2000) *Lyotard and the End of Grand Narratives*. Cardiff: University of Wales Press.

Bruce, A. and Jonsson, E. (1996) *Competition in the Provision of Health Care*. Aldershot: Arena and Ashgate Press.

Burch, M. and Wood, B. (1983) *Public Policy in Britain*. Oxford: Blackwell.

Burnham, P. (2001) 'New Labour and the politics of depoliticisation', *British Journal of Politics and International Relations*, 3(2): 127–49.

Burns, T. and Stalker, G. M. (1961) *The Management of Innovation*. London: Tavistock.

Butcher, T. (2002) *Delivering Welfare*, 2nd edn. Buckingham: Open University Press.

Butler, J. (1992) *Patients Policies and Politics Before and After 'Working for Patients'*. Buckingham: Open University Press.

Butler, J. (1994) 'Origins and early development', in R. Robinson and J. Le Grand (eds), *Evaluating the NHS Reforms*. London: King's Fund Institute.

Byrne, D.S. (2004) 'Evidence-based: what constitutes valid evidence?', in A.G. Gray and S. Harrison (eds), *Governing Medicine: Theory and Practice*. Buckingham: Open University Press.

Byrne, P. (1997) *Social Movements in Britain*. London: Routledge.

Cairns, J. (2006) 'Providing guidance to the NHS: the Scottish Medicines Consortium and the National Institute for Clinical Excellence compared', *Health Policy*, 76: 134–43.

Calabresi, G. and Bobbitt, P. (1978) *Tragic Choices*. New York: Norton.

Calman, K. (1998) *MMR - Parents' Concerns and Media Interest*. CEM/CMO/98/6. London: Department of Health.

Cameron, K.S. and Freeman, S.J. (1991) 'Culture, congruence, strength and type: relationship to effectiveness', *Research in Organisational Change and Development*, 5: 23–58.

Canadian Institute for Advanced Research (1997) 'CIAR estimated health impact of determinants of health on population health status', http://www.hc-sc.gc.ca/hppb/regions/ab-nwt/pdf/pop-health_e.ppt (accessed 8 October 2003).

Canadian Taskforce on the Periodic Health Examination (1979) 'Taskforce Report: the Periodic Health Examination', *Canadian Medical Association Journal*, 121(9): 1139–254.

Carley, M. (1980) *Rational Techniques in Policy Analysis*. London: Heinemann.

Carr-Saunders, A.M. and Wilson, P.A. (1933) *The Professions*. Oxford: Oxford University Press.

Carter, N. Klein, R.E. and Day, P. (1992) *How Organisations Manage Success: the Use of Performance Indicators in Government*. London: Routledge.

Castle, B. (1980) *The Castle Diaries 1974–76*. London: Weidenfeld and Nicholson.

Cawson, A. (1982) *Corporatism and Welfare: Social Policy and State Intervention in Britain*. London: Heinemann.

Cawson, A. (ed) (1985) *Organised Interests and the State: Studies in Meso-Corporatism*. London: Sage.

CDP (1977) *Gilding the Ghetto: the State and Poverty Experiments*. London: Community Development Programme.

Central Health Services Council (1959) *The Welfare of Children in Hospital* ('Platt Report'). London: HMSO.

Centre for Reviews and Dissemination (1996) *Undertaking Systematic Reviews on Effectiveness*, Report no 4. York: University of York.

Chalmers, I. (2002) 'MRC Therapeutic Trials Committee's Report on Serum Treatment of Lobar Pneumonia: BMJ 1934', www.jameslindlibrary.org/trial_records/20th_Century/1930s/MRC_trials_commentary.html (accessed 16 February 2007).

Chandler, D. (2001) 'Active citizens and the therapeutic state: the role of democratic participation in local government reform', *Policy and Politics*, 29: 3–14.

Chaney, P. and Drakeford, M. (2004) 'The primacy of ideology: social policy and the first term of the national Assembly for Wales', in N. Ellison, L. Bauld and M. Powell (eds) *Social Policy Review 16: Analysis and Debate in Social Policy 2004*. pp. 121–42. Bristol: Policy Press.

Cherry, S. (1996) *Medical Services and the Hospitals in Britain 1860–1939*. Cambridge: Cambridge University Press.

Child, J. (1984) *Organisation: A Guide to Problems and Practice*, 2nd edn. London: Harper and Row.

Clement, L. (2003) 'The great care fiasco', *Community Care*, 22 May: 3.

Coates, D. (2002) 'Strategic choices in the study of New Labour: a response to replies from Hay and Wickham-Jones', *British Journal of Politics and International Relations*, 4(3): 479–86.

Cobb, R.W. and Elder C.D. (1972) *Participation in American Politics: The Dynamics of Agenda Building*. Boston, MA: Allyn and Bacon.

Coburn, D. (1992) 'Freidson then and now: an "internalist" critique of Freidson's past and present views of the medical profession', *International Journal of Health Services*, 22(3): 497–512.

Coburn, D., Rapport, S. and Borgeault, I. (1997) 'Decline vs retention of medical power through restratification: an examination of the Ontario case', *Sociology of Health and Illness*, 19(1): 1–22.

Cochrane, A.L. (1972) *Effectiveness and Efficiency: Random Reflections on Health Services*. London: Nuffield Provincial Hospitals Trust.

Cohen, M.D., March, J.G. and Olsen, J.P. (1972) 'A garbage can model of organisational choice', *Administrative Science Quarterly*, 72(1): 1–25.

Coiera, E. (1996) 'The Internet's challenge to health and provision', *British Medical Journal*, 312: 3–4.

Cole, A. (2005) 'UK GP activity exceeds expectations', *British Medical Journal*, 331: 536.

Cole, A. (2006) 'England to consider shake-up of medical regulation', *British Medical Journal*, 333: 163.

Colebatch, H.K. (1998) *Policy*. Buckingham: Open University Press.

Coleman, A. (2003) 'Through the looking glass: the emergence of health scrutiny', *Primary Care Report*, 5(5): 34–5.

Coleman, A.J. (2006) 'Health scrutiny, democracy and integration: part of the same jigsaw?', *Local Government Studies*, 32(2): 123–38.

Coleman, J.S. (1988) 'Social capital in the creation of human capital', *American Journal of Sociology*, 94: S95–120.

Coleman, J.S., Katz, E. and Menzel, H. (1966) *Medical Innovation: a Diffusion Study*. Indianapolis: Bobbs-Merrill.

Colwill, J. (1998) 'Professionalism and control in health services provision: some lessons from the health service in Britain', *Journal of Contemporary Health*, 7: 71–6.

Comas Herrera, A., Pickard, L., Wittenberg, R., Davies, B. and Darton, R. (2003) *Future Demand for Long Term Care 2001-2031: Projections of Demand for Older People in England*. Canterbury: University of Kent Personal Social Services Research Unit.

Commission for Health Improvement (1999) *Holding up a Mirror to Ourselves*. London: CHI.

Commission for Health Improvement (2004) *Sharing the learning on patient and public involvement from CHI's work*. London: CHI.

Committee of Enquiry into the Cost of the National Health Service (1956) *Report*. Cmnd 663. ('Guillebaud Report'). London: HMSO.

Committee of Enquiry into the Regulation of the Medical Profession (1975) *Report*. Cmnd 6018. ('Merrison Report'). London: HMSO.

Committee of the Management of Local Government (1967) *Report (Maud)*. London: HMSO.

Committee on the Functions of the District General Hospital (1969) *Report*. London: HMSO.

Common, R. (1995) 'The agencification of the civil service', in M. Mullard (ed.), *Policy Making in Britain: an Introduction*. pp. 136–59. London: Routledge.

Consumers' Association (2001) *National Institute for Clinical Excellence: A Patient-centred Inquiry*, London: Consumers' Association.

Cooper, E., Coote, A., Davies, A. and Jackson, C. (1995) *Voices off: Tackling the Democratic Deficit in Health*. London: Institute for Public Policy Research.

Coote, A. (1993) 'Public participation in decisions about health care', *Critical Public Health*, 4(1): 36–48.

Coote, A. and Lenaghan, J. (1997) *Citizens' Juries: Theory into Practice*. London: Institute for Public Policy Research.

Cooter, R. and Pickstone, J.E. (eds) (2000) *Medicine in the 20th Century*. London: Harwood.

Coulter, A. and Ham, C.J. (eds) (2000) *The Global Challenge of Health Care Rationing*. Buckingham: Open University Press.

Courpasson, D. (2000) 'Managerial strategies of domination: power in soft bureaucracies', *Organization Studies*, 21(1): 141–61.

Crenson, M.A. (1971) *The Unpolitics of Air Pollution: A Study of Non-decision Making in the Cities*. Baltimore, MD: Johns Hopkins University Press.

Crinson, I. (2004) 'The politics of regulation within the "modernized" NHS: the case of Beta Interferon and the "cost-effective" treatment of Multiple Sclerosis', *Critical Social Policy*, 24: 30–49.

Crossley, N. (1999) 'Fish, field, habitus and madness: on the first wave mental health users movement in Britain', *British Journal Of Sociology*, 50(4): 647–70.

Crossman, R. (1972) *Inside View: Three Lectures on Prime Ministerial Government*. London: Jonathan Cape.

Crouch, C. (2000) *Coping With Post-Democracy*. London: Fabian Society.

Crowley, P., Green, J., Freake, D. and Drinkwater, C. (2002) 'Primary Care Trusts involving the community: is community development the way forward?', *Journal of Management in Medicine*, 16(4): 311–22.

Currie, C. (2003) 'Clinical arithmetic', *British Medical Journal*, 327: 1418–9.

Dalton, R.J. and Kuechler, M. (eds) (1990) *Challenging the Political Order: New Social and Political Movements in Western Democracies*. Cambridge: Polity Press.

Daly, J. (2005) *Evidence-based Medicine and the Search for a Science of Clinical Care*. Berkeley, CA: University of California Press.

Davidoff, F., Haynes, B., Sackett, D. and Smith, R. (1995) 'Evidence based medicine: a new journal to help doctors identify the information they need', *British Medical Journal*, 310: 1085–6.

Davies, C. (2002) 'Registering a difference: changes in the regulation of nursing', in J. Allsop and M. Saks (eds), *Regulating the Health Professions*, pp. 108–19. London: Sage.

Davies, C. (2007) 'Grounding governance in dialogue? Discourse, practice and the potential for a new organisational form in Britain', *Public Administration*, 85(1): 47–65.

Davies, C. and Beach, A. (2000) *Interpreting Professional Self-Regulation: A History of the United Kingdom Central Council for Nursing, Midwifery and Health Visiting*. London: Routledge.

Davies, C. Wetherell, M., Barnett, E. and Seymour-Smith, S. (2005) *Opening the Box: Evaluating the Citizens Council of NICE*. London: School of Health & Social Welfare and Psychology Discipline, The Open University.

Davies, H.T.O. (1999) 'Public trust and accountability for clinical performance: lessons from the national press reportage of the Bristol hearing', *Journal of Evaluation in Clinical Practice*, 5(3): 335–42.

Davies, H.T.O., Nutley, S. and Smith, P.C. (eds) (2000) *What Works? Evidence-Based Policy and Practice in Public Services*. Bristol: Policy Press.

Davis, P. (1997) *Managing Medicines: Public Policy and Therapeutic Drugs*. Buckingham: Open University Press.

Day, M. (2005) 'UK doctors protest at extension to nurses' prescribing powers', *British Medical Journal*, 331: 1159.

Day, P. and Klein, R. (1983) 'The mobilization of consent versus the management of conflict – decoding The Griffiths Report', *British Medical Journal*, 287(6407): 1813–16.

Day, P. and Klein, R.E. (1985) 'Central accountability and local decision making: towards the new NHS'. *British Medical Journal*, 290: 1676–8.

Day, P. and Klein, R.E. (1997) *Steering But Not Rowing? The Transformation of the Department of Health: a Case Study*. Bristol: Policy Press.

Department of the Environment (1972) *The New Local Authorities: Management and Structure (Bains)*. London: HMSO.

Department of Health (1996) *Promoting Clinical Effectiveness: A Framework for Action in and through the NHS*. London: Department of Health.

Department of Health (1997) 'Government takes action to reduce health inequalities', press release no 97/192, 11 August. London: Department of Health.

Department of Health (1998) *Our Healthier Nation: A New Contract for Health*. London: Stationery Office.

Department of Health (2000a) *National Service Framework for Coronary Heart Disease*. London: Department of Health.

Department of Health (2000b) *Report into Quality and Practice within the National Health Service Arising from the Actions of Rodney Ledward* ('Ritchie Report'). London: Department of Health.

Department of Health (2001a) *Shifting the Balance of Power: Securing Delivery*. London: Department of Health.

Department of Health (2001b) *The Expert Patient: A New Approach to Chronic Disease Management for the 21st Century*. London: Department of Health.

Department of Health (2002a) *A guide to NHS foundation trusts*. London: Department of Health.

Department of Health (2002b) *Reforming NHS Financial Flows: Introducing Payment by Results*. London: Department of Health.

Department of Health (2003a) Abolition of Community Health Councils: ministerial statement. Downloaded from: http://www.doh.gov.uk/involvingpatients/ministerialstatement.htm.

Department of Health (2003b) *Choice, Responsiveness and Equity in the NHS and Social Care: A National Consultation*. London: Department of Health.

Department of Health (2003c) *Tackling Health Inequalities: A Programme for Action*. London: Department of Health.

Department of Health (2004a) *"Choose & Book" – Patient's Choice of Hospital and Booked Appointment* London: Department of Health

Department of Health (2004b) *Choosing Health: Making Healthy Choices Easier*. Cm6374. London: Stationery Office.

Department of Health (2004c) *Getting Over the Wall: How the NHS is improving the patient's experience*. London: Department of Health

Department of Health (2004a) *National Standards, Local Action: Health and Social Care Standards and Planning Framework 2005/06–2007/08*. London: Department of Health.

Department of Health (2004e) *The NHS Improvement Plan: Putting People at the Heart of Public Services*. London: Department of Health.

Department of Health (2004f) *Practice Based Commissioning: Engaging Practices in Commissioning*. London: Stationery Office.

Department of Health (2004g) *Practice Based Commissioning. Promoting Clinical Engagement*. London: Department of Health.

Department of Health (2004h) *Reconfiguring the Department of Health's Arm's Length Bodies*. London: Department of Health

Department of Health (2005a) *Commissioning a Patient-Led NHS*. Gateway ref 5312. London: Department of Health.

Department of Health (2005b) *Creating a Patient-led NHS: Delivering the NHS Improvement Plan*. London: Department of Health.

Department of Health (2005c) *Tackling Health Inequalities: Status Report on the Programme for Action*. London: Department of Health.

Department of Health (2006) *A Stronger Local Voice: A Framework for Creating a Stronger Local Voice in the Development of Health and Social Care Services*. London: Department of Health.

Department of Health and Social Security (1970) *The Future Structure of the National Health Service* (The Crossman Green Paper). London: HMSO.

Department of Health and Social Security (1972a) *National Health Service Reorganisation: England*. Cmnd 5055. London: HMSO.

Department of Health and Social Security (1972b) *Management arrangements for the reorganised National Health Service*. London: HMSO.

Department of Health and Social Security (1974) Democracy in the NHS: Membership of Health Authorities. London: HMSO.

Department of Health and Social Security (1976) *Priorities for Health and Social Services in England*. London: HMSO.

Department of Health and Social Security (1977) *The Way Forward*. London: HMSO.

Department of Health and Social Security and Welsh Office (1979) *Patients First: Consultative Paper on the Structure and Management of the National Health Service in England and Wales*. London: HMSO.

Department of Health/HM Treasury (2002) *Tackling Health Inequalities: Summary of the 2002 Cross-Cutting Review*. London: Department of Health.

Department of Health, Welsh Office, Scottish Home and Health Department, and Northern Ireland Office (1989) *Working for Patients*. Cm 555. London: HMSO.

Dewar, S. (1999) 'Viagra; the political management of rationing', in J. Appleby and A. Harrison (eds), *Health Care UK 1999/2000*. London: King's Fund.

Dewar, S. and Finlayson, B. (2002) 'Regulating the regulators', *British Medical Journal*, 324: 378–9.

Dingwall, R. (2001) *Aspects of Illness*. Aldershot: Ashgate.

Dingwall, R., Rafferty, A.M. and Webster, C. (1988) *An Introduction to the Social History of Nursing*. London: Routledge.

Dixon, J., Goodwin, N. and Mays, N. (1998) *Accountability of Total Purchasing Pilot Projects*. London: King's Fund.

Dixon, T., Shaw, M., Frankel, S. and Ebrahim, S. (2004) 'Hospital admissions, age and death: retrospective cohort study', *British Medical Journal*, 328: 1288–90.

Dodds-Smith, I. (2000) 'NICE and the ultimate decision makers: the legal framework for the prescription and reimbursement of medicines', in A. Miles, J.R. Hampton and B. Hurwitz (eds), *NICE, CHI and the NHS Reforms: Enabling Excellence or Imposing Control?* pp. 103–25. London: Aesculapius Medical Press.

Dollery, C.T. (1993) *Medicine and the Pharmacological Revolution*. London: Royal College of Physicians.

Donaldson, C. and Gerard, K. (1993) *The Economics of Health Care Financing: the Visible Hand*. London: Macmillan.

Donaldson, C. and Gerard, K. with Jan, S., Mitton, C. and Wiseman, V. (2004) *The Economics of Financing Health Care: The Visible Hand*, 2nd edition. Basingstoke: Palgrave Macmillan.

Donnison, J. (1988) *Midwives and Medical Men*. London: Heinemann.

Dopson, S. and Fitzgerald, L. (eds) (2005) *Knowledge to Action? Evidence-based Health Care in Context*. Oxford: Oxford University Press.

Douglas, M. (1985) *Risk Acceptability According to the Social Sciences*. New York: Russell Sage Foundation.

Dowie, J. and Elstein, A. (eds) (1988) *Professional Judgement: a Reader in Clinical Decision Making*. Cambridge: Cambridge University Press.

Downs, A. (1957) *An Economic Theory of Democracy*. New York: Harper and Row.

Dowswell, T., Harrison, S., Lilford, R.J. and McHarg, K. (1995) 'Health authorities use panels to gather public opinion', letter in *British Medical Journal*, 311: 1168–9.

Dowswell, T., Harrison, S., Mort, M. and Lilford, R.J. (1997) *Health Panels: A Survey*. NHS Executive Northern and Yorkshire end of award report no HSR 015.

Drever, F., Whitehead, M. and Roden, M. (1996) 'Current patterns and trends in male mortality by social class (based on occupation)' *Population Trends*, 86: 15–20. London: The Stationery Office.

Dror, Y. (1964) 'Muddling though – "science" or inertia?' *Public Administration Review*, 24: 153–7.

Drummond, M.F., Sculpher, M.J., Torrance, G.W., O'Brien, B.J. and Stoddart, G.L. (2005) *Methods for the Economic Evaluation of Health Care Programmes*, 3rd edn. Oxford: Oxford University Press.

Du Gay, P. (2000) *In Praise of Bureaucracy: Weber, Organisation, Ethics*. London: Sage.

Dunleavy, P. (1991) *Democracy, Bureaucracy and Public Choice: Economic Explanations in Political Science*. New York: Harvester Wheatsheaf.

Dunleavy, P. and O'Leary, B. (1987) *Theories of the State: the Politics of Liberal Democracy*. London: Macmillan.

Dunsire, A. (1978) *Implementation in a Bureaucracy: the Executive Process Part 1*. London: Martin Robertson and Oxford University Press.

Dworkin, R. (1994) 'Will Clinton's plan be fair?', *New York Review of Books*, 13 January: 20–5.

Dyer, C. (1997) 'Ruling on interferon beta will hit all health authorities', *British Medical Journal*, 315: 143–8.

Dyer, C. (1998) 'Bristol doctors found guilty of serious professional misconduct', *British Medical Journal*, 316: 1924.

Dyer, C. (2000) 'Gynaecologist struck off the Medical Register', *British Medical Journal*, 321: 258.

Eckstein, H. (1958) *The English Health Service: Its Origins, Structure and Achievements*. Cambridge, MA: Harvard University Press.

Eckstein, H. (1960) *Pressure Group Politics: the Case of the British Medical Association*. London: Allen and Unwin.

Edelman, M. (1971) *Politics as Symbolic Action*. New York: Free Press.

Edelman, M. (1977) *Political Language: Words that Succeed and Policies that Fail*. New York: Free Press and Institute for the Study of Poverty.

Effective Health Care (1992) *The Treatment of Persistent Glue Ear in Children*. Leeds: University of Leeds.

Effective Health Care (1994) *Implementing Clinical Practice Guidelines*. Leeds: University of Leeds Nuffield Institute for Health and University of York Centre for Reviews and Dissemination.

Effective Health Care (1995) *The Management of Menorrhagia*. Leeds: University of Leeds Nuffield Institute for Health and University of York Centre for Reviews and Dissemination.

Effective Health Care (1999) *Getting Evidence Into Practice*, 5(1). York: University of York Centre for Reviews and Dissemination.

Efficiency Unit (1988) *Improving Management in Government: the Next Steps* ('Ibbs Report'). London: HMSO.

Elder, C.D. and Cobb, R.W. (1983) *The Political Uses of Symbols*. New York: Longman.

Elizabeth, S., New, B., Hanley, B., Sang, B. and Davies, S. (1998) *Ordinary Wisdom: Reflections on an Experiment in Citizenship and Health*. London: King's Fund.

Ellis, N.D. and Chisholm, J. (1993) *Making Sense of the Red Book*, 2nd edn. London: Routledge.

Elmore, R.F. (1979) 'Backward mapping: implementation research and policy decisions', *Political Science Quarterly*, 94(4): 601–16.

Elster, J. (ed.) (1998) *Deliberative Democracy*. Cambridge: Cambridge University Press.

Elston, M.A. (1991) 'The politics of professional power', In J. Gabe M.W. Calnan and M. Bury (eds), *The Sociology of the Health Service*. London: Routledge.

Elwood, J.M. (1988) *Causal Relationships in Medicine: a Practical System for Critical Appraisal*. Oxford: Oxford University Press.

England and Wales Court of Appeal (Civil Division) Decisions (2003), *B (a child) {2003} EWCA Civ 1148 (30 July 2003) Neutral Citation No: {2003} EWCA Civ 114 Judgment: Approved by the Court for Handing Down*, http://www.quackwatch.org/03HealthPromotion/immu/mmrappeal.html.

Enthoven, A.C. (1999) *In Pursuit of an Improved NHS*. London: Nuffield Trust.

Esland, G. (1980a) 'Professionals and professionalism' in G. Esland and G. Salaman (eds), *The Politics of Work and Occupations*, pp. 213–50. Milton Keynes: Open University Press.

Esland, G. (1980b) 'Diagnosis and therapy' in G. Esland and G. Salaman (eds), *The Politics of Work and Occupations*. pp. 251–78. Milton Keynes: Open University Press.

Etzioni, A. (1967) 'Mixed scanning: a third approach to decision making', *Public Administration Review*, 27: 385–92.

Etzioni, A. (ed.) (1969) *The Semi-Professions and their Organisation*. New York: Free Press.

Etzioni, A. (1993) *The Spirit of Community: Rights, Responsibilities and the Communitarian Agenda*. London: Fontana.

Etzioni, A. (1997) *The New Golden Rule: Community and Morality in a Democratic Society*. London: Profile Books.

Evans, M. and Cerny, P.G. (2003) 'Globalisation and social policy' in N. Ellison and C. Pierson (eds), *Developments in British Social Policy 2*, pp. 19–41. Basingstoke: Palgrave.

Evans, R.G. (1990) 'The dog in the night-time: medical practice variations and health policy' in T.F. Andersen and G. Mooney (eds), *The Challenge of Medical Practice Variations*. Basingstoke: Macmillan.

Expert Working Group on Cancer to the Chief Medical Officers of England and Wales (1999) *A Policy Framework for Commissioning Cancer Services* ('Calman-Hine Report'). London: Department of Health and Welsh Office.

Exworthy, M., Powell, M. and Mohan, J. (1999) 'The NHS: quasi-market, quasi-hierarchy and quasi-network?', *Public Money and Management*, 19(4): 15–22.

Fairclough, N. (1989) *Language and Power*. London: Longmans.

Fairclough, N. (2000) *New Labour, New Language?* London: Routledge.

Faulks, K. (1998) *Citizenship in Modern Britain*. Edinburgh: Edinburgh University Press.

Ferriman, S. (2001) 'Blair backtracks on meeting EU health spending', *British Medical Journal*, 323: 1325.

Feyerabend, P. (1993) *Against Method*, 3rd edn. London: Verso.

Field, M.J. and Lohe, K.N. (eds) (1992) *Guidelines for Clinical Practice: From Development to Use by Committee on Clinical Practice Guidelines*. Washington, DC: National Academy of Science, Institute of Medicine.

Fisher, R.A. (1935) *The Design of Experiments*. Edinburgh: Oliver and Boyd.

Fishkin, J.S. (1979) *Tyranny and Legitimacy: A Critique of Political Theories*. Baltimore, MD: Johns Hopkins University Press.

Fishkin, J.S. (1997) *Voice of the People: Public Opinion and Democracy, second edition*. New Haven, CT: Yale University Press.

Fitzpatrick, M. (2002) 'MMR: injection of fear', Spiked online, January 10, http://www.spiked-online.com/Articles/00000002D39E.htm (accessed 22 May 2005).

Flynn, R. (1988) 'Political acquiescence, privatisation and residualisation in British housing policy', *Journal of Social Policy*, 17(1): 3–13.

Flynn, R. (1997) 'Quasi-welfare, associationalism and the social division of citizenship', *Citizenship Studies*, 1: 3.

Flynn, R. (2002) 'Clinical governance and governmentality', *Health, Risk and Society* 4(2): 155–73.

Flynn, R. and Williams, G. (eds) (1997) *Contracting for Health: Quasi-Markets and the National Health Service*. Oxford: Oxford University Press.

Flynn, R., Williams, G. and Pickard, S. (1996) *Markets and Networks: Contracting in Community Health Services*. Buckingham: Open University Press.

Foot, M. (1973) *Aneurin Bevan 1945–1960*. London: Paladin.

Forbes, R.B., Lees, A., Waugh, N. and Swingler, R.J. (1999) 'Population based cost utility study of interferon beta-1b in secondary progressive multiple sclerosis', *British Medical Journal* 319: 1529–33.

Forbes, T.M. (1999) *Strategic Management and NHS Hospital Trusts: Empirical Evidence from the West of Scotland*, unpublished PhD thesis, University of Glasgow.

Foster, P. and Wilding, P. (2000) 'Whither welfare professionalism?', *Social Policy and Administration*, 34(2): 143–59.

Fotaki, M., Boyd, A., McDonald, R., Roland, M., Smith, L., Edwards, A. and Elwyn, G. (2005) *Patient Choice and the Organisation and Delivery of Health Services: Scoping Exercise*. London: SDO.

Foucault, M. (1976) *The Birth of the Clinic: an Archaeology of Medical Perception*. London: Tavistock.

Foucault, M. (1991) 'Governmentality', transl. R. Braidotti revised C. Gordon in G. Burchell, C. Gordon and P. Miller (eds), *The Foucault Effect: Studies in Governmentality*, pp. 87–104. Chicago, IL: University of Chicago Press (originally published in French, 1978).

Fox, A. (1974) *Man Mismanagement*. London: Hutchinson.

Fox, R.C. (2000) 'Medical uncertainty revisited', in G. Albrecht, R. Fitzpatrick and S. Scrimshaw (eds), *The Handbook of Social Studies in Health and Medicine*, pp. 409–25. New York: Sage.

Frances, J. (1991) 'Introduction' in G. Thompson, J. Frances, R. Levacic and J. Mitchell (eds), *Markets, Hierarchies and Networks: the Co-ordination of Social Life*, pp. 1–24. London: Sage.

Freeden, M. (1999) 'The ideology of New Labour', *Political Quarterly*, 70(1): 42–51.

Freeman, R. (2000) *The Politics of Health in Europe*. Manchester: Manchester University Press.

Freemantle, N. and Harrison, S. (1993) 'Interleukin 2: the public and professional face of rationing in the NHS', *Critical Social Policy*, 13(3): 94–117.

Freidson, E. (1970a) *Professional Dominance*. New York: Atherton Press.

Freidson, E. (1970b) *Profession of Medicine: a Study of the Sociology of Applied Knowledge*. Chicago: University of Chicago Press.

Freidson, E. (1984) 'The changing nature of professional control', *Annual Review of Sociology* 10: 1–20 (reprinted in Freidson, 1994, to which page references refer).

Freidson, E. (1988) *Profession of Medicine: a Study of the Sociology of Applied Knowledge*, 2nd edn. Chicago: University of Chicago Press.

Freidson, E. (1994) *Professionalism Reborn: Theory, Prophecy and Policy*. Oxford: Polity Press.

Friend, J. and Jessop, W. (1969) *Local Government and Strategic Choice: an operational research approach to the process of public planning*. London: Tavistock.

Fukuyama, F. (1995) *Trust: the Social Virtues and the Creation of Prosperity*. London: Hamish Hamilton.

Fuller, S. (1997) *Science*. Buckingham: Open University Press.

Gabe, J., Bury, M. and Elston, M.A. (2004) *Key Concepts in Medical Sociology*. London: Sage.

Gains, F. (2004) 'Hardware, software or network connection? Theorising crisis in the UK Next Steps agencies', *Public Administration*, 82(3): 547–66.

Gardner, E. (1992) 'Requests pouring in for AHCPR's new practice guidelines', *Modern Healthcare*, 31 August: 33.

Gaze, H. (2004) 'Forums lose 11 per cent of their members', *Health Service Journal*, 17th June: 8–9 online:

Giddens, A. (1982) *Profiles and Critiques in Social Theory*. London; Macmillan.

Giddens, A. (1990) *The Consequences of Modernity*. Cambridge: Polity Press.

Giddens, A. (1991) *Modernity and Self Identity: Self and Society in the Late Modern Age*. Cambridge: Polity Press.

Giddens, A. (1998) *The Third Way: The Renewal of Social Democracy*. Cambridge: Polity Press.

Giddens, A. (2000) *The Third Way and Its Critics*. Cambridge: Polity Press.

Gilpin, R. (2001) *Global Political Economy: Understanding the International Economic Order*. Oxford: Princeton University Press.

Gladstone, D. (ed.) (2000) *Regulating Doctors*. London: Institute for the Study of Civil Society.

Glendinning, C., Dowling, B. and Powell, M. (2005) 'Partnerships between health and social care under "New Labour'" smoke without fire? A review of policy and evidence', *Evidence and Policy*, 1(3): 365–81.

Glennerster, H. (ed.) (1981). 'From containment to conflict? Social planning in the seventies', *Journal of Social Policy*, 10 (1): 31–51.

Glennerster, H. (1992) *Paying for Welfare: the 1990s*. London: Harvester Wheatsheaf.

Glennerster, H. (2003) *Understanding the Finance of Welfare: What Welfare Costs and How to Pay for It*. Bristol: Policy Press.

Glennerster, H., Matsaganis, M., Owens, P. and Hancock, S. (1994) *Implementing GP Fundholding: Wild Card or Winning Card?* Buckingham: Open University Press.

Goldacre, M.J. Lee, A. and Don, B. (1987) 'Waiting list statistics: relation between admissions from waiting list and length of waiting list', *British Medical Journal*, 295: 1105–8.

Gomm, R. (2000) 'Understanding experimental design', in R. Gomm and C. Davies (eds), *Using Evidence in Health and Social Care*. pp. 46–64. London: Open University Press and Sage.

Goodin, R.E. and Niemeyer, S.J. (2003) 'When does deliberation begin? Internal reflection versus public discussion in deliberative democracy', *Political Studies*, 51(4): 627–49.

Goodin, R.E. and Wilenksy, P. (1984) 'Beyond efficiency: the logical underpinnings of administrative principles', *Public Administration Review*, 6: 512–17.

Gough, I. (1979) *The Political Economy of the Welfare State*. London: Macmillan.

Gouldner, A.W. (1954) *Patterns of Industrial Bureaucracy*. Glencoe, IL: Free Press.

Graham, H. (2000) 'The challenge of health inequalities' in H. Graham (ed.) *Understanding Health Inequalities*. Buckingham: Open University Press.

Granshaw, L. (1992) 'The rise of the modern hospital in Britain', in A. Wear (ed.), *Medicine in Society: Historical Essays*. pp. 197–218. Cambridge: Cambridge University Press.

Grant, W. (ed.) (1985) *The Political Economy of Corporatism*. London: Macmillan.

Grant, W. (2000) *Pressure Groups and British Politics*. London: Macmillan.

Gray, B.H. (1992) 'The legislative battle over health services research', *Health Affairs*, 11(4): 38–66.

Gray, J.A.M. (1997) *Evidence-based Healthcare: How to Make Health Policy and Management Decisions*. Oxford: Churchill Livingstone.

Greco, P.J. and Eisenberg, J.M. (1993) 'Changing physicians' practices', *New England Journal of Medicine*, 329(17): 1271–3.

Greener, I. (2003) 'Patient choice in the NHS: the view from economic sociology', *Social Theory and Health*, 1(1): 72–89.

Greener, I. (2004) 'Health service organisation in the UK: a political economy approach', *Public Administration*, 82(3): 657–76.

Greenhalgh, T., Robert, G., Bate, P., MacFarlane, F. and Kyriakidou, O. (2005) *Diffusion of innovations in health service organisations*. Oxford: Blackwell.

Greer, S.L. (2004) *Territorial Politics and Health Policy: UK Health Policy in Comparative Perspective*. Manchester: Manchester University Press.

Greer, S.L. and Jarman, H. (2007) *The Department of Health and the Civil Service: from Whitehall to Department of Delivery to Where?* London: Nuffield Trust.

Gregory, R. (1989) 'Political rationality or "incrementalism"? Charles E Lindblom's enduring contribution to public policy making theory', *Policy and Politics*, 17(2): 139–53.

Griffiths, R. (1988) *Community Care: Agenda for Action*. London: HMSO.

Grimshaw, J.M. and Russell, I.T. (1993) 'Effect of clinical guidelines on medical practice: a systematic review of rigorous evaluations', *Lancet*, 342: 1317–22.

Gruer, R. Gordon, D.S. Gunn, A.A. and Ruckley, C.V. (1986) 'Audit of surgical audit', *Lancet*, 4 January: 23–5.

Gunn, L. (1978) 'Why is implementation so difficult?', *Management Services in Government*, 33: 169–76.

Guyatt, G.H. and Rennie, D. (1993) 'Users' guide to the medical literature', *JAMA*, 270: 2096–7.

Gyford, J. (1991) *Citizens, Consumers and Councils: Local Government and the Public*. Basingstoke: Macmillan.

Haas, P.M. (1992) 'Epistemic communities and international policy co-ordination', *International Organisation*, 46(1): 1–35.

Hafferty, F. (1988) 'Theories at the crossroads: a discussion of evolving views on medicine as a profession', *Milbank Quarterly*, 66, supp 2: 202–25.

Hall, P. (1980) *Great Planning Disasters*. London, Weidenfeld.

Hall, S. (2001) 'Medical scandals leave trust in doctors unshaken', *Guardian*, 7 May. Available from http://society.guardian.co.uk/nhsperformance/story/0,,487612,00.html

Hall, P., Land, H., Parker, R. and Webb, A. (1975) *Change, Choice and Conflict in Social Policy*. London: Heinemann.

Hallas, J. (1976) *CHCs in Action*. London: Nuffield Provincial Hospitals Trust.

Ham, C.J. (1980) 'Community Health Council participation in the NHS planning system', *Social Policy and Administration*, 14(3): 221–31.

Ham, C.J. (1981) *Policy Making in the National Health Service*. London: Macmillan.

Ham, C.J. (1990) *Holding on While Letting Go: A Report on the Relationship Between Directly Managed Units and DHAs*. London: King's Fund College.

Ham, C.J. (1994) *Management and Competition in the New NHS*. Oxford: Radcliffe Medical.

Ham, C. J. (2004) *Health Policy in Britain, fifth edition*. London: Palgrave Macmillan.

Ham, C.J. and Pickard, S. (1998) *Tragic Choices in Health Care: the Case of Child B*. London: King's Fund.

Hargreaves, I., Lewis, J. and Speers, T. (2003) *Towards a Better Map: Science, the Public and the Media*. Swindon: Economic and Social Research Council. http://www.esrc.ac.uk/esrccontent/DownloadDocs/Mapdocfinal. pdf (accessed 27 November 2005).

Harpwood, V. (2001) 'Clinical governance, litigation and human rights', *Journal of Management in Medicine*, 15(3): 227–41.

Harrison, M.L. (1984) *Corporatism and the Welfare State*. London: Gower.

Harrison, S. (1981) 'The politics of health manpower', in A.F. Long and G. Mercer (eds), *Manpower Planning in the National Health Service*. Farnborough: Gower Press.

Harrison, S. (1982) 'Consensus decision making in the National Health Service: a review', *Journal of Management Studies*, 19(4): 337–94.

Harrison, S. (1988) *Managing the National Health Service: Shifting the Frontier?* London: Chapman and Hall.

Harrison, S. (1991) 'Working the markets: purchaser/ provider separation in English health care', *International Journal of Health Services*, 21(4): 625–35.

Harrison, S. (1994) *Managing the National Health Service in the 1980s: Policy Making on the Hoof?* Aldershot: Avebury.

Harrison, S. (1999) 'Clinical autonomy and health policy: past and futures', in M. Exworthy and S. Halford (eds), *Professionalism and the New Managerialism in the Public Sector*. Buckingham: Open University Press.

Harrison, S. (2001) 'Reforming the medical profession in the United Kingdom 1989–97: structural interests in health care', in M. Bovens B.G. Peters and P. t'Hart (eds), *Success and Failure in Public Governance*, pp. 277–92. Aldershot: Edward Elgar.

Harrison, S. (2002) 'New Labour, modernisation and the medical labour process', *Journal of Social Policy*, 31(3): 465–85.

Harrison, S. (2004) 'Governing medicine: governance, science and practice', in A.G. Gray and S. Harrison (eds), *Governing Medicine: Theory and Practice*, pp. 180–7. Buckingham: Open University Press.

Harrison, S. (2006) 'Changing welfare, changing states: new directions in social policy', *British Journal of Sociology*, 57(2): 312.

Harrison, S. and Ahmad, W.I.U. (2000) 'Medical autonomy and the UK state 1975 to 2025', *Sociology*, 34(1): 129–46.

Harrison, S. and Dowswell, G. (2002) 'Autonomy and bureaucratic accountability in primary care: what English General Practitioners say', *Sociology of Health and Illness*, 24(2): 208–26.

Harrison, S. and Hunter, D.J. (1994) *Rationing Health Care*. London: Institute for Public Policy Research.

Harrison, S. and Lim, J. (2000) 'Clinical governance and primary care in the English National Health Service: some issues of organisation and rules', *Critical Public Health*, 10(3): 321–9.

Harrison, S. and Lim, J. (2003) 'The frontier of control: doctors and managers in the NHS 1966 to 1997', *Clinical Governance International*, 8(2): 13–7.

Harrison, S. and Moran, M. (2000) 'Resources and rationing: managing supply and demand in health care', in G. Albrecht, R. Fitzpatrick and S. Scrimshaw (eds), *The Handbook of Social Studies in Health and Medicine*. pp. 493–508. New York: Sage.

Harrison, S. and Mort, M. (1998) 'Which champions, which people? Public and user involvement as a technology of legitimation', *Social Policy and Administration*, 32(1): 60–70.

Harrison, S. and Smith, C. (2003) 'Neo-bureaucracy and public management: the case of medicine in the National Health Service', *Competition and Change*, 7(4): 243–54.

Harrison, S. and Wistow, G. (1992) 'The purchaser/provider split in English health care: towards explicit rationing?', *Policy and Politics*, 20(2): 123–30.

Harrison, S. and Wood, B. (1999) 'Designing health service organisation in the UK, 1968 to 1998: from blueprint to bright idea and "manipulated emergence"', *Public Administration*, 77(4): 751–69.

Harrison, S., Hunter, D.J. and Pollitt, C.J. (1990) *The Dynamics of British Health Policy*. London: Unwin Hyman

Harrison, S., Hunter, D.J. Marnoch, G. and Pollitt, C. (1992) *Just Managing: Power and Culture in the National Health Service*. London: Macmillan.

Harrison, S., Small, N. and Baker, M.R. (1994) 'The wrong kind of chaos? The early days of an NHS trust', *Public Money and Management*, 14(1): 39–46.

Harrison, S., Barnes, M. and Mort, M. (1997) 'Praise and damnation: mental health groups and the construction of organisational legitimacy', *Public Policy and Administration*, 12(2): 4–16.

Harrison, S., Dowswell, G. and Wright, J. (2002a) 'Practice nurses and clinical guidelines in a changing primary care context: an empirical study', *Journal of Advanced Nursing*, 39(3): 1–10.

Harrison, S., Milewa, T. and Dowswell, G. (2002b) *Patient and Public Involvement in NHS Primary Care: Final Report of a Department of Health Research Study*. Manchester: University of Manchester Department of Applied Social Science.

Harrison, S., Moran, M. and Wood, B. (2002c) 'Policy emergence and policy convergence: the case of "scientific–bureaucratic medicine" in the USA and UK', *British Journal of Politics and International Relations*, 4(1): 1–24.

Haug, M. (1973) 'Deprofessionalisation: an alternative hypothesis for the future', *Sociological Review Monograph*, 2: 195–211.

Haug, M. (1988) 'A re-examination of the hypothesis of deprofessionalisation', *Millbank Quarterly*, Supplement 2: 48–56.

Hay, C. (2002) 'Globalisation, "EU-isation" and the space for social democratic alternatives: pessimism of the intellect: a reply to Coates', *British Journal of Politics and International Relations*, 4(3): 452–64.

Hay, C. and Richards, D. (2000) 'The tangled web of Westminster and Whitehall: the discourse, strategy and practice of networking within the British core executive', *Public Administration*, 78(1): 1–27.

Hayek, F.A. (1988) *The Fatal Conceit: the Errors of Socialism*. London: Routledge.

Haywood, S. and Alaszewski, A. (1980) *Crisis in the National Health Service*. London: Croom Helm.

Heald, D. (1997) 'Privately financed capital in public services', *Manchester School*, LXV(4).

Heater, D. (1990) *Citizenship: the Civic Ideal in World History, Politics and Education*. London: Longman.

Hebert, K. (2004) 'Life expectancy in Great Britain rises – but later years are still spent in poor health', *British Medical Journal*, 329: 250.

Held, D. (1996) *Models of Democracy*, 2nd edn. Oxford: Polity.

Heller, T., Heller, D. and Pattison, S. (2001) 'Vaccination against mumps, measles and rubella: is there a case for deepening the debate?', *British Medical Journal*, 323: 838–40.

Hennessy, P. (1989) *Whitehall*. London: Fontana.

Hickson, D.J. and McMillan, C.J. (1981) *Organisation and Nation the Aston Programme IV*. Farnborough: Gower.

Hill, M. and Hupe, P. (2002) *Implementing Public Policy*. London: Sage.

Hindess, B. (2001) 'Power, government, politics' in K. Nash and A. Scott (eds), *The Blackwell Companion to Political Sociology*. Oxford: Blackwell.

Hirst, P. and Thompson, G. (1996) *Globalization in Question: The International Economy and the Possibilities of Governance*. Cambridge: Polity Press.

Hoffenberg, R. (1992) 'Letter to the editor', *British Medical Journal*, 304: 182.

Hoggett, P. (1990) *Modernisation, Political Strategy and the Welfare State: an Organisational Perspective*. Bristol: School for Advanced Urban Studies, University of Bristol.

Hoggett, P. (1997) 'Contested communities', in P. Hoggett (ed.), *Contested Communities*. Bristol: Policy Press.

Hogwood, B.W. (1987) *From Crisis to Complacency? Shaping Pubic Policy in Britain*. Oxford: Oxford University Press.

Hogwood, B.W. and Gunn, L.A. (1984) *Policy Analysis for the Real World*. Oxford: Oxford University Press.

Holliday, I. (1992) *The NHS Transformed*. Manchester: Baseline Books.

Hood, C. (1976) *The Limits of Administration*. London: Wiley.

Hood, C. (1991) 'A public management for all seasons?', *Public Administration*, 69: 3–19.

Hood, C., James, O. and Scott, C. (2000) 'Regulation of government: has it increased, is it increasing, should it be diminished?', *Public Administration*, 78(2): 283–304.

House of Lords Select Committee on Science and Technology (1988) *Third Report: Priorities in Medical Research*. HL Paper 54-1. London: HMSO.

Hoyes, L., Jeffers, S., Lart, R., Means, R. and Taylor, M. (1993) *User Empowerment and the Reform of Community Care*. Bristol: University of Bristol School for Advanced Urban Studies.

Hughes, E.C. (1958) *Men and their Work*. New York: Free Press.

Hunter, D.J. (1993) 'Rationing and health gain', *Critical Public Health*, 4(1): 27–32.

Hunter, D.J. (1997) *Desperately Seeking Solutions: Rationing Health Care*. London: Longmans.

Hunter, D.J. and Harrison, S. (1997) 'Democracy, accountability and consumerism', in J. Munro and S. Iliffe (eds), *Health Choices Future Options for Health Policy*, pp. 120–54. London: Lawrence and Wishart.

Hutton, W. (2000) *New Life for Health: the Commission on the NHS*. London: Vintage.

Jacobzone, S. (2004) 'Resource and service implications of short waiting times: the French experience', in J. Appleby, N. Devlin and D. Dawson (eds), *How Much Should We Spend on the NHS? Issues and Challenges Arising from the Wanless Review of Future Health Care Spending*, pp. 76–93. London: King's Fund.

James, S. (1997) *British Government: a Reader in Policy Making*. London: Routledge.

Jamous, H. and Peloille, B. (1970) 'Changes in the French university-hospital system', in J.A. Jackson (ed.), *Professions and Professionalisation*, pp. 111–52. Cambridge: Cambridge University Press.

Jaques, E. (ed.) (1978) *Health Services: Their Nature and Organisation and the Role of Patients, Doctors, and the Health Professions*. London: Heinemann.

Jay, P. (ed.) (1996) *The Oxford Dictionary of Political Quotations*. Oxford: Oxford University Press.

Jenkin, P. (1980) 'Foreword' in D. Black, J. Morris, C. Smith and P. Townsend (eds), *Inequalities in Health: Report of a Research Working Group*. London: Department of Health and Social Security.

Jenkins, W.I. (1978) *Policy Analysis: a Political and Organisational Perspective*. Oxford: Martin Robertson.

Jessop, B. (1999) 'The changing governance of welfare: recent trends in its primary functions, scale, and modes of co-ordination', *Social Policy and Administration*, 33(4): 348–59.

John, P. (1998) *Analysing Public Policy*. London: Continuum.

John, P. (2001) 'Policy networks' in K. Nash and A. Scott (eds), *The Blackwell Companion to Political Sociology*, pp. 139–48. Oxford: Blackwell.

Johnson, T.J. (1972) *Professions and Power*. London: Macmillan.

Johnson, T.J. (1995) 'Governmentality and the institutionalisation of expertise', in T.J. Johnson, G. Larkin and M. Saks (eds), *Health Professions and the State in Europe*. London: Routledge.

Jones, B., Kavanagh, D., Moran, M. and Norton, P. (2001) *Politics UK*, 4th edn. London: Longmans.

Kahn, C.N. (1998) 'The AHCPR after the battles', *Health Affairs*, 17(1): 109–10.

Kahssay, H.M. and Oakley, P. (1999) *Community Involvement in Health Development: a Review of the Concept and Practice*. Geneva: World Health Organisation.

Kennedy, A., Gately, C., Rogers, A. and the EPP Evaluation Team (2004) *Assessing the Process of Embedding EPP in the NHS: Preliminary Survey of Expert Patients Programme PCT Pilot Sites*. Manchester, National Primary Care Research and Development Centre: 1–46.

Keohane, R.O. (1984) *After Hegemony: Cooperation and Discord in the World Political Economy.* Princeton, NJ: Princeton University Press.

Keynes, J.M. (1936) *The General Theory of Employment, Interest and Money.* London: Macmillan.

Khan, U. and Everitt, S. (1996) *An Evaluative Study of the North Beds 500 Consumer Panel.* Luton: University of Luton Centre for the Study of Public Participation.

Kingdon, J.W. (1984) *Agendas, Alternatives and Public Policy.* Boston: Little, Brown.

Kirk, S., Bailey, J. and Glendinning, C. (1997) 'Involving communities in health service planning in primary care', *Health and Social Care in the Community*, 5(6): 398–407.

Klein, R.E. (1983) *The Politics of the National Health Service.* London: Longman.

Klein, R.E. (1984) 'Who makes decisions in the NHS?', *British Medical Journal*, 288: 1706–8.

Klein, R.E. (1990) 'The state and the profession: the politics of the double bed', *British Medical Journal*, 301: 700–2.

Klein, R.E. (1995) *The New Politics of the National Health Service.* London: Longman.

Klein, R.E. (1998) 'Competence, professional self-regulation and the public interest', *British Medical Journal*, 316: 1740–2.

Klein, R.E. (2000) 'The crises of the welfare states', in R. Cooter and J.E. Pickstone (eds), *Medicine in the 20th Century*, pp. 155–70. London: Harwood.

Klein, R.E. (2001) *The New Politics of the NHS.* Harlow: Pearson.

Klein, R. (2004) 'The first wave of NHS foundation trusts', *British Medical Journal* 328: 1332.

Klein, R.E. (2005) 'Transforming the NHS' in M. Powell, L. Bauld and K. Clarke (eds), *Social Policy Review 17: Analysis and Debate in Social Policy 2005*, pp. 51–68. Bristol: Policy Press.

Klein, R.E. (2006) *The New Politics of the NHS*, 5th edn. Oxford: Radcliffe Publishing.

Klein, R.E. and Lewis, J. (1976) *The Politics of Consumer Representation.* London: Centre for Studies in Social Policy.

Klein, R.E., Day, P. and Redmayne, S. (1996) *Managing Scarcity: Priority Setting and Rationing in the National Health Service.* Buckingham: Open University Press.

Kneebone, R. and Darzi, A. (2005) 'New professional roles within surgery', *British Medical Journal*, 330: 803–4.

Knoke, D. and Kuklinski, J.H. (1982) *Network Analysis.* Beverly Hills, CA: Sage.

Kuhn, T.S. (1962) *The Structure of Scientific Revolutions.* Chicago, IL: University of Chicago Press.

Labour Party (1994) *Health 2000: the Health and Wealth of the Nation in the 21st Century.* London: Labour Party.

Labour Party (1995) *Renewing the NHS: Labour's Agenda for a Healthier Britain.* London: Labour Party.

Laing, R.D. (1969) *The Divided Self.* New York: Random House.

Larkin, G.V. (1983) *Occupational Monopoly and Modern Medicine.* London: Tavistock.

Larkin, G.V. (2002) 'The regulation of the professions allied to medicine', in J. Allsop and M. Saks (eds), *Regulating the Health Professions*, pp. 120–33. London: Sage.

Larner, W. and Walters, W. (2000) 'Privatisation, governance and identity: the United Kingdom and New Zealand compared', *Policy and Politics*, 28(3): 361–77.

Larsen, T., Taylor-Gooby, P. and Kananen, J. (2006) 'New Labour's policy style: a mix of policy approaches', *Journal of Social Policy*, 35(4): 629–49.

Lasswell, H.D. (1956) *The Decision Process: Seven Categories of Functional Analysis.* College Park, MD: University of Maryland.

Latour, B. (1987) *Science in Action: How to Follow Scientists and Engineers through Society.* Cambridge, MA: Harvard University Press.

Laver, M. (1986) *Social Choice and Public Policy.* Oxford: Blackwell.

Laver, M. (1997) *Private Desires, Political Action: An Introduction to the Politics of Rational Choice.* London: Sage.

Lawrence, C. (1994) *Medicine and the Making of Modern Britain 1700–1920.* London: Routledge.

Learmonth, M. (2005) 'Doing things with words: the case of management and administration', *Public Administration*, 83(3): 617–37.

Lee, K. and Mills, A. (1982) *Policy-Making and Planning in the Health Sector.* London: Croom Helm.

Lee-Potter, J. (1997) *A Damn Bad Business: the NHS Deformed.* London: Gollancz.

LeGrand, J. (1991) 'Quasi-markets and social policy', *Economic Journal*, 101: 1256–67.

Leonard, O., Allsop, J., Taket, A. and Wiles, R. (1997) *User Involvement in Two Primary Health Care Projects in London.* London: South Bank University School of Education, Politics and Social Science.

Levacic, R. (1991) 'Markets and government: an overview', in G. Thompson, J. Frances, R. Levacic and J. Mitchell (eds), *Markets, Hierarchies and Networks: the Co-ordination of Social Life.* London: Sage.

Levin, P. (1997) *Making Social Policy: The Mechanisms of Government and Politics and How to Investigate Them.* Buckingham: Open University Press.

Levitt, R. (1976) *The Reorganised National Health Service.* London: Croom Helm.

Levitt, R. (1979) *The Reorganised National Health Service*, 2nd edn. London: Croom Helm.

Levitt, R. (1980) *The People's Voice in the NHS.* London: King Edward's Hospital Fund for London.

Levitt, R. and Wall, A. (1984) *The Reorganised National Health Service*, 3rd edn. London: Croom Helm.

Levitt, R. and Wall, A. (1992) *The Reorganised National Health Service*, 4th edn. London: Chapman and Hall.

Levitt, R., Wall, A. and Appleby, J. (1995) *The Reorganised National Health Service*, 5th edn. London: Chapman and Hall.

Levitt, R., Wall, A. and Appleby, J. (1999) *The Reorganised National Health Service,* 5th edn. London: Stanley Thornes Publishers.

Lewis, J. (1986) *What Price Community Medicine? The Philosophy, Practice and Politics of Public Health Since 1919.* Brighton: Wheatsheaf.

Lewis, J. (1992) 'Providers, "consumers", the state and the delivery of health-care services in twenti-eth- century Britain', in A. Wear (ed.), *Medicine in Society.* pp. 317–46. Cambridge: Cambridge University Press.

Lewis, J. (2000) 'Health and health care in the progressive era', in R. Cooter and J.E. Pickstone (eds), *Medicine in the 20th Century*, pp. 81–96. London: Harwood.

Lewis, S., Saulnier, M. and Renaud, M. (2000) 'Reconfiguring health policy: simple truths, com-plex solutions', in G. Albrecht, R. Fitzpatrick and S. Scrimshaw (eds), *The Handbook of Social Studies in Health and Medicine*, pp. 509–22. New York: Sage.

Light, D.W. (1995) 'Countervailing powers: a framework for professions in transition', in T.J. Johnson, G. Larkin and M. Saks (eds), *Health Professions and the State in Europe*, pp. 25–43. London: Routledge.

Light, D.W. Levine, S. (1988) 'The changing character of the medical profession: a theoretical overview', *Milbank Quarterly*, 66, supp 2: 10–32.

Lijphart, A. (1999) *Patterns of Democracy: Governance Forms and Performance in 36 Countries.* New Haven, CT: Yale University Press.

Likierman, A. (1988) *Public Expenditure: Who Really Controls it and How?* Harmondsworth: Pelican.

Lilienfield, A.M. and Lilienfield, D.E. (1979) 'A century of case-controlled studies: progress?', *Journal of Chronic Diseases*, 32: 5–13.

Lindblom, C.E. (1959) 'The science of muddling through', *Public Administration Review*, 19: 78–88.

Lindblom, C.E. (1965) *The Intelligence of Democracy*. New York: Free Press.

Lindblom, C.E. (1977) *Politics and Markets*. New York: Basic Books.

Lindblom, C.E. (1979) 'Still muddling, not yet through', *Public Administration Review*, 39(6): 517–25.

Lipsey, R.G. (1966) *An Introduction to Positive Economics*. London: Weidenfeld and Nicholson.

Lipsky, M. (1980) *Street-Level Bureaucracy: Dilemmas of the Individual in Public Services*. New York: Sage.

LMCA (2003) *Annual Review*. London: LMCA.

Lohr, L. (1973) 'The concept of organisational goal', *American Political Science Review*, 67: 470–81.

Loney, M. (1983) *Community Against Government: the British Community Development Project 1968–78*. London: Heinemann.

Loudon, I. (1992) 'Medical practitioners 1750–1850 and the period of medical reform in Britain', in A. Wear (ed.), *Medicine in Society: Historical Essays*, pp. 219–47. Cambridge: Cambridge University Press.

Lowi, T.J. (1972) 'Four systems of policy, politics and choice', *Public Administration Review*, 32(4): 298–310.

Lupton, C., Buckland, S. and Moon, G. (1995) 'Consumer involvement in health care purchasing: the role and influence of Community Health Councils', *Health and Social Care in the Community*, 3(4): 215–26.

Lyon, D. (1999) *Postmodernity*, 2nd edn. Buckingham: Open University Press.

Lyotard, J.F. (1984) *The Postmodern Condition: A Report on Knowledge*. Manchester: Manchester University Press.

Mahmood, K. (2002) 'Clinical governance and professional restratification in medicine', *Journal of Health, Organisation and Management*, 15(3): 242–52.

Maidment, R. and Thompson, G. (eds) (1993) *Managing the United Kingdom: an Introduction to its Political Economy and Public Policy*. London: Sage.

Majone, G. (1986) 'Mutual adjustment by debate and persuasion', in F.X. Kaufman, G. Majone and V. Ostrom (eds), *Guidance, Control and Evaluation in the Public Sector: the Bielefeld Interdisciplinary Project*. Berlin: De Gruyter.

Mannion, R. (2005) *Practice-based Budgeting: Lessons from the Past, Prospects for the Future*. University of York: Centre for Health Economics.

Mannion, R., Davies, H.T.O. and Marshall, M.N. (2005) *Cultures for Performance in Health Care*. Maidenhead: Open University Press.

March, J.G. and Simon, H.A. (1958) *Organisations*. New York: Wiley.

Marinetto, M. (1999) *Studies of the Policy Process: a Case Analysis*. London: Prentice Hall.

Marks, H.M. (1997) *The Progress of Experiment: Science and Therapeutic Reform in the United States, 1900–1990*. Cambridge: Cambridge University Press.

Marnoch, G. (2003) 'Scottish devolution: identity and impact and the case of community care for the elderly', *Public Administration*, 81(2): 253–73.

Marquand, D. (1988) *The Unprincipled Society: New Demands and Old Politics*. London: Jonathan Cape.

Marris, P. and Rein, M. (1974) *Dilemmas of Social Reform*, 2nd edn. Harmondsworth: Penguin.

Marsh, D. and Rhodes, R.A.W. (eds) (1992) *Policy Networks in British Government*. Oxford: Oxford University Press.

Marshall, M. and Roland, M. (2002) 'The new contract: renaissance or requiem for general practice?', *British Journal of General Practice*, 52: 531–2.

Marshall, M., Sheaff, R., Rogers, A., Campbell, S., Halliwell, S., Pickard, S., Sibbald, B. and Roland, M. (2002) 'A qualitative study of the cultural changes in primary care organisations needed to implement clinical governance', *British Journal of General Practice*, 52: 641–5.

Marshall, T.H. (1950) *Citizenship and Social Class and Other Essays*. Cambridge: Cambridge University Press.

Mayor, S. (2001) 'Health department to fund interferon beta despite institute's ruling', *British Medical Journal*, 323: 1087.

McDonald, R. (2000) 'Just say no? Drugs, politics and the UK National Health Service', *Policy and Politics*, 28(4): 563–76.

McDonald, R. (2002) *Using Health Economics in Health Services: Rationing Rationally?* Buckingham: Open University Press.

McDonald, R. and Harrison, S. (2004) 'The micropolitics of clinical guidelines: an empirical study', *Policy and Politics*, 32(2): 223–38.

McDonald, R., Waring, J.J., Harrison, S. Walshe, K. and Boaden, R. (2005a) 'Guidelines and trust in the operating theatre: a qualitative study of doctors' and nurses' views', *Quality and Safety in Health Care*, 14: 290–4.

McDonald, R., Waring, J.J. and Harrison, S. (2005b) 'Balancing risk, that is my life: the politics of risk in a hospital operating theatre', *Health, Risk and Society*, 7(4): 397–411.

McDonald, R., Harrison, S., Checkland, K., Campbell, S. and Roland, M. (forthcoming) 'Impact of financial incentives on clinical autonomy and internal motivation in primary care: an ethnographic study', *British Medical Journal*.

McIver, S. (1998) *Independent Evaluation of Citizens' Juries in Health Authority Settings*. London: King's Fund.

McKeown, T. (1980) *The Role of Medicine: Dream, Mirage or Nemesis?* Oxford: Blackwell.

McKinlay, J. and Arches, J. (1985) 'Towards the proletarianisation of physicians', *International Journal of Health Services*, 15: 161–95.

McKinlay, J.B. and Marceau, L. (2002) 'The end of the golden age of doctoring', *International Journal of Health Services*, 32(2): 379–416.

McKinlay, J. and Stoeckle, J. (1988) 'Corporatisation and the social transformation of doctoring', *International Journal of Health Services*, 18: 191–205.

McLean, I. and McMillan, A. (2003) 'The distribution of public expenditure across the UK regions', *Fiscal Studies*, 24: 45–71.

McPherson, K. (2004) 'UK evidence on "healthy lifestyles" and their effect on the demand for health care', in J. Appleby, N. Devlin and D. Dawson (eds), *How Much Should we Spend on the NHS? Issues and Challenges Arising from the Wanless Review of Future Health Care Spending*, pp. 44–54. London: King's Fund.

Means, R., Richards, S. and Smith, R. (2003) *Community Care: Policy and Practice*. Basingstoke: Palgrave Macmillan.

Mechanic, D. (1991) 'Sources of countervailing power in medicine', *Journal of Health Politics, Policy and Law*, 16(3): 485–98.

Mechanic, D. (1992) 'Professional judgement and the rationing of medical care', *University of Pennsylvania Law Review*, 140: 1713–54.

Meehan, E. (1993) 'Citizenship and the European Community', *Political Quarterly*, 64(2): 172–86.

Meikle, J. (2002) 'Demand surges for MMR single vaccines', *Guardian*, 7 August http://www.guardian.co.uk/uk_news/story/0,,770393,00.html (accessed 22 May 2005).

Melia, K.M. (1987) *Learning and Working: the Occupational Socialisation of Nurses*. London: Tavistock.

Merton, R.K. (1949) *Social Theory and Social Structure*. New York: Free Press.

Midwinter, A. and McGarvey, N. (2001) 'In search of the regulatory state: evidence from Scotland', *Public Administration*, 79(4): 825–50.

Milewa, T. (2004) 'Local participatory democracy in Britain's health service: innovation or fragmentation of a universal citizenship?', *Social Policy and Administration*, 38(3): 240–52.

Milewa, T., Valentine, J. and Calnan, M. (1999) 'Community participation and citizenship in British health care planning', *Sociology of Health and Illness*, 21(4): 445–65.

Miliband, R. (1977) *Marxism and Politics*. Oxford: Oxford University Press.

Millerson, G. (1964) *The Qualifying Associations: a Study in Professionalism*. London: Routledge and Kegan Paul.

Milward, H.B. and Provan, K.G. (1998) 'Measuring network structure', *Public Administration*, 76(2): 387–407.

MIND (2006) 'Mind celebrates 60 years of speaking out', press release, http://www.mind.org.uk/News+policy+and+campaigns/Press/60thanniversarylaunch.htm

McDonald, R., Harrison, S., Checkland, K., Campbell, S. and Roland, M. (in press) 'Impact of financial incentives on clinical autonomy and internal motivation in primary care: an ethnographic study', *British Medical Journal*.

Ministry of Health (1962) *A hospital plan for England and Wales*, Cmnd 1604. London: HMSO.

Ministry of Health (1966) *Report Of The Committee On Senior Nursing Staff Structure*. London: HMSO.

Ministry of Health (1967) *First Report of the Joint Working Party on the Organisation of Medical Work in Hospitals*. London: HMSO.

Ministry of Health, (1968) *National Health Service: the Administrative Structure of the Medical and Related Services in England and Wales*. London: HMSO.

Ministry of Health and Department of Health for Scotland (1944) *A National Health Service*, Cmnd 6502. London: HMSO.

Mintzberg, H. (1991) 'The professional organisation', in H. Mintzberg and J.B. Quinn (eds), *The Strategy Process: Concepts, Contexts, Cases*, 2nd edn. London: Prentice Hall.

Mishra, R. (1984) *The Welfare State in Crisis: Social Thought and Social Change*. Brighton: Harvester.

Mohan, J. (2002) *Planning, Markets and Hospitals*. London: Routledge.

Moran, M. (1999) *Governing the Health Care State: a Comparative Study of the United Kingdom, the United States and Germany*. Manchester: University of Manchester Press.

Moran, M. (2003) *The British Regulatory State: High Modernism and Hyper-Innovation*. Oxford: Oxford University Press.

Moran, M. (2004) 'Governing doctors in the British regulatory state' in A.G. Gray and S. Harrison (eds), *Governing Medicine: Theory and Practice*, pp. 27–36. Buckingham: Open University Press.

MORI (2003) Whom Do We Trust? http://www.ipsos-mori.com/publications/rmw/whomdowetrust.shtml (accessed 14 April 2007).

Mort, M. and Harrison, S. (1999) 'Healthcare users, the public and the consultation industry' in T. Ling (ed.), *Reforming Health Care by Consent: Involving Those Who Matter,* pp. 107–20. Oxford: Radcliffe Medical Press.

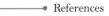

Mort, M., Harrison, S. and Wistow, G. (1996) 'The user card: picking through the organisational undergrowth in health and social care', *Contemporary Political Studies*, 2: 1133–40.

Mort, M., Harrison, S. and Dowswell, T. (1999) 'Public health panels: influence at the margin', in U.A. Khan (ed.), *Participation Beyond the Ballot Box: European Case Studies in State-Citizen Political Dialogue*, pp. 94–109. London: UCL Press.

Mossialos, E., Dixon, A., Figueras, J. and Kutzin, J. (2002) *Funding Health Care: Options for Europe.* Buckingham: Open University Press.

Mossialos, E., Mrazek, M. and Walley, T. (eds) (2004) *Regulating Pharmaceuticals in Europe: Striving for Efficiency, Equity and Quality.* London: Sage.

Mouzelis, N.P. (1967) *Organisation and Bureaucracy: An Analysis of Modern Theories.* London: Routledge and Kegan Paul.

Mouzelis, N.P. (1975) *Organisation and Bureaucracy: An Analysis of Modern Theories.* London: Routledge & Kegan Paul.

Moynihan, R. and Smith, R. (2002) 'Too much medicine? Almost certainly', *British Medical Journal*, 309: 859–60.

Mukamel, D.B., Weimer, D.L., Zwanziger, J., Gorthy, S.F.H. and Mushlin, A.I. (2004) 'Quality report cards, selection of cardiac surgeons, and racial disparities: a study of the publication of the New York State Cardiac Surgery Reports', *Inquiry – the Journal of Health Care Organization Provision and Financing*, 41: 435–46.

Mulrow, C. (1994) 'Rationale for systematic reviews', *British Medical Journal*, 309: 597–9.

Murphy, R. (1988) *Social Closure.* Oxford: Oxford University Press.

National Audit Office Wales (2005) *NHS Waiting Times in Wales.* Cardiff: NAO.

National Statistics (2004) *Preventive Measures. Turning point in MMR vaccinations?* http://www. statistics.gov. uk/cci/nugget.asp?id=923

Navarro, V. (1988) 'Professional dominance or proletarianisation? Neither', *Millbank Quarterly*, 66, supp2: 57–75.

Needham, G. (2000) 'Research and practice: making a difference', in R. Gomm and C. Davies (eds), *Using Evidence in Health and Social Care*, pp. 131–52. London: Open University Press and Sage.

New, B. (1996) 'The rationing agenda in the NHS', *British Medical Journal*, 312: 1593–1601.

New, B. and Le Grand, J. (1996) *Rationing in the NHS: Principles and Pragmatism.* London: King's Fund.

Newman, J. and Vidler, E. (2006) 'Discriminating customers, responsible patients, empowered users: consumerism and the modernisation of health care', *Journal of Social Policy*, 35(2): 193–209.

Newman, J., Barnes, M., Sullivan, H. and Knops, A. (2004) 'Public participation and collaborative governance', *Journal of Social Policy*, 33(2): 203–23.

NHS Confederation/British Medical Association (2003) *The New GMS Contract - Investing in General Practice.* London: The NHS Confederation.

NHS Executive (1996a) *Clinical Guidelines: Using Clinical Guidelines to Improve Patient Care Within the NHS.* London: Department of Health.

NHS Executive (1996b) *Promoting Clinical Effectiveness: a Framework for Action in and Through the NHS.* London: Department of Health.

NHS Executive (1998) *A First Class Service: Quality in the New NHS.* London: Department of Health.

NHS Management Executive (1992) *Local Voices: Views of Local People in Purchasing for Health.* London: HMSO.

NHS Management Executive (1993) *Improving Clinical Effectiveness*. Leeds: NHS Management Executive (EL(93)115).

NHS Management Inquiry (1983) *Report* (Chairman Mr ER Griffiths). London: Department of Health.

NICE (1999) *Patient Voices*. London: National Institute for Clinical Excellence.

NICE (2001) NICE appraisal of beta interferon and glatiramer for MS, Process to October 2001, http://www.nice.org.uk/page.aspx?o=18751

NICE (2002) 'NICE issues guidance on drugs for multiple sclerosis', press release. http://www.nice.org.uk/ page.aspx?o=38119 (accessed 13 April 2006).

Nicolson, T. and Milne, R. (1999) *Beta Interferons (1a and 1b) in Relapsing-remitting and Secondary Progressive Multiple Sclerosis*. Development and Evaluation Committee Report No 98. Southampton: Wessex Institute for Health Research and Development.

Niskanen, W.A. (1971) *Bureaucracy and Representative Government*. Chicago, IL: Aldine-Atherton.

Oakley, A. (2000) *Experiments in Knowing: Gender and Method in the Social Sciences*. Cambridge: Polity Press.

O'Connor, J. (1973) *The Fiscal Crisis of the State*. New York: St Martin's Press .

O'Connor, J. (1984) *Accumulation Crisis*. New York: Basil Blackwell.

O'Day, R. (2000) *The Professions in Early Modern England 1450–1800: Servants of the Commonwealth*. London: Longmans.

OECD (1993) *Managing With Market-Type Mechanisms*. Paris: Organisation for Economic Co-operation and Development.

Oeppen, J. and Vaupel, J.W. (2002) 'Broken limits to life expectancy', *Science*, 296: 1029–31.

Offe, C. (1984) *Contradictions of the Welfare State*. London: Hutchinson.

Office of Health Economics (2003) *Compendium of Health Statistics 2003/04*. London: Office of Health Economics.

Office of Health Economics (2005) *Compendium of Health Statistics 2005/06*. London: Office of Health Economics.

Office of Health Economics (2007) *Compendium of Health Statistics 2007/08*. London: Office of Health Economics.

Office of Technology Assessment (1978) *Assessing the Efficacy and Safety of Medical Technology*. Washington: Congress of the United States.

O'Keefe, E. and Hogg, C. (1999) 'Public participation and marginalized groups: the community development model', *Health Expectations*, 2: 245–54.

O'Neill, O. (2002) *A Question of Trust: the BBC Reith Lectures 2002*. Cambridge: Cambridge University Press.

Osborne, D. and Gaebler, T. (1993) *Reinventing Government: How the Entrepreneurial Spirit is Transforming the Public Sector*. New York: Plume.

Ouchi, W.G. (1980) 'Markets, bureaucracies and clans', *Administrative Science Quarterly*, 25: 129–41.

Ouchi, William (1981) *Theory Z: How American Business Can Meet the Japanese Challenge*. Reading, MA: Addison Wesley.

Oxman, A.D., Thomson, M.A., Davis, D.A. and Haynes, R. B. (1995) No magic bullets: a systematic review of 102 trials of interventions to improve professional practice, *Canadian Medical Association Journal*, 153: 1423–31.

Parker, D. and Lawton, R. (2000) 'Judging the use of clinical protocols by fellow professionals', *Social Science and Medicine*, 51: 669–77.

Parkin, D.W., McGuire, A.J. and Yule, B.F. (1989) 'What do international comparisons of health care expenditures really show?', *Community Medicine*, 11(2): 116–23.

Parkin, D.W., McNamee, P., Jacoby, A., Miller, P., Thomas, S. and Bates, D. (1998) 'A cost-utility analysis of interferon beta for multiple sclerosis', *Health Technology Assessment*, 2(4).

Parkin, F. (1982) *Max Weber*. London: Tavistock Publications.

Parkinson, C.N. (1957/1972) *Parkinson's Law*. London: John Murray.

Parkinson, J. (2006) *Deliberating in the Real World: Problems of Legitimacy in Deliberative Democracy*. Oxford: Oxford University Press.

Parson, W. (1995) *Public Policy: an Introduction to the Theory and Practice of Policy Analysis*. Aldershot: Edward Elgar.

Pateman, C. (1970) *Participation and Democratic Theory*. Cambridge: Cambridge University Press.

Pater, J.E. (1981) *The Making of the National Health Service*. London: King's Fund.

Patulin Clinical Trials Committee (1944) 'Clinical trial of patulin in the common cold', reprinted in *International Journal of Epidemiology*, 33: 243–6, 2004.

Pauly, M.V. (1968) 'The economics of moral hazard', *American Economic Review*, 58: 531–57.

Pawson, R.D. and Tilley, N. (1997) *Realistic Evaluation*. London: Sage.

Peckham, S. and Exworthy, M. (2003) *Primary Care in the UK: Policy, Organisation and Management*. Basingstoke: Palgrave.

Perkin, H. (1989) *The Rise of Professional Society: England Since 1880*. London: Routledge.

Peters, B.G. (1998) 'Managing horizontal government: the politics of co-ordination', *Public Administration*, 76(2): 295–312.

Peters, T.J. and Waterman, R.H. (1982) *In search of Excellence: Lessons from America's Best-Run Companies*. New York: Harper and Row.

Pickard, S. (1997) 'The future organisation of Community Health Councils' *Social Policy and Administration*, 32: 226–44.

Pickstone, J.V. (2000) 'Production, community and consumption: the political economy of twentieth-century medicine', in R. Cooter and J.V. Pickstone (eds), *Medicine in the 20th Century*. London: Harwood.

Pierre, J. and Peters, B.G. (2000) *Governance, Politics and the State*. London: Macmillan.

Plant, R. (1992) 'Citizenship, rights and welfare', in A. Coote (ed.), *The Welfare of Citizens: Developing New Social Rights*. London: Rivers Oram Press.

Polanyi, K. (1944) *The Great Transformation*. New York: Rhinehardt.

Polanyi, M. (1967) *The Tacit Dimension*. London: Routledge and Kegan Paul.

Pollitt, C.J. (1984) *Manipulating the Machine: Changing the Pattern of Ministerial Departments 1960–83*. London: Allen and Unwin.

Pollitt, C.J. (1985) 'Measuring performance: a new system for the National Health Service', *Policy and Politics*, 13(1): 1–15.

Pollitt, C.J. (1993) *Managerialism and the Public Services*, 2nd edn. Oxford: Blackwell.

Pollitt, C.J. (2003a) *The Essential Public Manager*. Maidenhead: Open University Press.

Pollitt, C.J. (2003b) 'Joined-up government: a survey', *Political Studies Review*, 1(1): 34–49.

Pollitt, C.J., Bathgate, K., Caulfield, J., Smullen, A. and Talbot, C. (2001) 'Agency fever: analysis of an international policy fashion', *Journal of Comparative Policy Analysis: Research and Practice*, 3: 271–90.

Pollock, A.M., Leys, C., Rowland, D. and Gnani, S. (2004) *NHS plc: The Privatisation of our Health Care*. London: Verso.

Porter, R. (1997) *The Greatest Benefit to Mankind: A Medical History of Humanity from Antiquity to the Present*. London: Harper Collins.

Powell, M.A. (ed.) (2002) *New Labour's Welfare Reforms*. Bristol: Policy Press.

Powell, M.A. (2003) 'Quasi-markets in British health policy: a long duree perspective', *Social Policy and Administration*, 37(7): 725–41.

Powell, J.E. (1966) *Medicine and Politics*. London: Pitman Medical.

Power, M. (1997) *The Audit Society: Rituals of Verification*. Oxford: Oxford University Press.

Pressman, J.L. and Wildavsky, A. (1979) *Implementation: How Great Expectations in Washington are Dashed in Oakland; Or, Why it's Amazing that Federal Programs Work at All, This being a Saga of the Economic Development Administration as Told by Two Sympathetic Observers Who Seek to Build Morals on a Foundation of Ruined Hopes*, 2nd edn. Berkeley, CA: University of California Press.

Prior, D., Stewart, J. and Walsh, K. (1995) *Citizenship, Rights, Community and Participation*. London: Pitman.

Pritchard, L. (2004) 'BMA alarm as ruling poses "retrial" threat', *BMA News Review*, 17 April: 2.

Propper, C., Wilson, D. and Burgess, S. (2006) 'Extending choice in English health care: the implications of the economic evidence', *Journal of Social Policy* 35 (4): 537–557.

Public Inquiry into Children's Heart Surgery at the Bristol Royal Infirmary 1985–1995 (2001) *Learning from Bristol*, Cmnd 5207 ('Kennedy Report'). London: The Stationery Office.

Putnam, R.D. (1993) *Making Democracy Work: Civic Traditions in Modern Italy*. Princeton, NJ: Princeton University Press.

Quennell, P. (2003) 'Getting a word in edgeways? Patient group participation in the appraisal process of the National Institute for Clinical Excellence', *Clinical Governance International*, 8(2): 39–45.

Rafferty, A.M. (2000) 'Nurses' in R. Cooter and J.E. Pickstone (eds), *Medicine in the 20th Century*, pp. 519–30. London: Harwood.

Raftery, J. (2001) 'NICE: faster access to modern treatments? Analysis of guidance on health technologies', *British Medical Journal*, 323: 1300–3.

Raftery, J. (2006) 'Review of NICE's recommendations, 1999–2005', *British Medical Journal*, 332: 1266–8.

Ramsay, R. (2002) *The Rise of New Labour*. Harpenden: Pocket Essentials.

Rayner, B. (1994) *History of the Department of Health*. London: Department of Health.

Reddy, S.G. (1996) 'Claims to expert knowledge and the subversion of democracy: the triumph of risk over uncertainty', *Economy and Society*, 25(2): 222–54.

Redfern, M. (2001) *The Royal Liverpool Children's Inquiry Report*. London: The Stationery Office.

Reed, M. (1994) 'Expert power and organisation in high modernity: an empirical review and theoretical synthesis', paper presented at ESRC seminar, Cardiff, 14 April.

Rees, A.M. (1995) 'The promise of social citizenship', *Policy and Politics*, 23(4): 313–25.

Reinhardt, U.E. (1985) 'The theory of physician-induced demand: reflections after a decade', *Journal of Health Economics*, 4: 187–93.

Resource Allocation Working Party (1976) *Sharing Resources for Health in England*. London: HMSO.

Rhodes, R.A.W. (1997) *Understanding Governance: Policy Networks, Governance, Reflexivity and Accountability*. Buckingham: Open University Press.

Richards, D. and Smith, M. (2002) *Governance and Public Policy in the UK*. Oxford: Oxford University Press.

Richardson, A. (1983) *Participation*. London: Routledge and Kegan Paul.

Richardson, J.J. (ed.) (1982) *Policy Styles in Western Europe*. London: Allen and Unwin.

Richardson, J.J. and Jordan, G. (1979) *Governing Under Pressure: the Policy Process in a Post-Parliamentary Democracy*. Oxford: Martin Robertson.

Ritzer, G. (2000) *The McDonaldisation of Society*. Thousand Oaks, CA: Pine Forge Press.

Rivett, G. (1998) *From Cradle to Grave: Fifty Years of the NHS*. London: King's Fund.

Roberts, F. (1949) 'The population problem', *The British Medical Bulletin*, 6(3): 257–260.

Roberts, F. (1952) *The Cost of Health*. London: Turnstile Press.

Robinson, J.C. (1999) *The Corporate Practice of Medicine*. Berkeley, CA: University of California Press.

Robinson, R. and Steiner, A. (1998) *Managed Health Care: US Evidence and Lessons for the National Health Service*. Buckingham: Open University Press.

Rogers, L. and O'Reilly, J. (2004) 'Baby Blair had MMR jab after outcry', *The Times online* 29 February, http://www.timesonline.co.uk/article/0,,2087-1020509,00.html (accessed 22 May 2005).

Rogers, A. and Pilgrim, D. (2001) *Mental Health Policy in Britain,* 2nd edn. Basingstoke: Palgrave.

Roland, M. (2004) 'Linking physician pay to quality of care: a major experiment in the UK', *New England Journal of Medicine*, 351: 1488–54.

Rose, R. (1993) *Lesson-drawing in Public Policy: A Guide to Learning Across Time and Space*. New York: Chatham House.

Rose, N. (1996) 'The death of the social? Refiguring the territory of government', *Economy and Society*, 25(3): 327–56.

Rose, R. (1973) 'Comparing public policy: an overview', *European Journal of Political Research*, 1: 67–94.

Rowbottom, R.W., Balle, J., Cang, S., Dixon, M., Jaques, E., Packwood, T. and Tolliday, H. (1973) *Hospital Organisation*. London: Heinemann.

Royal Commission on Local Government (1969) *Report*, Cmnd 4040 (Chairman: Lord Radcliffe-Maud). London: HMSO.

Royal Commission on Long-Term Care of the Elderly (1998) *In Respect of Old Age* (Chairman: Sir Stewart Sutherland). London: The Stationery Office.

Royal Commission on the National Health Service (1979) *Report*, Cmnd 7615 (Chairman: Sir Alec Merrison). London: HMSO.

Rummery, K. (2002) *Disability, Citizenship and Community Care: A Case for Welfare Rights?* Aldershot: Ashgate.

Sabatier, P.A. (ed.) (1999) *Theories of the Policy Process*. Boulder, CO: Westview Press.

Sackett, D.L. and Straus, S.E. (1998) 'Finding and applying evidence during clinical rounds', *JAMA*, 280: 1336–8.

Sackett, D.L., Rosenberg, W., Gray, J.A., Haynes, R.B. and Richarsdon, W.S. (1996) 'Evidence-based medicine: what it is and what it isn't', *British Medical Journal*, 312: 71–2.

Sackett, D.L. and Straus, S., Richardson, W.S., Rosenberg, W. and Haynes, R.B. (2000) *Evidence-based Medicine: How to Practise and Teach EBM*, 2nd edn. Edinburgh: Churchill Livingstone.

Saks, M. (2003) *Orthodox and Alternative Medicine*. London: Sage.

Saks, M. and Allsop, J. (2007) 'Professional regulation and health support work in the United Kingdom', *Social Policy and Society*, 6: 165–177.

Salter, B. (2000) 'Change in the governance of medicine: the politics of self-regulation', in D. Gladstone (ed.), *Regulating Doctors*. pp. 8–27. London: Institute for the Study of Civil Society.

Salter, B. (2001) 'Who rules? The new politics of medical regulation', *Social Science and Medicine*, 52: 871–83.

Salter, B. and Jones, M. (2006) 'Change in the policy community of human genetics: a pragmatic approach to open governance', *Policy and Politics*, 34(2): 347–66.

Scally, G. and Donaldson, L. (1998) 'Clinical governance and the drive for quality improvement in the new NHS in England', *British Medical Journal*, 317: 61–5.

Schmitter, P.C. (1974) 'Still the century of corporatism', *Review of Politics*, 36: 85–131.

Schon, D.A. (1983) *The Reflective Practitioner: How Professionals Think in Action*. Aldershot: Ashgate and Basic Books.

Schulz, R.I. and Harrison, S. (1983) *Teams and Top Managers in the National Health Service*. London: King's Fund.

Schulz, R.I. and Harrison, S. (1986) 'Physician autonomy in the Federal Republic of Germany, Great Britain and the United States', *International Journal of Health Planning and Management*, 1(5): 1213–28.

Schumpeter, J.A. (1976) *Capitalism, Socialism and Democracy*. London: Allen and Unwin (first published 1943).

Scottish Executive (1999) *Introduction of Managed Clinical Networks Within the NHS in Scotland*. NHS MEL 10.

Scottish Executive (2005a) *Delivering for Health*. Edinburgh: Scottish Executive.

Scottish Executive (2005b) *Building a Health Service Fit for the Future: a National Framework for Service Change in the NHS in Scotland*. Edinburgh: Scottish Executive.

Secretary of State for Communities and Local Government (2006) *Strong and Prosperous Communities*. Cm 6939. London: The Stationery Office.

Secretary of State for Health (1992) *The Health of the Nation: A Strategy for Health in England*. Cm 1986. London: HMSO.

Secretary of State for Health (1997) *The New NHS: Modern, Dependable*. Cm 3807. London: The Stationery Office.

Secretary of State for Health (1998) *A First Class Service: Quality in the New NHS*. London: The Stationery Office.

Secretary of State for Health (1999) *Saving Lives: Our Healthier Nation*. Cm 4386. London: The Stationery Office.

Secretary of State for Health (2000) *The NHS Plan: A Plan for Investment, A Plan for Reform*. Cm 4818-1. London: The Stationery Office.

Secretary of State for Health (2005) Speech to HR in the NHS Conference, 13 May, http://www.dh.gov.uk/ en/News/Speeches/Speecheslist/DH_4110963

Secretary of State for Health (2006) *Our Health, Our Care, Our Say: a New Direction for Community Health Services*. Cm 6737. London: The Stationery Office.

Secretaries of State for Health, Wales, Northern Ireland and Scotland (1989) *Working for Patients*. Cm 555. London: HMSO.

Secretaries of State for Social Services, Wales, Northern Ireland Office and Scotland (1987) *Promoting Better Health: the Government's Programme for Improving Primary Health Care*. London: HMSO.

Segall, S. (2005) 'Political participation as an engine of social solidarity: a sceptical view', *Political Studies*, 53(2): 362–78.

Self, P. (1972) *Administrative Theories and Politics,* 2nd edn. London: Unwin Hyman.

Seshamani, M. and Gray, A. (2004) 'Age, proximity to death and future demands on the NHS', in J. Appleby, N. Devlin and D. Dawson (eds), *How Much Should We Spend on the NHS? Issues and Challenges Arising from the Wanless Review of Future Health Care Spending*, pp. 56–69. London: King's Fund.

Shaw, G.B. (1932) *The Doctor's Dilemma*, 2nd edn. London: Constable.

Shaw, M., Dorling, D., Gordon, D. and Davey Smith, G. (1999) *The Widening Gap: Health Inequalities and Policy in Britain*. Bristol: Policy Press.

Sheaff, R., Pickard, S. and Smith, K. (2002) 'Public service responsiveness to users' demands and needs: theory, practice and primary healthcare in England', *Public Administration*, 80(3): 435–52.

Silverman, D. (1970) *The Theory of Organisations*. London: Heinemann.

Simon, H.A. (1957) *Administrative Behaviour; A Study of Decision Making Process in Administrative Organisation*, 2nd edn. New York: Macmillan.

Simpson, P. (2004) 'Changing practice', *British Medical Journal*, 328: 248.

Sinclair, S. (1997) *Making Doctors: an Institutional Apprenticeship*. Oxford: Berg.

Skelcher, C. (1998) *The Appointed State: Quasi-Governmental Organisations and Democracy*. Buckingham: Open University Press.

Skocpol, T. (1996) *Boomerang: Clinton's Health Security Effort and the Turn Against Government in US Politics*. New York: Norton.

Smethurst, D.P. and Williams, H.C. (2001) 'Power laws: are hospital waiting lists self-regulating?', *Nature*, 410: 652–3.

Smith, A. (1979) *The Wealth of Nations Books I-III*, 3rd edn. London: Penguin (originally published 1776).

Smith, C. (2001) 'Trust and confidence: possibilities for social work in "high modernity"', *British Journal of Social Work*, 31: 287–305.

Smith, M. and Beazley, M. (2000) 'Progressive regimes: partnerships and the involvement of local communities: a framework for evaluation', *Public Administration*, 78(4): 855–78.

Solesbury, W. (1976) 'The environmental agenda: an illustration of how situations may become political issues and issues may demand responses from government: or how they may not', *Public Administration*, 54(4): 379–97.

Soroka, S.N. and Lim, E.T. (2003) 'Issue definition and the public policy link: public preferences and health care spending in the US and UK', *British Journal of Politics and International Relations*, 5(4): 576–93.

Spiers, M. (1975) *Techniques and Public Administration: a Contextual Evaluation*. London: Fontana.

Stacey, M. (1992) *Regulating British Medicine: the General Medical Council*. Chichester: Wiley.

Stacey, M. (2000) 'The General Medical Council and professional self-regulation', in D. Gladstone (ed.), *Regulating Doctors*, pp. 28–39. London: Institute for the Study of Civil Society.

Stalker, K. (1997) 'Choices or voices? A case study of a self-advocacy group', *Health and Social Care in the Community*, 5(4): 246–54.

Starr, P. (1982) *The Social Transformation of American Medicine: the Rise of a Sovereign Profession and the Making of a Vast Industry*. New York: Basic Books.

Stewart, J.D. (1995) *Innovation in Democratic Practice*. Birmingham: University of Birmingham, Institute of Local Government Studies.

Stewart, J.D. (1996) 'A dogma of our times: the separation of policy-making and implementation', *Public Money and Management*, 16: 33–40.

Stewart, J.D. (1997) *More Innovation in Democratic Practice. Occasional Paper No 9*. Birmingham: University of Birmingham School of Public Policy.

Stewart, J.D. (2004) 'Scottish solutions to Scottish problems?', in N. Ellison L. Bauld and M. Powell (eds), *Social Policy Review 16: Analysis and Debate in Social Policy 2004*, pp. 101–20. Bristol: Policy Press.

Stewart, J.D., and Davis, H. (1994) 'A new agenda for local governance', *Public Money and Management*, 14(4): 29–36.

Stewart, J.D., Kendall, E. and Coote, A. (1994) *Citizens' Juries*. London: Institute for Public Policy Research.

Stoker, G. (1988) *The Politics of Local Government*. Basingstoke: Macmillan.

Stoker, G., Gains, F., John, P., Rao, N. and Harding, A. (2003) *Implementing the 2000 Act with Respect to New Council Constitutions and the Ethical Framework: First Report*. London: Office of the Deputy Prime Minister (http://www.elgce.org.uk).

Stone, D. (1980) *The Limits of Professional Power: National Health Care in the Federal Republic of Germany*. Chicago: University of Chicago Press.

Sudlow, C. and Counsell, C. (2003) 'Problems with UK government's risk sharing scheme for assessing drugs for multiple sclerosis', *British Medical Journal*, 326: 388–92.

Summerfield, C. and Babb, P. (2003) *Social Trends, 33*. London: The Stationery Office.

Syrett, K. (2003) 'A technocratic fix to the "legitimacy" problem? The Blair government and health care rationing in the United Kingdom', *Journal of Health Politics, Policy and Law*, 28(4): 715–46.

Szasz, T. (1970) *The Manufacture of Madness*. New York: Harper and Row.

Tanenbaum, S.J. (1994) 'Knowing and acting in medical practice: the epistemological politics of outcomes research', *Journal of Health Politics, Policy and Law*, 19(1): 27–44.

Taylor, B., Miller, E., Farrington, C.P., Petropoulos, M.C., Favot-Mayaud, I., Li, J. and Waight, P.A. (1999) 'Autism and measles, mumps and rubella vaccine: no epidemiological evidence for a causal association', *Lancet*, 353: 2026–9.

Taylor, G.R. (1997) *Labour's Renewal: the Policy Review and Beyond*. London: Macmillan.

Taylor, M., Hoyes, L., Lart, R. and Means, R. (1992) *User Empowerment in Community Care: Unravelling the Issues*. Bristol: University of Bristol School for Advanced Urban Studies.

Taylor-Gooby, P. and Dale, J. (1981) *Social Theory and Social Welfare*. London: Edward Arnold.

Thomas, D.N. (1983) *The Making of Community Work*. London: Allen and Unwin.

Thompson, G. (1993) 'Network co-ordination', in R. Maidment and G. Thompson (eds), *Managing the United Kingdom: an Introduction to its Political Economy and Public Policy*, pp. 51–74. London: Sage.

Thompson, J.D. and Tuden, A. (1956) 'Strategies, structures and processes of organisational decision', in J.D. Thompson (ed.), *Comparative Studies in Administration*, pp. 195–216. Pittsburg, PA: University of Pittsburgh Press.

Thorogood, N. (2002) 'Regulating dentistry', in J. Allsop and M. Saks (eds), *Regulating the Health Professions*, pp. 108–19. London: Sage.

Tingle, J. and Foster, C. (2002) *Clinical Guidelines: Law, Policy and Practice*. London: Cavendish.

Titmuss, R.M. (1973) *The Gift Relationship*. Harmondsworth: Penguin.

Tolliday, H. (1978) 'Clinical autonomy' in E. Jaques (ed.), *Health Services: Their Nature and Organisation and the Role of Patients, Doctors, Nurses and the Complementary Professions*. London: Heinemann.

Townsend, P. and Davidson, N. (eds) (1982) *Inequalities in Health: the Black Report*. Harmondsworth: Penguin.

Townsend, P. and Davidson, N. Whitehead, M. (1988) *Inequalities in Health: the Black Report and the Health Divide Single Volume*. Harmondsworth: Penguin.

Towse, A. (2004) 'Introduction' in J. Appleby N. Devlin and D. Dawson (eds), *How Much Should We Spend on the NHS? Issues and Challenges Arising from the Wanless Review of Future Health Care Spending*, pp. 6–13. London: King's Fund.

Trinder, L. and Reynolds, S. (eds) (2000) *Evidence-Based Practice: A Critical Appraisal*. Oxford: Blackwell.

Tullock, G. (1976) *The Vote Motive* (Hobart Paper No. 9). London: Institute of Economic Affairs.

Turner, B.S. (1996) 'Introduction' in B.S. Turner (ed.), *The Blackwell Companion to Social Theory*. Oxford: Blackwell.

Turner, S.P. (2003) *Liberal Democracy 3.0*. London: Sage.

Twine, F. (1994) *Citizenship and Social Rights: the Interdependence of Self and Society*. London: Sage.

Unnamed (2001) 'Government campaign to inform parents about MMR vaccine safety', *Pharmaceutical Journal*, 266: 7132:103.

Wakefield, A. and Montgomery, S.M. (2000) 'Measles, mumps and rubella vaccine: through a glass, darkly', *Adverse Drug Reaction and Toxicological Reviews*, 19(4): 265–83.

Wakefield, A.J., Murch, S.H., Anthony, A., Linnell, J., Casson, D.M., Malik, M., Berelowitz, M., Dhillon, A.P., Thomson, M.A., Harvey, P., Valentine, A., Davies, S.E. and Walker-Smith, J.A. (1998) 'Ileal-lymphoid-nodular hyperplasia, non-specific colitis, and pervasive developmental disorder in children', *Lancet* 351: 637–41.

Walsh, N. Allen, L., Baines, D. and Barnes, M. (1999) *Taking Off: a First Year Report of the Personal Medical Services Pilots in England*. Birmingham: University of Birmingham Health Services Management Centre.

Walsh, N., Maybin, J. and Lewis, R. (2007) 'So where are the alternative providers in primary care?', *British Journal of Healthcare Management*, 13: 43–6.

Walshe, K. (2003) *Regulating Health Care: a Prescription for Improvement?* Maidenhead: Open University Press.

Wanless, D. (2001) *Securing our Future Health: Taking a Long-Term View. Interim Report*. London: HM Treasury.

Wanless, D. (2002) *Securing our Future Health: Taking a Long-Term View. Final Report*. London: HM Treasury.

Wann, M. (1995) *Building Social Capital: Self Help in a Twenty-First Century Welfare State*. London: Institute for Public Policy Research.

Watkin, B. (1975) *Documents on Health and Social Services: 1834 to the Present Day*. London: Methuen.

Watkin, B. (1978) *The NHS: the First Phase – 1948–1974 and After*. London: Allen and Unwin.

Watkins, S. (1987) *Medicine and Labour: the Politics of a Profession*. London: Lawrence and Wishart.

Watts, G. (2006) 'Are the Scots getting a better deal on prescribed dugs than the English?', *British Medical Journal*, 333: 875.

Webb, E. (1996) 'Trust and crisis' in R.M. Kramer and T.R. Tyler (eds), *Trust in Organisations: Frontiers of Theory and Research*. Thousand Oaks, CA: Sage.

Weber, M. (1947) *The Theory of Social and Economic Organisation*, trans. A.M. Henderson and T. Parsons. New York: Free Press.

Webster, C. (1988) *The Health Services Since the War: Volume I: Problems of Health Care – the National Health Service Before 1957*. London: HMSO.

Webster, C. (1996) *The Health Services Since the War: Volume II – Government and Health Care: the British National Health Service 1958–1979*. London: HMSO.

Webster, C. (1998) *The National Health Service: a Political History*. Oxford: Oxford University Press.

Webster, C. (2002) *The National Health Service: a Political History,* 2 edn. Oxford: Oxford University Press.

Wennberg, J.E. (1984) 'Dealing with medical practice variations: a proposal for action', *Health Affairs*, 3(2): 6–32.

Wensing, M., Van der Weijden, T. and Grol, R. (1998) 'Implementing guidelines and innovations in general practice: which interventions are effective?', *British Journal of General Practice*, 48: 991–7.

White, C. (2004) 'NICE guidance has failed to end "postcode prescribing"', *British Medical Journal*, 328: 1277.

Whitehead, M. (1990) *The Concepts and Principles of Equality and Health.* Copenhagen: WHO Regional Office for Europe.

Whitehead, M. (1992) 'The Health Divide', in P. Townsend, M. Whitehead and N. Davidson (eds), *Inequalities in Health: the Black Report and the Health Divide,* 2nd edn. London: Penguin.

Whitehead, M. (1997) 'Life and death across the millennium', in F. Drever and M. Whitehead (eds), *Health Inequalities: Decennial Supplement.* DS Series, no15. London: The Stationery Office.

Wilding, P.R. (1967) 'The genesis of the Ministry of Health', *Public Administration*, 67(3): 149–68.

Willcocks, A.J. (1967) *The Creation of the National Health Service.* London: Routledge and Kegan Paul.

Wilkinson, E. (2007) MMR vaccine confidence 'growing', BBC News, http://news.bbc.co.uk/1/hi/health/6449485.stm

Williamson, A. and Room, G. (eds) (1983) *Health and Welfare States of Britain: An Inter-Country Comparison.* London: Heinemann.

Williamson, C. (1992) *Whose Standards? Consumer and Professional Standards in Health Care.* Buckingham: Open University Press.

Williamson, O.E. (1975) *Markets and Hierarchies: Analysis and Anti-Trust Implications.* New York: Free Press.

Williamson, O.E. (1996) *The Mechanisms of Governance.* Oxford: Oxford University Press.

Wilmott, P. (1989) *Community Initiatives: Patterns and Prospects.* London: Policy Studies Institute.

Wistow, G. and Harrison, S. (1998) 'Rationality and rhetoric: the contribution to social care policy making of Sir Roy Griffiths 1986–1991', *Public Administration,* 76(4): 649–68.

Wolfe, R.M. and Sharp, L.K. (2002) 'Anti-vaccinationists past and present', *British Medical Journal*, 325: 430–2.

Wood, B. (1976). *The Process of Local Government Reform: 1966–1974.* London: HMSO.

Wood, B. (2000) *Patient Power? Patients Associations in Britain and America.* Buckingham: Open University Press.

Woolf, S.H. (1992) 'Practice guidelines: a new reality in medicine - II', *Archives of Internal Medicine*, 152: 946–52.

Wright, J., Reeves, J., Warren, E., Bibby, J., Harrison, S., Dowswell, G., Russell, I.T. and Russell, D. (2003) 'Effectiveness of multifaceted implementation of guidelines in primary care', *Journal of Health Services Research and Policy*, 8(3): 142–8.

Yoshioka, A. (1998) 'Use of randomisation in the Medical Research Council's clinical trial of streptomycin for pulmonary tuberculosis in the 1940s', *British Medical Journal*, 317: 1220–3.

Index